Strategic Air Command

Strategic Air Command
People, Aircraft, and Missiles

Second Edition

Edited by Norman Polmar and
Timothy M. Laur

The Nautical & Aviation Publishing Company of America
Baltimore, Maryland

Copyright © 1979, 1990 by The Nautical & Aviation Publishing Company of America, Inc.

Published by The Nautical & Aviation Publishing Company of America, Inc., 101 W. Read Street, Suite 314, Baltimore, Maryland 21201.

All photographs are official U.S. Air Force unless otherwise noted.

Library of Congress Catalog Card Number: 90-35105

ISBN: 0-933852-77-0

Printed in the United States of America

Library of Congress Cataloging In Publication Data
Strategic Air Command: people, aircraft, and missiles / edited by Norman Polmar and Timothy
    M. Laur; chronology (1976-1985) compiled by the Office of the Historian of the Strategic
    Air Command—2nd ed.
        p.   cm.
    ISBN 0-933852-77-0
    1. United States. Air Force. Strategic Air Command—History—Chronology.
    I. Polmar, Norman. II. Laur, Timothy. III. United States. Air Force.
    Strategic Air Command. Office of the Historian.
    UG633.S79   1990
    358.4'2'0973—dc20

90-35105
CIP

Contents

Preface to Second Edition

This book is a chronological history of the people, aircraft, weapons systems, and significant activities of the U.S. Air Force's Strategic Air Command. The first edition covered the period 1946 through 1976. This edition continues the history of SAC into 1990.

Since the publication of the first edition, many significant developments with SAC's weapon systems—bombers and strategic missiles—have taken place. Most notable has been the controversial B-1 bomber, now operational since 1986, and the even more controversial B-2 Stealth bomber still under development. The primary bombers of the SAC fleet, the B-52G and H have an average age of about 30 years, and based on their present roles, are expected to continue in their missions until the year 2030.

The development of new missiles for SAC has been almost as controversial. The Peacekeeper MX and the still-to-be-developed Small ICBM (SICBM) have caused debate since their inception, especially with respect to the potential bombing options against them.

The dramatic reduction in the defense budget that is occurring in the early 1990s has significant impact on the future strength and operations of SAC. However, a suggestion late in 1989 that the Looking Glass flights be reduced to save operational funds was refused by President George Bush.

Since the first edition of this book was written in 1979, phenomenal changes have occurred in the strategic posture of the superpowers and the strategic weapons they operate. In the last decade of the 20th century, the military structure of the nations which engaged in the cold war continues to change at a rapid rate.

The tremendous economic burden of modern weapon systems, the era of *glasnost*, or openness, of the Soviet Union and the Warsaw Pact nations, and the apparent amelioration of tensions between the United Sates and the Soviet Union all dictate the most judicious development of future strategic systems.

Sources for *Strategic Air Command* include fact sheets and histories published by SAC, the Air Force Association's *Air Force* magazine, and press releases issued by various Air Force and Department of Defense activities. Some of the specific data provided in the first edition and in this edition through the mid-1980s were not available from the command for the last part of the decade. For the descriptions of the aircraft and missiles, the U.S. Naval Institute Military Database, part of the United Communications Group's Periscope Defense Information Service, was the primary source of current data. Individual appreciation is extended to Jeffrey Rhodes of the Air Force Association who helped with some last-minute facts on SAC, and to Beth Laur, who, more than once, ensured that final copies were personally delivered to the publishers to meet their deadlines.

Preface to the First Edition

Silently, at a score of air bases throughout the United States, sentries patrol before giant aircraft, their wings bent low by heavy fuel loads; inside their mammoth fuselages rest several thermo-nuclear weapons. Nearby the bomber crews relax or sleep, only 15 minutes or less from takeoff.

Simultaneously, at scores of underground missile control centers, other Air Force officers live day to day in the presence of controls for launching more than a thousand intercontinental missiles.

At the same time, high above the United States, a large aircraft circles continuously, always relieved "on station," to keep a SAC general airborne with a command staff, with communications available to control all SAC bombers and missiles should the primary SAC command center near Omaha, Nebraska, be destroyed.

These are the principal elements of the land-based strategic striking forces of the United States, the Strategic Air Command. With the U.S. Navy's submarine-launched ballistic missiles, SAC provides the nation's strategic deterrence against nuclear war. These three strategic striking forces—which form the so-called TRIAD—are a primary factor in U.S. defense strategy.

This book describes the land-based components of the TRIAD, the Strategic Air Command. This publication is based largely on the excellent chronology entitled *Development of Strategic Air Command, 1946–1976*, prepared by the Office of the Historian, Headquarters, SAC. The chronology was written by Mr. J.C. Hopkins, assisted by Mr. Sheldon A. Goldberg and Mrs. Marcena R. Clifford of Headquarters, SAC, under the overall direction of Mr. John T. Bohn, Command Historian.

Mr. Norman Polmar, the Editor of this volume, has prepared considerable complementary material to the basic chronology, including material on the leadership, current order of battle and organization of SAC, and detailed descriptions of SAC's principal aircraft and missiles from 1946 onward. Indeed, the aircraft descriptions are probably unique in that this is believed to be the only volume to catalogue all variants of the principal SAC bomber and reconnaissance aircraft.

Although not an actual component of SAC, British strategic forces are highlighted in this volume because of the joint U.S.-British deployment of* the Thor intermediate range ballistic missile, and the regular participation of British aircraft from Bomber Command (later Strike Command) in SAC aircraft competitions. Also, the Royal Air Force was the only foreign service to operate U.S.-built strategic aircraft, flying 88 B-29 Superfortresses during the early 1950s.

The Editor is in debt to several individuals for their assistance in the preparation of this volume, including Messrs. William Green and Gordon Swanborough, Editors of *Air International*; H.D. Hollinger of Boeing Wichita Company; Lieutenant Colonel Michael McRaney, USAF, formerly with Department of Defense's Public Affairs Directorate; Alvin Spivak and Rob Mack of General Dynamics/Fort Worth Division; J.W.R. Taylor, Editor, *Jane's All the World's Aircraft*; and Miss Kathy Cassity of the Air Force Museum.

Several of the photographs used in this volume are from the collection of the late James C. Fahey.

Introduction

The U.S. Strategic Air Command (SAC) directs two of the three "legs" of the U.S. strategic deterrence force, popularly known as the "strategic triad." The SAC components are the land-based Intercontinental Ballistic Missiles (ICBM) and the air-breathing bomber components, the land-based manned bombers themselves and air-launched cruise missiles that they deliver. (The U.S. Navy operates the third leg of the triad, the submarine-launched ballistic and cruise missiles).

Although SAC was established in 1946, specifically to deliver nuclear weapons against the Soviet Union (or other potential aggressors in time of war), U.S. strategic bombers were employed extensively in a conventional bombing role in the Korean War (1950-1953) and the Vietnam War (1964-1973). In addition, SAC bomber aircraft have demonstrated an extensive capability for maritime patrol, anti-shipping, and minelaying activities, in keeping with the U.S. Air Force's secondary mission of supporting the navy in sea control.

Thus, SAC has developed a variety of military capabilities to supplement its primary mission—strategic offensive operations to deter a potential aggressor.

General George C. Kenney was appointed the first commander of SAC and was given a mandate to build an organization for long-range offensive operations in any part of the world. He began with 100,000 military personnel and 1,300 aircraft, including about 300 B-29 bombers. In 1948 deliveries began of two new aircraft—the B-36 and B-50. General Curtis E. LeMay took command of SAC that year, and the headquarters moved from Andrews AFB, Maryland, to Offutt AFB, Nebraska.

While some of SAC's B-29s were being used for conventional bombing in Korea, new aircraft were introduced to replace old and obsolete systems. During the Korean War, B-29s dropped 167,000 tons of conventional bombs and destroyed all North Korean strategic targets in three months. By the mid-1950s, SAC was operating its first all-jet bomber, the B-47. The KC-97 was the main refueling tanker. Before General LeMay's reassignment in 1957, SAC had received its first B-52 Stratofortresses and KC-135 Stratotankers, giving it an all-jet capability. A nonstop, around-the-world flight by three B-52s in 1957 demonstrated the command's worldwide capability.

By 1960, one-third of the bomber force was on 15-minute ground alert, and airborne alert and dispersal concepts were being tested to overcome shorter warning times. The B-36 was gone, but SAC had added the B-58 Hustler, the nation's first bomber capable of supersonic speeds.

General Thomas S. Power, SAC's third commander, supervised the entry of the ICBM into the force. Atlas and Titan ICBM wings were activated in 1958, and Snark, Thor, Hound Dog, and the short-lived Jupiter soon became familiar terms in describing the mixed force of unmanned systems. Later, the Minuteman gradually replaced the Atlas.

During the mid-1960s, the B-47 bomber and KC-97 tanker were retired, and by 1971 the B-58 medium bomber had been replaced by the FB-111, a variable sweep-wing bomber. The Minuteman force continued to improve in quality as earlier versions were replaced by multiple warhead Minuteman IIs.

From 1964 to 1973, B-52s, KC-135s, and reconnaissance aircraft flew thousands of bombing, air refueling, and reconnaissance missions, respectively, in Southeast Asia. SAC forces helped to lift the siege at Khe Sanh and helped stop the 1972 North Vietnamese spring offensive in An Loc, Kontum, and Quang Tri. Additionally, SAC's Linebacker II campaign assisted in forcing the North Vietnamese back to the negotiation table in December 1972. The operations of KC-135 tankers, meanwhile, increased fighter flexibility and range responsiveness, decreasing the need to base fighters at exposed forward airfields.

In April 1975, SAC started transferring 128 KC-135 tankers to three Air Force Reserve and 13 Air National Guard units. In wartime mobilization SAC would control those units, which would become full partners with their active duty counterparts under the Air Force's total force policy. On a day-to-day basis, each of the 16 SAC-gained units was responsible for one line of tanker alert.

In November 1975, Headquarters U.S. Air Force transferred command of the 1st Airborne Command and Control Squadron at Andrews AFB, Maryland, from the Headquarters Command to Headquarters SAC. With this action, SAC acquired the new E-4, a modified Boeing 757. The 1st ACCS had three E-4s outfitted with special communications equipment to serve as the National Emergency Airborne Command Post (NEACP).

The Minuteman force modernization program was also completed in 1975. The project replaced Minuteman I ICBMs with Minuteman IIs and Minuteman IIIs. Conversion of a squadron of Minuteman II missiles to Peacekeeper missiles at F. E. Warren AFB, Wyoming, was completed in December 1988.

Global Shield

To test SAC's readiness and capability in response to an attack on the United States, it is necessary to simulate a wartime environment. In July 1979, SAC conducted its largest and most comprehensive exercise in more than 20 years—Global Shield '79. The exercise was the first comprehensive test of all SAC and associated Air Reserve Forces units to carry out their assigned wartime missions.

Now an annual exercise, Global Shield demonstrates the readiness and effectiveness of SAC's nuclear deterrent forces. Participating aircrews, missile crews, and support people train in wartime tasks, and they experience the link between their operations and the jobs of others.

New Responsibilities

A new SAC responsibility came from the 1979 reorganization of the Aerospace Defense Command. Already the operational manager for space surveillance and missile warning, SAC also assumed responsibility for its organization, training, equipment, and operations. However, operational control of air defense, space surveillance, and missile warning assets remained with the commander-in-chief, North American Defense Command. When the Air Force Space Command was formed 1 October 1983, SAC transferred its space warning and surveillance systems to the new organization. The transfer was complete by 1 January 1984.

A new organization, the Joint Strategic Connectivity Staff, was established in 1980 at Headquarters SAC. The commander-in-chief of SAC was made the director of this Joint Chiefs of Staff agency. Its purpose was to analyze strategic connectivity systems and procedures and to make recommendations concerning them to the joint staff. The joint chiefs assumed responsibility for the connectivity staff and its functions on 15 September 1983. This agency moved from Headquarters SAC to the Washington, DC, area.

In 1983, the Joint Chiefs of Staff formed the Rapid Deployment Joint Task Force, designated the U.S. Central Command. The national command authorities directed U.S. forces to be capable of self-sustained or integrated missions during a time-sensitive crisis. To accomplish the new requirements, the SAC commander-in-chief developed the command's strategic projection force to provide worldwide combat support.

New Systems

In addition to accepting new responsibilities, SAC expanded its inventory of weapons systems. In late 1981, SAC received its first Air-Launched Cruise Missiles (ALCM), designed to increase the B-52's effectiveness as a standoff platform. The ALCM is an unmanned, winged air vehicle capable of sustained subsonic flight. After being launched from an aircraft, it determines its own location and guides itself to a predetermined target. Cruise missiles first became operationally capable at Griffiss AFB, New York, in December 1982.

To enhance its air refueling mission, SAC augmented its existing KC-135 tanker force with the KC-10A. The KC-10A primarily supports contingency operations by refueling fighter aircraft and strategic airlifters such as the C-5 and C-141. It also carries people and more pallets of cargo than two newer "stretch" C-141s. The first KC-10 was delivered to SAC in 1981, and the last production model rolled off the assembly line in 1989.

As part of the SAC modernization effort, re-engining the KC-135 fleet with modern, efficient turbofan engines began in 1982. Re-engining not only improved the aircraft's safety, environmental impact, and survivability, but also increased its refueling capability by 50 percent, almost doubled its effective range, and greatly improved its takeoff performance. KC-135R procurement will continue into the 1990s, enabling SAC to use the aircraft well into the 21st century.

SAC also began to augment its reconnaissance force of U-2s and SR-71s with the TR-1 aircraft in 1981. The TR-1 is a single-engine, fixed-wing aircraft designed for high-altitude surveillance and reconnaissance. In 1990, the last operational flight of the SR-71 was flown in record-breaking style, and the Blackbird was retired, its mission taken over by satellites.

The delivery of the first B-1B in July 1985 marked a new era in SAC's ability to penetrate enemy defenses and carry out the Single Integrated Operational Plan. SAC plans the serial production of the Northrop-built bomber, the B-2, and two ICBM systems, the Peacekeeper Rail Garrison and the Small ICBM (nicknamed "Midgetman").

The new international posture that is evolving in the 1990s will bring the role of the Strategic Air Command under close scrutiny. Budget considerations will dictate critical decisions concerning weapons systems, rather than strategic imperatives or threat perceptions. The decision to retire the much-acclaimed SR-71 "Blackbird" was as much financial as it was related to the aircraft's capabilities or mission.

The congressional defense hearings in 1990 brought on a fierce competition in the military for funds. The new concept of a "peace dividend" will certainly exert tremendous pressure on all aspects of the defense budget. Although strategic systems generally fared well for 1991 in the original Bush Administration budget, the president later suggested that he was ready to consider a no-growth budget. The high cost of SAC's bombers and missiles will undoubtedly be debated, as will high value systems of the Navy. Every description of the B-2 places emphasis on its feature of being the "most expensive aircraft in history" rather than its high technological development, its capabilities and performance.

Since its formation, the Strategic Air Command has made a reality of its motto "Peace is our Profession." The strategic deterrence mission of SAC has certainly played a significant role in ensuring the peace since the end of World War II. Moreover, SAC demonstrated flexibility during the Vietnam War by adapting its strategic bombing role to contribute to the combat effort. With the most dramatic changes in history occurring with the Warsaw Pact members and in the strategic balance between East and West, SAC must again adjust its mission to fit the national and global strategies of the 21st century. Low-intensity conflict, international terrorism, and regional conflicts will take the place (if they haven't already) of the East-West strategic balance. How SAC defines its mission to meet these new defense issues will determine its survival.

Air Order of Battle 1989-1990

Bomber Aircraft

178	B-52G Stratofortress
96	B-52H Stratofortress
61	FB-111A
97	B-1B

Tanker Aircraft

640	KC-135 Stratotanker
60	KC-10A Extender

Reconnaissance Aircraft

28	U-2/TR-1
~27	RC-135

Command Aircraft

4	E-4B National Emergency Airborne Command Post (NEACP)
13	EC-135 Airborne Command Post ("Looking Glass")

Intercontinental Ballistic Missiles (ICBM)

450	Minuteman II
500	Minuteman III (200 with 335 kt warhead/300 with 300 kt)
50	MX Peacekeeper

Attack Missiles

~1,500	SRAM (B-52s and FB-111s)
~1,715	Air Launched Cruise Missile (ALCM) (B-52s and B-1s)

**HEADQUARTERS
STRATEGIC AIR COMMAND
OFFUTT AFB, NEBRASKA**

1st Combat Eval. Group
Barksdale AFB, La.

8th Air Force
Barksdale AFB, La.

7th Air Division*
Ramstein AB
W. Germany

12th Air Division
Ellsworth AFB
S.D.

42d Air Division
Grand Forks AFB
N.D.

2d Bomb Wing
Barksdale AFB, La.
(B-52, KC-10, KC-135)

306th Strategic Wing*
RAF Mildenhall, UK

28th Bomb Wing
Ellsworth AFB, S.D.
(B-1B, KC-135)

319th Bomb Wing
Grand Forks AFB, N.D.
(B-1B, KC-135)

7th Bomb Wing
Carswell AFB, Tex.
(B-52, KC-135)

11th Strategic Group*
RAF Fairford, UK

44th Strat. Missile Wing
Ellsworth AFB, S.D.
(Minuteman)

321st Strat. Missile Wing
Grand Forks AFB, N.D.
(Minuteman)

42d Bomb Wing
Loring AFB, Me.
(B-52, KC-135)

17th Recon. Wing*
RAF Alconbury
UK

380th Bomb Wing
Plattsburgh AFB, N.Y.
(FB-111, KC-135)

509th Bomb Wing
Pease AFB, N.H.
(KC-135)

97th Bomb Wing
Eaker AFB, Ark.
(B-52, KC-135)

379th Bomb Wing
Wurtsmith AFB, Mich.
(B-52, KC-135)

410th Bomb Wing
K.I. Sawyer AFB, Mich.
(B-52, KC-135)

416th Bomb Wing
Griffis AFB, N.Y.
(B-52, KC-135)

351st Strat. Mis. Wng.*
Whiteman AFB, Mo.
(Minuteman)

19th Air Refuel. Wing*
Robins AFB, Ga.
(KC-135)

68th Air Refuel. Wing*
S. Johnson AFB, N.C.
(KC-10)

305th Air Refuel. Wing
Grissom AFB, Ind.
(KC-135)

*Tenant Units

2

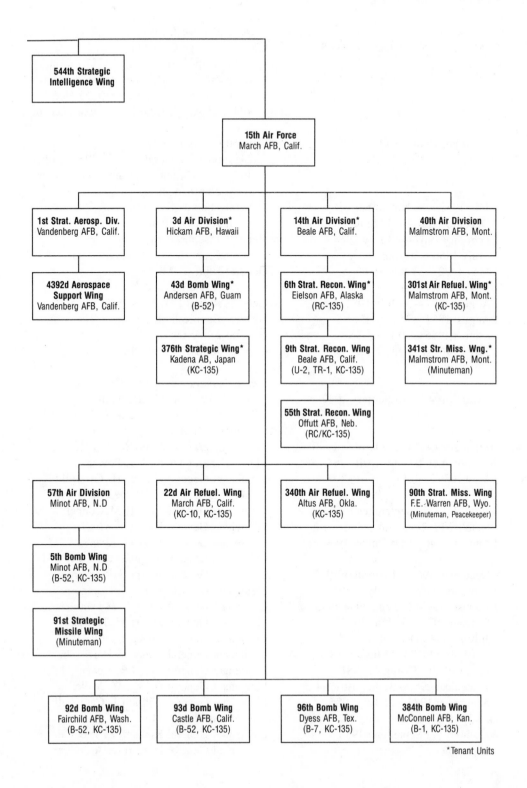

544th Strategic Intelligence Wing

15th Air Force
March AFB, Calif.

1st Strat. Aerosp. Div.
Vandenberg AFB, Calif.

3d Air Division*
Hickam AFB, Hawaii

14th Air Division*
Beale AFB, Calif.

40th Air Division
Malmstrom AFB, Mont.

4392d Aerospace Support Wing
Vandenberg AFB, Calif.

43d Bomb Wing*
Andersen AFB, Guam
(B-52)

6th Strat. Recon. Wing*
Eielson AFB, Alaska
(RC-135)

301st Air Refuel. Wing*
Malmstrom AFB, Mont.
(KC-135)

376th Strategic Wing*
Kadena AB, Japan
(KC-135)

9th Strat. Recon. Wing
Beale AFB, Calif.
(U-2, TR-1, KC-135)

341st Str. Miss. Wng.*
Malmstrom AFB, Mont.
(Minuteman)

55th Strat. Recon. Wing
Offutt AFB, Neb.
(RC/KC-135)

57th Air Division
Minot AFB, N.D

22d Air Refuel. Wing
March AFB, Calif.
(KC-10, KC-135)

340th Air Refuel. Wing
Altus AFB, Okla.
(KC-135)

90th Strat. Miss. Wing
F.E. Warren AFB, Wyo.
(Minuteman, Peacekeeper)

5th Bomb Wing
Minot AFB, N.D
(B-52, KC-135)

91st Strategic Missile Wing
(Minuteman)

92d Bomb Wing
Fairchild AFB, Wash.
(B-52, KC-135)

93d Bomb Wing
Castle AFB, Calif.
(B-52, KC-135)

96th Bomb Wing
Dyess AFB, Tex.
(B-7, KC-135)

384th Bomb Wing
McConnell AFB, Kan.
(B-1, KC-135)

*Tenant Units

3

Command Leadership

*Commanders-in-Chief**

21 March 1946 — 19 October 1948
General George C. Kenney
Retained position as senior U.S. military representative, Military Staff Committee of the United Nations, until 15 October 1946, at which time he became head of SAC.

19 October 1948 — 30 June 1957
General Curtis E. LeMay
Lieutenant general until 29 October 1951; longest tenure of any U.S. military force commander.

1 July 1957 — 30 November 1964 — General Thomas S. Power
1 December 1964 — 31 January 1967 — General John D. Ryan
1 February 1967 — 28 July 1968 — General Joseph J. Nazzaro
29 July 1968 — 30 April 1972 — General Bruce K. Holloway
1 May 1972 — 31 July 1974 — General John C. Meyer
1 August 1974 — 31 July 1977 — General Russell E. Dougherty
1 August 1977 — 31 July 1981 — General Richard H. Ellis
1 August 1981 — 31 July 1985 — General Bennie L. Davis
1 August 1985 — 30 June 1986 — General Larry D. Welch
1 July 1986 — Present — General John T. Chain, Jr.

*Vice Commanders-in-Chief***

21 March 1946 — 10 January 1947
Major General St. Clair Streett
Served as acting commander until General Kennedy reported for duty.

10 January 1947 — 26 October 1948 — Major General Clements McMullen
26 October 1948 — 14 April 1954 — Major General Thomas S. Power
3 May 1954 — 30 June 1961
Lieutenant General Francis H. Griswold
Major general until 31 December 1957

1 July 1961 — 30 September 1962 — Lieutenant General John P. McConnell
1 October 1962 — 31 July 1964 — Lieutenant General Hunter Harris, Jr.
1 August 1964 — 1 December 1964
Lieutenant General John D. Ryan
To general upon assignment as CINCSAC

1 December 1964 — 1 February 1967 — Lieutenant General Joseph J. Nazzaro
1 February 1967 — 31 July 1969 — Lieutenant General Keith K. Compton
1 August 1969 — 30 September 1973 — Lieutenant General Glen W. Martin
1 October 1973 — 30 June 1977 — Lieutenant General James M. Kewck
1 July 1977 — 3 December 1977 — Lieutenant General James E. Hill
6 December 1977 — 27 June 1978 — Lieutenant General Edgar S. Harris, Jr.
28 June 1978 — 31 August 1981 — Lieutenant General Lloyd R. Leavitt, Jr.
1 September 1981 — 31 August 1984 — Lieutenant General George C. Miller
1 September 1984 — 25 July 1985 — Lieutenant General William J. Campbell
26 July 1985 — 30 January 1987 — Lieutenant General Monroe W. Hatch
30 January — 1 September 1988 — Lieutenant General Kenneth L. Peek, Jr.
1 September 1988 — Present — Lieutenant General Donald D. Aldridge

General George C. Kenney

General Curtis E. LeMay   **General Richard H. Ellis**

9 July 1962 — 16 June 1963	Major General Hewitt T Wheless
17 June 1963 — 31 July 1964	Major General Keith K. Compton
1 August 1964 — 2 July 1966	Major General Charles M. Eisenhart
5 July 1966 — 21 January 1969	Major General James B. Knapp
22 January 1969 — 31 May 1972	Major General Timothy J. Dacey, Jr.
	Brigadier general until 1 August 1969
1 June 1972 — 23 April 1973	Major General Warren D. Johnson
24 April 1973 — 13 September 1973	Major General George H. McKee
17 September 1973 — 10 January 1974	Major General James R. Allen
27 February 1974 — 26 May 1975	Major General Martin G. Colladay
27 May 1975 — 1 July 1976	Major General Andrew B. Anderson, Jr.
1 August 1976 — 5 December 19677	Major General Edgar S. Harris
9 January 1978 — 27 June 1978	Major General Lloyd R. Leavitt, Jr.
28 June 1978 — 31 July 1980	Major General Earl G. Peck
1 August 1980 — 31 July 1982	Major General Andrew Pringle, Jr.
1 August 1982 — 27 January 1983	Major General Christopher S. Adams, Jr.
28 July 1983 — 30 September 1984	Major General Monroe W. Hatch, Jr.
1 October 1984 — 28 October 1985	Major General John A. Brashear
29 October 1985 — 5 July 1987	Major General Robert D. Beckel
5 July 1987 — 1 October 1989	Major General Randall D. Peat
1 October 1989 — Present	Major General Donadl L. Marks

---

* Originally commanding general; changed to commander in June 1953; changed to commander-in-chief in April 1955.

** Originally deputy commander; changed to vice commander in October 1952; changed to vice commander-in-chief in April 1955.

1946

Resources

Personnel	37,092 (4,319 officers, 27,871 airmen, 4,902 civilians)
Tactical Aircraft	279 (148 B-29, 85 P-51, 31 F-2, 15 C-54)*
Aircraft Units	Nine Very Heavy Bomb Groups (30 UE), six with B-29s and three without aircraft assigned
	Two Fighter Groups (75 UE), one with P-51s and one without aircraft assigned
	One Reconnaissance Wing with F-2s and one Reconnaissance Squadron with F-13s
	One Air Transport Unit (10 UE) with C-54s
Active Bases	18 in the continental limits of the United States (CONUS)

Organization

Establishment of SAC. On 21 March, the Strategic Air Command was established as one of the three major combat commands of the U.S. Army Air Forces. General Carl Spaatz, Commanding General of the Army Air Forces, issued the new command's first mission:

The mission. "The Strategic Air Command will be prepared to conduct long-range offensive operations in any part of the world either independently or in cooperation with land and Naval forces; to conduct maximum range reconnaissance over land or sea either independently or in cooperation with land and naval forces; to provide combat units capable of intense and sustained combat operations employing the latest and most advanced weapons; to train units and personnel for the maintenance of the Strategic Forces in all parts of the world; to perform such special missions as the Commanding General, Army Air Force may direct."

Command status, 21 March. Creation of the new command was achieved by redesignating Headquarters Continental Air Forces as Headquarters Strategic Air Command. Resources of the Continental Air Forces were divided among three new commands—Strategic Air Command, Tactical Air Command, and Air Defense Command.

---

*About 30 of the B-29s were configured to carry nuclear weapons.

The B-29 Superfortress was the outstanding heavy bomber of World War II. At the end of the war it was the only aircraft that could carry the atomic bomb and became the backbone of the newly formed Strategic Air Command. (Boeing photo)

SAC received most of these resources, including the headquarters at Bolling Field, Washington, D. C.; Second Air Force, whose headquarters was located at Colorado Springs, Colorado; the 311th Reconnaissance Wing, with its headquarters at MacDill Field, Florida; and approximately 100,000 personnel, 22 major installations and over 30 minor bases, and a conglomerate of bomber, fighter, reconnaissance, and support aircraft numbering about 1,300. With postwar demobilization still in process, these resources would be drastically reduced by the end of the year.

Headquarters. On 21 October, Headquarters SAC officially opened at Andrews Field, Maryland, having moved there from Bolling during the period from 15 through 20 October.

Fifteenth Air Force. Effective 31 March, Headquarters Fifteenth Air Force, which had been assigned to the Strategic Air Command on 21 March, was activated at Colorado Springs and absorbed the personnel and functions of Headquarters Second Air Force. The latter was inactivated and assigned in an inactive status to the Air Defense Command.

Effective 1 May, the 311th Reconnaissance Wing, which had been assigned directly to Headquarters SAC since 21 March, was further assigned to Fifteenth Air Force.

Eighth Air Force. On 7 June, in preparation for the assignment of a second numbered air force to the Strategic Air Command, Headquarters Eighth Air Force was relieved from assignment to the United States Army Forces, Pacific and moved to MacDill Field, Florida, and assigned to SAC. On 1 August, Headquarters Eighth Air Force was attached for administrative purposes to headquarters Fifteenth Air Force.

Having been relieved from attachment to Headquarters Fifteenth Air Force, Headquarters Eighth Air Force moved from MacDill to Fort Worth Army Air Field, Texas, on 1 November. Headquarters Eighth Air Force was manned largely with personnel from Headquarters 58th Bombardment Wing, Very Heavy, which was also located at Fort Worth. Approximately one-half of the fully equipped combat units of Fifteenth Air Force were transferred to the Eighth on 1 November, but they remained under the Fifteenth's administrative control until 19 November, at which time Headquarters Eighth Air Force became operational.

Operations

Operation Crossroads. In developing an atomic bombing force, SAC relied heavily upon the 509th Composite Group (redesignated a very heavy bomb group on 30 July). When SAC began operations, the 509th was the only group capable of delivering the A-bomb, having delivered two weapons at Hiroshima and Nagasaki. It had just been committed to drop a third one as part of the Operation Crossroads test at Bikini Atoll in July of 1946.

Approved by President Truman in early January, Operation Crossroads was a gigantic peacetime exercise. It involved the efforts of approximately 42,000 people, including Army and Navy personnel and civilian scientists, operating under a provisional organization called Task Force One. The objective was to study the nuclear effects of two A-bombs, one to be dropped from a B-29 and exploded in the air and the other to be attached to a ship and exploded underwater.

Task Group 1.5, the Army Air Force's element of this gigantic force, consisted of approximately 2,200 people drawn largely from SAC and placed under the command of Brigadier General Roger M. Ramey, Commanding General of the 58th Bomb Wing. General Ramey's group was responsible for delivering the first A-bomb and providing aircraft to photograph the explosion and collect scientific data.

On 1 July, "Dave's Dream," a B-29 piloted by Major Woodrow P. Swancutt and assigned to the 509th Group, temporarily stationed at Kwajalein, dropped a Nagasaki-type A-bomb on 73 ships lying off Bikini. Five ships were sunk and nine badly damaged. Task Group 1.5 also participated in the second phase of Operation Crossroads, the underwater explosion on 25 July, by providing numerous aircraft for photographic, data collection, and support functions.

So successful were these two explosions that plans for a third detonation, another underwater explosion of greater depth, were shelved.

First TDY of an entire wing. In October, the 28th Bomb Group, a B-29 unit stationed at Grand Island Army Air Field, Nebraska, deployed to Elmendorf, Alaska, for six months temporary duty (TDY) training in arctic operations. This was the first time an entire SAC bomb group was sent outside the continental limits of the United States. In April 1947, the 28th returned to its new home at Rapid City Army Air Field, South Dakota.

SAC bombers as instrument of international diplomacy—In mid-November, Colonel James C. Selser, Jr., Commander of the 43d Bomb Group at Davis-Monthan Field, Arizona, led a flight of six B-29s to Rhein-Main Airfield, Germany. Two C-54s of the 1st Air Transport Unit, Roswell Field, New Mexico, accompanied the B-29s with spare parts and supplies. The aircraft remained in Europe for almost two weeks.

The Superfortresses flew along the border of Soviet-occupied territory, visited capitals of several free European countries, and surveyed numerous airdromes for possible use by B-29s. This flight, which was planned and executed after two U.S. Army C-47s were shot down over Yugoslavia, is regarded as the first instance in which SAC bombers were used as an instrument of international diplomacy. While the flight could not be regarded as a direct threat to Russia, the presence of B-29s and their reputation as carriers of the A-bomb served notice that the United States was not abandoning Western Europe to the Communists. In early December, the Selser flight returned home.

1947

Resources

Personnel	49,589 (5,175 officers, 39,307 airmen, 5,107 civilians)
Tactical Aircraft	713 (319 B-29, 230 P-51, 120 P-80, 9 C-54, and 35 F-2, F-9, F-13, and FB-17)
Aircraft Units	16 Very Heavy Bomb Groups (30 UE), 11 with B-29s and five without aircraft
	Five Fighter Groups (75 UE), three with P-51s and two with P-80s
	Two Reconnaissance Groups, one (12 UE) equipped with F-9s and one (24 UE) without aircraft, and one Reconnaissance Squadron (24 UE) with F-13s
	One Air Transport Unit (10 UE) with C-54s
Active Bases	16 CONUS bases

Organization

Creation of the Air Force 18 September. The Department of the Air Force was created as a military service coequal to the Department of the Army and the Department of the Navy under the Department of Defense.

Reorganization of SAC. SAC inherited the organizational machinery of the Continental Air Forces, designed primarily to support a peacetime demobilization program. General Kenney soon found it necessary to make major adjustments throughout the command. He assigned the reorganization job to Major General Clements McMullen, who was brought in from the Eighth Air Force to become Deputy Commander. Imbued with his own ideas of economy and spurred on by an austere defense budget, which forced the Air Force to adopt a 55 rather than a 70-group program, McMullen immediately began to reorganize the command, to trim manpower at all levels, and to centralize command jurisdiction functions in Headquarters SAC. By subordinating small special staff agencies under larger general staff agencies, A-1 through A-6, he reduced from 23 to six the number of staff agencies reporting directly to the command section.

In reorganizing the headquarters, General McMullen abolished several positions. He personally took over the duties of Chief of Staff in addition to his own duties as Deputy Commander. In the move to centralize control, several units were relieved from command jurisdiction to Fifteenth Air Force and assigned directly to Headquarters SAC. These included the 311th Reconnaissance Wing; the 4th, 56th, and 82d Fighter Groups; and the 307th Bomb Group. Fifteenth Air Force was left as strictly a bomber command, controlling the fully equipped 28th, 93d, and 97th Bomb Groups and the partially equipped 92d, 98th and 301st Bomb Groups. Eighth Air Force, which was left untouched by the centralization action, controlled three B-29 groups, the 7th, 43d, and 509th, the newly activated 2d Bomb Group, the 27th and 33d Fighter Groups, and the 1st Air Transport Unit.

Hobson Reorganization Plan. In October and December, SAC combat units began reorganizing under the Hobson Plan. Under this plan, wing headquarters bearing the same numerical designation as the bombardment and fighter groups were organized and placed in a supervisory capacity over all combat and support elements on a base. Prior to this reorganization, the base or installation commander, who was often a non-flying administrator, was the immediate superior of the combat group commander.

The Hobson Plan reversed this unwieldy arrangement. It elevated the wing headquarters to the highest echelon of command and placed the wing commander in the position of directing rather than requesting that his flying activities be supported. The flying activities remained assigned to the combat group, which was normally composed of three combat squadrons and a headquarters. The group commander was directly responsible to the wing commander. The remaining functions were divided among three groups, maintenance and supply, airdrome, and medical, each of which was assigned to the wing.

Operations

Aerial mapping missions. Although the total number of personnel assigned to SAC increased only moderately during the year, the scope and volume of operations expanded considerably. The 311th Reconnaissance Wing was involved in Operation Eardrum, the aerial mapping of Greenland, and in surveying an Iceland to Alaska "top-of-the-world" air route.

Between May and October, B-29 squadrons trained on a rotational basis at Yokota Air Base, Japan.

SAC goodwill flights. SAC units flew training and "goodwill" flights to England, West Germany, Italy, France, Holland, and Belgium. A Good Neighbor Flight was made to South America in conjunction with the inauguration of the new Uruguayan President, Tomas Beretta, on 1 March. This flight of six B-29s of the 97th Bomb Group, Smoky Hill Army Air Field, Kansas, was led by Major General Charles F. Born, Commanding General of the Fifteenth Air Force.

First SAC maximum effort mission. Within the United States, SAC units flew many simulated attacks on major metropolitan areas, such as Los Angeles, Chicago, and New York. The most significant flight was over New York on 16 May, when 101 B-29s theoretically dropped their bombs in a maximum effort mission. Another 30 B-29s remained at their home bases; they were unable to take off because of maintenance and supply problems.

1948

Resources

Personnel 51,965 (5,562 officers, 40,038 airmen, 6,365 civilians)

Tactical Aircraft 837 (35 B-36, 35 B-50, 486 B-29, 131 F-51, 81 F-82, 24 RB-17, 30 RB-29, 4 RC-45, 11 C-54)

Aircraft Units Two Heavy Bomb Groups (18 UE), one with B-36s and one without aircraft

12 Medium Bomb Groups, 11 (five 45 UE and six 30 UE) equipped with B-29s and one (45 UE) equipped with both B-29s and B-50s

Two Fighter Groups (75 UE), one with F-51s and one with F-82s

Two Strategic Reconnaissance Groups (12 UE) and two Reconnaissance Squadrons (12 UE) with RB-17s and RB-29s

One Strategic Support Unit (10 UE) with C-54s

Two Medium Air Refueling Squadrons (20 UE) which were beginning to receive KB-29 tankers

Active Bases 21 CONUS bases; Effective 13 January, all installations formerly designated U.S. Army airfields were redesignated as U.S. Air Force bases. This slightly belated action was a consequence of the creation of the Department of the Air Force as one of the three coequal services of the Department of Defense, which had been effected on 18 September 1947.

Organization

Headquarters SAC moved to Offutt. Movement of Headquarters Strategic Air Command from Andrews Air Force Base, Maryland, to Offutt Air Force Base, Nebraska, was made on 9 November.

Effective 16 April, Headquarters 311th Reconnaissance Wing was redesignated Headquarters 311th Air Division, Reconnaissance. On 20 July, the organization moved from Andrews Air Force Base, Maryland, to Topeka Air Force Base, Kansas.

Operations

First B-50 delivered. On 20 February, the first B-50, "A" model serial number 46-017, was delivered to the 43d Bomb Wing at Davis-Monthan Air Force Base, Arizona. The B-50 was essentially an improved version of the B-29 Superfortress with more powerful engines and a taller fin and rudder. Like some B-29s it was equipped for inflight refueling.

First B-36 delivered. On 26 June, the first B-36, "A" model serial number 44-92004, was delivered to the 7th Bomb Group at Carswell Air Force Base, Texas. Nicknamed "The Peacemaker," the B-36 was the world's largest bomber. It measured 160 feet in length and had a wing span of 230 feet.

The early models, those delivered in 1948 and throughout most of 1949, were powered by six pusher-type, propeller-driven engines, while those models produced in late 1949 and thereafter were also outfitted with four turbojet engines paired in pods under each wing. The B-36 had many "bugs" that had to be worked out and it did not become fully operational until 1951. The introduction of the B-36 as an operational aircraft brought about a change in the designation of bombardment aircraft. The B-29s and the B-50s, which had been designated as "very heavy," were designated "medium" aircraft, while the new B-36 was designated a "heavy" bomber. The term "very heavy" was dropped.

First air refueling squadrons. In preparation for the assignment of tanker aircraft, the 43d and 509th Air Refueling Squadrons were activated at Davis-Monthan Air Force Base, Arizona, and Roswell Air Force Base, New Mexico, on 18 June. Assigned to the 43d and 509th Bomb Groups, these two squadrons were the first air refueling units in the United States Air Force. They began receiving tanker aircraft in late 1948.

These first tankers were simply B-29s modified to carry and dispense fuel in the air. Employing the British-developed system of inflight refueling, that is,

The prototype XB-36 dwarfs a B-29, the largest combat aircraft of World War II. The prototype XB-36 flew for the first time on 8 August 1946, with deliveries to SAC beginning two years later.

14

A B-29 fitted as a "flying boom" tanker refuels another B-29 during early trials of in-flight refueling for strategic bombers. The Air Force adopted the rigid-boom technique over the flexible hose concept because the boom permitted a faster fuel flow rate and higher altitude refuelings. (Boeing photo)

the use of trailing hoses and grapnel hooks, these tankers were designated KB-29Ms.

Berlin Blockade. When the Berlin Blockade began in late June, one B-29 squadron of the 301st Bomb Group was on rotational training at Furstenfeldbruck, Germany. SAC immediately ordered the 301st Group's other two B-29 squadrons to move to Goose Bay, Labrador, in preparation for movement to Germany. Two additional B-29 Groups, the 28th and 307th, were placed on alert and ordered to be ready to deploy within 12 and three hours, respectively, after notice, while the rest of the SAC force was placed on 24-hour alert. By early July, the 301st Group's other two B-29 squadrons were in place at Furstenfeldbruck. Later in the month, the 28th Bomb Group moved from Rapid City Air Force Base, South Dakota, to RAF Scampton, England, and the 307th deployed from MacDill Air Force Base, Florida, to RAF Stations Marham and Waddington, England.

Around-the-world flight. On 22 July, three B-29s of the 43d Bomb Group departed Davis-Monthan Air Force Base, Arizona, on a round-the-world flight attempt. The flight was scheduled to take 14 days, but one extra day was required due to the crash of one B-29 in the Arabian Sea. The other two aircraft made eight en route stops and completed the 20,000 mile flight in 103 hours and 50 minutes of actual flight time. The two aircraft completing the flight were "Gas Gobbler," commanded by Lt. Col. R. W. Kline, and "Lucky Lady," commanded by 1st Lt. A. M. Neal. They landed at Davis-Monthan on 6 August.

B-36 and B-50 nonstop flights to Hawaii. From 7 to 9 December, a B-36B and a B-50A, two of SAC's newly assigned bombers, completed round-trip non-stop flights from Carswell Air Force Base, Texas, to Hawaii. The B-36, assigned to the 7th Bomb Group and commanded by Major J. D. Bartlett, flew over 8,000 miles without landing in 35 hours and 30 minutes. The B-50, a 43d Bomb Group aircraft, was able to make the flight over a much longer route of 9,870 miles in 41 hours and 40 minutes. It received three inflight refuelings from KB-29 tankers of the 43d and 509th Air Refueling Squadrons.

Bombing Competition

Confronted with serious manning, supply, and administrative problems throughout its first two years of existence, the Strategic Air Command was unable to devote much time to bombing practice. Bombing accuracy fell far below desired standards. Hoping to stimulate interest in improving bombing accuracy, General Kenney decided to hold a bombing tournament, which came to be called the SAC Bombing Competition. The first competition was held at Castle Air Force Base, California, from 20 to 27 June. Ten B-29 groups participated, with each group being represented by three crews. Each crew accomplished three visual bomb releases and three radar releases from 25,000 feet altitude. Eighth Air Force's five entries swept the first five places in the competition, with the 43d Bomb Group being the top unit. Trophies were presented to the 43d and to the winning crew, a 509th Bomb Group entry commanded by 1st Lt. M. J. Jones.

1949

Resources

Personnel	71,490 (10,050 officers, 53,460 airmen, 7,980 civilians)
Tactical Aircraft	868 (390 B-29, 36 B-36, 99 B-50, 67 KB-29, 62 RB-29, 18 RB-17, 19 C-54, 11 C-82, 5 YC-97, 80 F-86, 81 F-82)
Aircraft Units	Three Heavy Bomb Groups (18 UE), one with B-36s and two in process of equipping with B-36s
	11 Medium Bomb Groups, eight (three 45 UE and five 30 UE) with B-29s and three (45 UE) with B-29s and B-50s
	Two Fighter Groups (75 UE), one with F-86s and one with F-82s
	Three Reconnaissance Groups, one (48 UE) with RB-29s, RB-17s, and C-82s and two (one 36 UE and one 18 UE) with RB-29s
	Two Strategic Support Squadrons (12 UE) with C-54s and YC-97s
	Six Air Refueling Squadrons (20 UE), two with KB-29s, two partially equipped with KB-29s, and two with no aircraft assigned
Active Bases	17 CONUS bases

Organization

On 6 April, the Strategic Air Command assumed jurisdiction over the 3d Air Division "for activities pertaining to Strategic Air Command units on rotational duty in the United Kingdom." Major General Leon W. Johnson, Commanding General of the 3d Air Division, reported directly to General LeMay on matters pertaining to the rotational units. The 3d Air Division was assigned directly to Headquarters USAF.

Second Air Force assigned to SAC. Effective 1 November, the Second Air Force was established and assigned to SAC and Headquarters Second Air Force was activated at Barksdale Air Force Base, Louisiana. It was manned from the personnel resources of Headquarters 311th Air Division, which had relocated from Forbes Air Force Base, Kansas, to Barksdale in late October. The 311th Air Division was discontinued.

Movement of Fifteenth Air Force. On 7 November, Headquarters Fifteenth Air Force began operations at March Air Force Base, California, having moved there from Ent Air Force Base, Colorado.

Operations

The Air Force gave top priority to manning and equipping the SAC force. Training of the medium-range B-29 and B-50 bombers was intensified. In order to familiarize personnel with operating conditions outside the United States, units were deployed on a rotational schedule for limited periods of time to selected overseas bases. Accuracy of high altitude bombing was substantially improved. Combat crew proficiency was raised through the system of "lead crew" training which had proved so successful during World War II. The SAC Lead Crew School was established at Walker Air Force Base, New Mexico.

The tempo of the command's operations and the constantly recurring rotational flights greatly increased SAC's effectiveness, but they subjected flight personnel to tensions that in many ways resembled those of combat.

In spite of arduous duty and extended absences from their families, about 50 percent of the command's airmen discharged at the end of their term of service reenlisted to fill their own vacancies. Although the reenlistment rate was far below the desired level, it was exceptionally high when viewed against the background of frequent movement and inadequate housing.

"Lucky Lady II" flight and first Mackay Trophy. On 2 March, the "Lucky Lady II," a B-50A (serial number 46-010) of the 43d Bomb Group, completed the first nonstop round-the-world flight, having covered 23,452 miles in 94 hours and one minute. The crew of 14 was commanded by Captain James Gallagher. Carswell Air Force Base, Texas, was the place of origin and return. "Lucky Lady II" was refueled four times in the air by KB-29 tankers of the 43d Air Refueling Squadron.

For this outstanding flight, the "Lucky Lady II" crew received numerous awards and decorations. Foremost among the awards was the Mackay Trophy, given annually by the National Aeronautic Association for the outstanding flight of the year.

B-36 record flight. On 12 March, a B-36 of the 7th Bomb Group set a long distance record when it completed a 9,600-mile flight in 43 hours and 37 minutes without refueling. The flight began and ended at Fort Worth, Texas. The aircraft, with a crew of 12, was piloted by Captain Roy Showalter.

In addition to this long-range flight demonstration, numerous test flights were conducted in order to evaluate the speed, altitude performance, weight-carrying capacity, armament, and ability of the B-36 to penetrate a realistic air defense system.

SAC continued to play an important role in the field of atomic energy through the development of strategies, tactics, techniques, and logistics to assure the most effective combat employment of atomic weapons in the national interest. Secretary of the Air Force W. Stuart Symington pointed out

18

at the end of the year: "Existence of this strategic atomic striking force is the greatest deterrent in the world today to the start of another global war."

Bombing Competition

Second competition. Convinced that the first competition had produced better bombing and a competitive spirit among crews, General LeMay decided to make it an annual affair. Held from 3 through 7 October, the second competition included 12 bomb groups: three B-36, seven B-29, and two B-50. Competition headquarters was at Davis-Monthan Air Force Base, Arizona, which was also the staging base for B-29s and B-50s. The B-36 crews operated out of their home bases. Ground rules and bombing requirements were the same as in 1948. Deprived of any major honors in the first meet, the Fifteenth Air Force's groups were ready for the 1949 competition and won top honors. The 93d Bomb Group, which had to switch to B-29s after fuel leaks developed in its new B-50s, won the unit award for bombing. A 28th Bomb Group B-36 crew won the individual crew trophy.

Spot Promotions Initiated. After the October Bombing Competition, General LeMay obtained approval to promote "on-the-spot" 237 outstanding aircraft commanders and other crew members who held the grade of first lieutenant to the temporary grade of captain. Expanded in 1950 and 1951 to include temporary promotions to major, lieutenant colonel, technical sergeant, and master sergeant, spot promotions soon became closely associated with SAC combat crew duty. They were designed to increase crew stability and proficiency and to reward outstanding combat crews. They were awarded to all eligible members of a combat crew. Winning crews in the top events of the SAC Bombing Competition usually received spot promotions. Loss of the temporary promotions by the entire crew or individual members followed failure to maintain high standards of performance.

1950

Resources

Personnel 85,473 (10,600 officers, 66,600 airmen, 8,273 civilians)

Tactical Aircraft 962 (38 B-36, 286 B-29, 196 B-50, 126 KB-29, 20 RB-36, 19 RB-50, 46 RB-29, 27 RB-45, 4 C-82, 14 C-97, 19 C-124, 167 F-84)

Aircraft Units Two Heavy Bomb Groups (18 UE) with B-36s

Two Heavy Reconnaissance Groups, one (18 UE) with RB-36s, and one (22 UE) converting from B-29s to RB-36s

12 Medium Bomb Groups, (45 UE), four with B-50s, seven with B-29s, and one with B-29s and B-50s

Two Medium Strategic Reconnaissance Groups, one (36 UE) with RB-45s and one (45 UE), with RB-29s, RB-50s, and C-82s

One RB-29 Reconnaissance Squadron (12 UE) on temporary duty with Far East Air Forces

Three Fighter Groups (75 UE), two fully equipped with F-84s and one partially equipped with F-84s

Three Strategic Support Squadrons (12 UE), one with C-97s, one with C-124s, and one partially equipped with C-124s

12 Medium Air Refueling Squadrons (eight 20 UE and four 12 UE), four fully equipped with KB-29s, five in process of equipping with KB-29s, and three with no aircraft assigned

Active Bases 19 CONUS bases and one overseas (Puerto Rico)

Organization

In early 1950, SAC's three numbered air forces differed significantly: The Eighth was primarily medium and heavy bombers, the Fifteenth concentrated on medium bombers, and the Second was devoted almost exclusively to reconnaissance activities. Expansion and the integration of B-36s and B-50s into the command created the need for a more balanced organization.

Geographic factors also prompted the need for reorganization. Headquarters Second Air Force, located in Louisiana, controlled units at Fairfield-

Suisun Air Force Base, California, while Headquarters Fifteenth Air Force, located in California, controlled units at MacDill Air Force Base, Florida.

On 1 April, SAC forces were realigned: Each numbered air force was assigned both bomber and reconnaissance aircraft and was assigned units and bases in rather specific geographical regions of the United States—the Second in the Eastern part, the Eighth in the Central region, and the Fifteenth in the Western area.

Operations

Korean War. The invasion of South Korea by North Korea on 25 June brought part of the SAC force into combat for the first time. On 3 July, General Hoyt S. Vandenberg, USAF Chief of Staff, ordered the 22d and 92d Bomb Groups to deploy their B-29s to the Far East to carry out conventional bombing operations north of the 38th parallel. The 22d went to Kadena Air Base, Okinawa, and the 92d deployed to Yokota Air Base, Japan. Upon arrival at these bases, the two groups joined the 19th Bomb Group, another B-29 unit that was assigned to the Far East Air Forces (FEAF), to form the FEAF Bomber Command (Provisional). Organized on 8 July 1950 by Lieutenant General George E. Stratemeyer, FEAF Commander, the Bomber Command was manned largely by SAC personnel. Its first commander was Major General Emmett "Rosie" O'Donnell, Jr., who was temporarily pulled out of his

A modified YRF-84F fighter approaches its "mother" RB-36D for an in-flight "landing." The concept permitted B-36s to carry a limited fighter escort on long-range missions. Note the twin turbojet pods under the B-36 wings.

B-29s enroute to targets in North Korea in 1950. All "strategic" targets in North Korea were destroyed early in the war that began in June 1950. Subsequently, the B-29s were used to bomb rail lines and "tactical" targets during the war.

job as commander of the Fifteenth Air Force to direct the bombing effort in Korea. SAC's 31st Strategic Reconnaissance Squadron (RB-29s) was on temporary duty at Kadena when the Korean conflict began. It was also attached to the FEAF Bomber Command.

FEAF Bomber Command's first strike was on 13 July, when fifty B-29s of the 19th, 22d, and 92d Bomb Groups hit Wonsan, an important North Korean port.

Three B-29 groups soon proved to be insufficient to carry out strategic bombing and provide the more immediate tactical support to ground troops. In early August, General Douglas MacArthur, Supreme Commander Allied Powers, accepted a Joint Chiefs of Staff offer of two more SAC B-29 groups, the 98th and 307th. The 98th flew its first combat mission from Yokota on 7 August, five days after leaving Fairchild Air Force Base, Washington; and the 307th launched its first strike from Kadena on 8 August, one week after leaving MacDill Air Force Base, Florida.

By late September, the strategic bombardment offensive was finished. The FEAF Bomber Command had destroyed all significant strategic targets and enemy airfields in North Korea, and General MacArthur allowed the 22d and 92d Bomb Groups to return home. The 98th and 307th remained in the Far East under the operational control of FEAF.

Effective 16 November, the 91st Strategic Reconnaissance Squadron moved without personnel and equipment from Barksdale Air Force Base, Louisiana, to Yokota Air Base, Japan. The 91st absorbed personnel and aircraft of the 31st Strategic Reconnaissance Squadron, which returned to Travis Air Force Base, California.

27th Fighter Wing in Korean War, first F-84E. On 8 November, the 27th Fighter-Escort Wing was directed to deploy to the Far East. Movement of the 27th's 75 F-84Es (the first F-84E was delivered in early 1950) was accomplished by aircraft carriers. It took approximately two weeks to make the trip from San Diego Naval Air Station, California, to Yokosuka, Japan. Upon arrival in Japan, Colonel Ashley B. Packard, the wing commander, established a rear echelon at Itazuke and took his fighters to Taegu Air Field in South Korea. The first F-84 mission was launched from Taegu on 6 December. The F-84s were used primarily for reconnaissance and close support missions. The 27th was still in the Far East at the end of the year.

Fox Able Three and the second Mackay Trophy. In September and October, the 27th Fighter-Escort Wing flew 180 F-84E fighters from Bergstrom Air Force Base, Texas, to Furstenfeldbruck, Germany. Nicknamed Fox Able Three, this gigantic ferry mission was divided into two almost equal flights. The first contingent of 90 aircraft left Bergstrom on 15 September. One aircraft aborted the flight before the first leg was completed, but the other 89 fighters continued the mission, stopping five times en route for fuel. On 18 September, 84 fighters landed at Furstenfeldbruck, having covered approximately 5,858 miles in 16 hours and three minutes, actual flying time. The other five fighters, held up for mechanical troubles at Keflavik, Iceland, landed in Germany on 19 September.

Airlifted back to Bergstrom by Military Air Transport Service aircraft, the 27th's crews began getting ready for the second phase of Fox Able Three. On 15 October, 92 F-84s took off from Bergstrom, following the same route as the first flight. Bad weather hampered this phase of the flight, and it was not until 28 October that 91 fighters (one aircraft had trouble on the first leg and landed at Memphis, Tennessee) finally landed in Germany. Colonel Cy Wilson, the 27th commander, directed the two flights as task force commander, flying in the lead aircraft.

For this flight, the 27th Wing received the Mackay Trophy for 1950. General Hoyt S. Vandenberg, USAF Chief of Staff, made the presentation to Colonel Raymond F. Rudell, the wing commander, at Bergstrom on 11 December 1951.

First KB-29P. On 1 September, the 97th Air Refueling Squadron, Biggs Air Force Base, Texas, received the first KB-29P tanker (serial number 44-86427). Prior to delivery of this aircraft, all SAC tankers were KB-29Ms, equipped with British-developed hose refueling equipment. The British system involved trailing a hose from the tanker to the receiver and transferring fuel by means of gravity. In the flying boom system, as developed by the Boeing Airplane Company, a telescopic pipe was lowered from the tanker, connected to a socket in the receiver aircraft, and the fuel transfer was made with the aid of a pump.

First RB-45. On 26 August, SAC's first RB-45, a "C" model, four-engine jet reconnaissance aircraft was delivered to the 91st Strategic Reconnaissance Wing at Barksdale Air Force Base, Louisiana.

1951

Resources

Personnel   144,525 (19,747 officers, 113,224 airmen, 11,554 civilians)

Tactical Aircraft   1,186 (340 B-29, 219 B-50, 98 B-36, 12 B-47, 187 KB-29, 21 KC-97, 38 B/RB-45, 65 RB-36, 40 RB-50, 30 RB-29, 4 C-82, 36 C-124, and 96 F-84)

Tactical Units   Three Heavy Bomb Wings (30 UE), two with B-36s and one in process of converting from B-29s to B-36s

19 Medium Bomb Wings (45 UE), 12 with or equipping with B-29s (including two TDY with FEAF), four with B-50s, one with both B-29s and B-50s, one with B-47s and one converting from B-29s to B-47s

Two Heavy Reconnaissance Wings (30 UE) with RB-36s

Four Medium Reconnaissance Wings, one (45 UE) with RB-50s, RB-29s, and C-82s, one (45 UE) with B/RB-45s, and two (36 UE) with or equipping with RB-29s

One RB-29 Reconnaissance Squadron (12 UE) TDY with FEAF

Three Fighter Escort Wings (75 UE) being equipped with F-84Gs

16 Medium Air Refueling Squadrons (13 20 UE and three 12 UE), ten with KB-29s, two partially equipped with KC-97s, and four without aircraft assigned

Three Strategic Support Squadrons (12 UE) with C-124s

Active Bases   22 in CONUS and 11 overseas (North Africa, Puerto Rico, and United Kingdom)

Organization

In January, Headquarters USAF approved General LeMay's proposal to reorganize SAC's combat forces at base level. Prior to this reorganization, each combat wing consisted of a wing headquarters, a combat group of tactical squadrons, a maintenance and supply group, an air base group (air base groups had replaced airdrome groups in 1948), and a medical group. This standard structure existed in most combat wings, including those on both single and double-wing bases. On two-wing bases (these were becoming more

24

prevalent with the tremendous expansion brought about by the Korean conflict) the senior wing commander exercised control over the junior wing commander.

Under the new system which was effected in February, each wing was reorganized to consist of a wing headquarters; a combat group of tactical squadrons and, where applicable, air refueling and aviation squadrons; three maintenance squadrons; and an air base group of housekeeping squadrons, a supply squadron, and a medical squadron. Medical and maintenance and supply groups were discontinued. The combat group headquarters was not discontinued at this time but continued to exist in name only. The wing commander served as the combat group commander. Gradually, the term "group" was falling into disuse and the term "wing" was becoming more popular.

Air divisions assigned. In conjunction with this reorganization, SAC received authority from Headquarters USAF to organize air division headquarters on double-wing bases and to operate only one air base group on these installations. Composed of approximately 17 people, representing the functions of command, operations, materiel, and administration, the air division headquarters served as an intermediate echelon of command between the combat wings and the numbered air force headquarters. The air division commander exercised direct control over the two wing commanders and the air base group commander. The first five air divisions were organized on 10 February at the indicated bases: 4th, Barksdale; 6th, MacDill; 12th, March; 14th, Travis; and 47th, Walker.

5th Air Division established in French Morocco. Effective 14 January, Headquarters 5th Air Division was activated at Offutt Air Force Base, Nebraska, with Major General Archie J. Old, Jr., being named commander. General Old began forming a new staff and making preparations to move to French Morocco in June. Instead of going directly to French Morocco as planned, General Old and his staff were sent to England in late April to open Headquarters 7th Air Division, the staff of which had been lost in a plane crash.

In late May, with a new 7th Air Division commander in place and another staff being formed, General Old and his staff moved on to Rabat, French Morocco, where Headquarters 5th Air Division was opened on 14 June. The primary mission of the new air division headquarters was to conclude negotiations for use of bases in French Morocco, to monitor construction of these facilities, and to supervise training of SAC units at these bases.

7th Air Division established in England. After the outbreak of hostilities in Korea, the U.S. and Great Britain decided jointly to build a number of bases in England to accommodate USAF aircraft. Pending completion of these bases, other airfields were earmarked for use by SAC. These included several bases that had been supporting SAC rotational units since 1948. In early 1951, Headquarters USAF approved General LeMay's proposal to establish an air division headquarters in England to monitor the base development program and to supervise SAC units rotating there. Effective 20 March, Headquarters 7th Air Division was activated at South Ruislip, London, England. On the same day, at Headquarters SAC, a briefing was held for Brigadier General Paul T. Cullen, who had been selected to command the new air division.

General Cullen and about 50 members of his new staff left for England on 23 March, but they were lost en route when their C-124 crashed somewhere in the Atlantic. On 26 April, Major General Archie J. Old, Jr. assumed temporary command of the 7th Air Division and opened the new headquarters. General Old remained in this position until 24 May, at which time Major General John P. McConnell assumed command and began forming a new staff. General Old and his people moved on to French Morocco.

Operations

Korean War. Throughout 1951, the 98th and 307th Bomb Wings remained in the Far East under the operational control of the FEAF Bomber Command. Their B-29s were engaged primarily in attacking bridges, marshalling yards, supply and troop camps, and various other targets. The 91st Strategic Reconnaissance Squadron also remained in the Far East and supported the FEAF Bomber Command effort with photographic and surveillance missions. In June, the 27th Fighter-Escort Wing began training its replacements from other major air commands and by the end of August it had returned to Bergstrom, leaving its F-84Es in the Far East. Upon returning to Bergstrom, the 27th began making preparations to receive the F-84G Thunderjet fighters (first aircraft delivered on 23 September), which were equipped for inflight refueling. No additional SAC fighter wings were called upon to serve in Korea.

First B-47. Committed to production in 1949, the B-47 medium bomber first made its appearance in the 306th Bomb Wing on 23 October. On that day, Colonel Michael N. W. McCoy, Wing Commander, flew the first operational B-47 (serial number 50-008) from the Boeing Airplane Company plant at Wichita, Kansas, to MacDill Air Force Base, Florida. On 19 November, in a ceremony at MacDill, this B-47 was named "The Real McCoy." The B-47 was a revolutionary aircraft. It was powered by six jet engines, strut-mounted under the wings, and was categorized as a 600-mph bomber. The authorized complement was 45 for each wing.

First KC-97. The 306th Air Refueling Squadron, MacDill Air Force Base, Florida, was the first unit to begin equipping with the KC-97 tanker. Its first aircraft, a KC-97E, was delivered on 14 July. Outfitted with a flying boom and loaded with fuel tanks, the four-engine, propeller-driven KC-97 could fly fast enough to match the minimum speed of the B-47. It transformed the B-47 into an intercontinental bomber. Each KC-97 squadron was authorized 20 aircraft. Serial number of first KC-97 was 51-183.

Rotational training. Seven medium bombardment groups, two strategic reconnaissance groups, and selected squadrons deployed to overseas locations, with most of the units going to the United Kingdom. However, rotations were also made to Japan, Guam, and Tripoli.

First B-36 flight to England. On 16 January, the first B-36s arrived in England. Six B-36Ds of the 7th Bomb Wing, Carswell Air Force Base, Texas, landed at Lakenheath RAF Station, England, having staged through Limestone Air Force Base, Maine. The flight returned to Carswell on 20 January.

First B-36 flight to French Morocco. On 3 December 1951, the first B-36s arrived in French Morocco. Six B-36s of the 11th Bomb Wing landed at Sidi Slimane, French Morocco, having flown nonstop from Carswell Air Force Base, Texas. The flight returned on 6 December.

The Daedalian Trophy. For its flying safety record in 1951, the Strategic Air Command received the Daedalian Trophy. First awarded for calendar year 1950, this trophy was established by the Order of the Daedalians, an organization of World War I pilots. It was administered by Headquarters USAF and awarded to the major air command with the lowest aircraft accident rate.

Bombing Competition

Third competition. With abatement of the threat of World War II developing out of the Korean conflict, the bombing competition was resumed and expanded. To stress the importance of celestial navigation and to enable reconnaissance wings to compete, navigation was included as a separate phase of the meet. MacDill Air Force Base, Florida, served as the competition headquarters as well as the staging base for medium aircraft, while Carswell Air Force Base, Texas, was the staging base for heavy aircraft. Held from 13 through 18 August, the third meet was attended by 45 SAC crews representing 12 bomb wings and three reconnaissance wings and flying B/RB-36, B/RB-29, and B-50 aircraft.

Two Royal Air Force crews using standard B-29s also participated. Bombing requirements included three visual releases and four radar runs, and the navigation phase included three night celestial navigation legs.

Fairchild Trophy awarded. In addition to numerous trophies for separate fields of bombing and navigation, the Fairchild Trophy was presented for the first time to the outstanding bomb unit in the combined fields of navigation and bombing. Named in honor of General Muir S. Fairchild, a former USAF vice chief of staff, this trophy bore the inscription: "In honor of General Muir S. Fairchild and to promote national security, this trophy is presented to the Strategic Air Command by the Hughes Aircraft Company." The first recipient of this trophy was the 97th Bomb Wing, a B-50 unit of the Eighth Air Force.

1952

Resources

Personnel	166,021 (20,282 officers, 134,072 airmen, 11,667 civilians)
Tactical Aircraft	1,638 (154 B-36, 114 RB-36, 62 B-47, 224 B-50, 39 RB-50, 230 F-84, 417 B-29, 18 RB-29, 36 C-124, 22 RB-45, 4 C-82, 179 KB-29, 139 KC-97)
Tactical Units	Five Heavy Bomb Wings (30 UE), three with B-36s, one being equipped with B-36s, and one without aircraft
	Four Heavy Strategic Reconnaissance Wings (30 UE), two with RB-36s and two in process of being equipped with RB-36s
	21 Medium Bomb Wings, eleven (45 UE); five with B-50s, two with B-29s, and four equipping with B-47s, and ten (30 UE), nine with and one equipping with B-29s (includes two TDY with FEAF)
	Five Medium Strategic Reconnaissance Wings, three (45 UE), one with RB-50s and C-82s, one with RB-45s, and one to be equipped with RB-47s, and two (30 UE) with B/RB-29s
	One squadron (10 UE) of RB-29s TDY with FEAF
	Four Strategic Fighter Wings (75 UE) with F-84s
	Three Strategic Support Squadrons (12 UE) with C-124s
	19 Medium Air Refueling Squadrons (20 UE), ten with KB-29s, six with KC-97s, and three in process of equipping with KC-97s
Active Bases	26 in CONUS and 10 overseas (Puerto Rico, North Africa, and United Kingdom)

Organization

Combat groups inactivated. Effective 16 June, all bombardment, fighter, and reconnaissance groups were inactivated. Simultaneously, the combat squadrons were assigned to the wings. For all practical purposes, the combat groups had ceased to exist in 1951 when the wings were reorganized and the group headquarters were left unmanned.

Medical groups activated. Effective 14 February, medical squadrons were redesignated medical groups and assigned to wings.

SAC insignia approved. On 4 January, Headquarters USAF approved an insignia for the Strategic Air Command. The design for the insignia evolved out of a contest conducted in late 1951. With a $100 U.S. Defense Bond as the prize, the contest drew entries from 60 military and civilian personnel scattered throughout the command. The judges, Generals LeMay, Power, and Kissner, selected the design submitted by Staff Sergeant R. T. Barnes, who was assigned to the 92d Bomb Wing, Fairchild Air Force Base, Washington. The significance of the insignia:

> The blue sky is representative of the Air Force operations. The arm and armor is a symbol of strength, power and loyalty and represents the science and art of employing far-reaching advantages in securing the objectives of war. The olive branch, a symbol of peace, and the lightning flashes, symbols of speed and power, are qualities underlying the mission of the Strategic Air Command.

Operations

Korean War. B-29s of the 98th and 307th Bomb Wings and RB-29s of the 91st Strategic Reconnaissance Squadron continued to support the UN efforts in Korea.

RB-45 flight Alaska to Japan and third Mackay Trophy. On 29 July, a 91st Strategic Reconnaissance Wing RB-45C (serial number 48-042), commanded by Major Louis H. Carrington, made the first nonstop, transpacific flight from Elmendorf Air Force Base, Alaska, to Yokota Air Base, Japan. This flight, which was made possible by two KB-29 inflight refuelings, earned Major Carrington and his two-man crew the Mackay Trophy for 1952.

Fox Peter One and Fox Peter Two. The use of inflight refueling as a means of speeding up mass flights of fighters was tested during two significant deployments to Japan.

In early July, Colonel David C. Schilling led 58 F-84Gs of the 31st Fighter-Escort Wing from Turner Air Force Base, Georgia, to Misawa and Chitose Air Bases, Japan. This flight, nicknamed Fox Peter One, was the first mass fighter deployment to be supported by inflight refueling. KB-29 tankers of the 2d and 91st Air Refueling Squadrons refueled the fighters on the first leg of the flight from Turner to Travis Air Force Base, California. The second refueling, conducted by tankers of the 2d, 91st, and 93d Air Refueling Squadrons, was carried out on the Travis to Hawaii leg of the flight. From Hickam Air Force Base, Hawaii, the fighters island-hopped to Japan, with en route stops at Midway, Wake, Eniwetok, Guam, and Iwo Jima.

It took approximately ten days to complete that portion of the flight from California to Japan. In late 1950, it had taken over two weeks to move the 27th Wing's F-84Es by aircraft carriers from California to Japan, and it took several more days to uncrate the fighters and get them ready for combat. For this 10,919-mile flight, the 31st Wing was awarded the Air Force Outstanding Unit Award in early 1954. The 31st was the first unit to receive this USAF award. The 27th Fighter-Escort Wing was selected to replace the 31st Wing in Japan under the 90-day rotational training program. Nicknamed Fox Peter Two, this deployment involved 75 F-84Gs under the command of Colonel Donal J. M. Blakeslee. The 7,800-mile flight, much shorter than Fox Peter One, began at Bergstrom Air Force Base, Texas, on 3 October and terminated at Misawa Air Base, Japan, on 14 October. En route stops were made at Travis, Hickam, and Midway, and inflight refuelings were accomplished on the Travis to Hickam and the Midway to Misawa legs. Aircraft were grounded one day at Hickam and held over another day at Midway because of bad weather.

The Daedalian Trophy. For the second consecutive year, the Strategic Air Command had the lowest aircraft accident rate in USAF. It received the Daedalian Trophy.

Bombing Competition

Held from 13 through 18 October, the fourth Bombing Competition involved ten B-29, five B-50, and four B-36 wings. Medium bombers staged out of Davis-Monthan Air Force Base, Arizona, and the heavy bombers operated out of Walker Air Force Base, New Mexico. The Royal Air Force entered the meet with four crews, two flying Washington (B-29) medium bombers and two flying Lincoln heavy bombers. Ground rules were altered somewhat for this meet. Each SAC wing sent only two crews instead of three as in previous years. Eighth Air Force's 97th Bomb Wing and Fifteenth's 93d Bomb Wing, both flying B-50Ds, tied for the Fairchild Trophy, and Major General Thomas S. Power, Vice Commander of SAC, flipped a coin to decide which would gain possession of the trophy for the first half of the ensuing year. The 93d won this privilege.

Reconnaissance Competition

Planned as an annual event, the initial SAC Reconnaissance, Photo, and Navigation Competition was held between 23 October and 1 November. Twelve crews representing four wings, two RB-36, one RB-50, and one RB-45, participated. The RB-45s and RB-50s staged out of Lockbourne Air Force Base, Ohio, while the RB-36s flew from Rapid City Air Force Base, South Dakota. The 28th Strategic Reconnaissance Wing, an RB-36 unit of the Eighth Air Force, had the highest score in the combined areas of photo-reconnaissance and navigation and won the P. T. Cullen Award. This impressive sterling silver trophy was named in honor of Brigadier General Paul T. Cullen. Prior to his death in a C-124 crash on 23 March 1951, General Cullen had been one of the leading photo-reconnaissance authorities in the United States.

1953

Resources

Personnel 170,982 (19,944 officers, 138,782 airmen, 12,256 civilians)

Tactical Aircraft 1,830 (185 B-36, 137 RB-36, 329 B-47, 138 B-50, 38 RB-50, 235 F-84, 110 B-29, 8 RB-29, 49 C-124, 143 KB-29, 359 KC-97, 88 YRB-47, 11 RB-47)

Tactical Units Six Heavy Bomb Wings (30 UE) with B-36s

Four Heavy Strategic Reconnaissance Wings (30 UE) with RB-36s

22 Medium Bomb Wings, 17 45 UE, seven with and six in process of equipping with B-47s, three equipped with B-50s, and one with B-29s, and five 30 UE with B-29s (includes two TDY with FEAF)

Five Medium Strategic Reconnaissance Wings, four 45 UE, one equipped with RB-50s, two partially equipped with YRB-47s, and one partially equipped with RB-47s, and one (30 UE) partially equipped with RB-29s

One RB-29 Strategic Reconnaissance Squadron (10 UE) TDY with FEAF

Six Strategic Fighter Wings (75 UE), five with F-84s and one with no aircraft

28 Medium Air Refueling Squadrons (20 UE), 20 equipped or equipping with KC-97s and eight equipped or equipping with KB-29s

Four Strategic Support Squadrons (12 UE) with C-124s

Active Bases 29 CONUS bases and 10 overseas (North Africa, Puerto Rico, and United Kingdom)

Organization

Although SAC continued to grow throughout 1953, this growth was tempered somewhat by the USAF wing program being reduced slightly from a goal of 143 to 120 combat wings.

Strategic fighter wings. Effective 20 January, SAC's four fighter-escort wings (12th, 27th, 31st, and 508th) were redesignated strategic fighter wings in recognition of their developing an atomic bombing capability. Two additional F-84 strategic fighter wings were activated in 1953.

Korean War. The 98th and 307th Bomb Wings and the 91st Strategic Reconnaissance Squadron continued to serve in a combat capacity with the FEAF Bomber Command until the fighting ended on 27 July. With exception of FEAF's own 19th Bomb Wing, the FEAF Bomber Command was composed entirely of SAC units and was commanded by SAC personnel. Through the three-year conflict, the Bomber Command's B-29s flew 21,328 effective combat sorties, including 1,995 reconnaissance sorties and 797 psychological warfare sorties. The B-29s dropped 167,100 tons of bombs on various targets ranging from front line enemy troop emplacements to airfields on the banks of the Yalu River. The 98th and 307th Bomb Wings and the 91st Strategic Reconnaissance Squadron were included in the South Korean Presidential Unit Citation that was bestowed upon the FEAF Bomber Command, Provisional. These units remained in the Far East throughout 1953.

Operations

Operation Longstride and fourth Mackay Trophy. The deployment of F-84Gs across the Atlantic became equally important to SAC operations, particularly since the F-84 had been converted to a fighter-bomber with a nuclear bombing capability. Nicknamed Operation Longstride, the first mass nonstop fighter flight over the Atlantic was a dual mission conducted by the 31st and 508th Strategic Fighter Wings, located at Turner Air Force Base, Georgia. These wings were assigned to the 40th Air Division.

The first phase of Operation Longstride began at 0743, ZULU time, on 20 August, when Colonel David C. Schilling, 31st Wing Commander, led a flight of nine F-84s off the runway at Turner Air Force Base. One Thunderjet spare accompanied the flight as far as Savannah, Georgia, and then returned home, while the main flight of eight continued on its way to North Africa. Three inflight refuelings by KC-97 aircraft were required to get the fighters across the Atlantic.

Operating out of Kindley Air Force Base, Bermuda, KC-97s of the 305th Air Refueling Squadron furnished the first two refuelings, while KC-97s of the 26th Air Refueling Squadron positioned at Lajes Air Force Base, Azores, provided the third refueling. The formation of eight landed at Nouasseur Air Base, French Morocco, approximately 10 hours and 20 minutes after leaving Turner. After spending a few days at Lakenheath RAF Station, England, the flight returned to Turner on 2 September.

Within a few minutes after Colonel Schilling's flight was on its way to North Africa, the second phase of Operation Longstride began. This flight of 20 Thunderjets was led by Colonel Thayer S. Olds, 40th Air Division Commander, and Colonel Cy Wilson, 508th Wing Commander. Using the North Atlantic route, the 508th's fighters were also refueled three times, once over Boston by KB-29 tankers of the 100th Air Refueling Squadron, once near Labrador by KC-97s of the 26th Air Refueling Squadron, and once near Iceland by KC-97s of the 306th Air Refueling Squadron, which was TDY to England. The main flight of 17 landed at Lakenheath RAF Station, England,

A trio of Washingtons in flight with RAF markings during the early 1950s. Britain borrowed 88 B-29 and B-29A aircraft from USAF storage to provide a strategic strike capability pending arrival of jet-propelled bombers. The first aircraft were flown to the United Kingdom in March 1950. A total of eight RAF bomber squadrons plus a special signals unit, No. 192 Squadron, flew the Washingtons. By the end of 1954, most had been retired from the bomber role, although a few continued in RAF service until early 1958. (Ministry of Defence photo)

approximately 11 hours and 20 minutes after leaving Turner. Three Thunderjets were held over one day at Keflavik before completing the flight. The flight returned to Turner on 12 September.

The 40th Air Division received the Mackay Trophy for Operation Longstride.

First B-47 wing deployment. From 22 January through 20 February, the 306th Bomb Wing, the first B-47 wing, was subjected to an exhaustive exercise, Sky Try, in which the B-47 was tested under simulated combat conditions.

Shortly after completion of Sky Try, SAC decided the 306th was ready for a 90-day rotational training mission to England. B-29 and B-50 wings had been rotating there since 1948. The 306th's deployment originated at MacDill Air Force Base, Florida, and involved equal flights of 15 B-47s on 3, 4, and 5 June. The B-47s staged through Limestone Air Force Base, Maine, where they remained overnight before going on the next day. They landed at Fairford RAF Station on the 4th, 5th, and 6th of June. The B-47 record of five hours and 38 minutes over the 3,120 mile route from Limestone to Fairford, established by Colonel Michael N. W. McCoy, 306th Wing Commander, on a 6 April indoctrination flight was broken nine times before the deployment was over. The best time was recorded by the last B-47 to land on 6 June. It completed the trip in five hours and 22 minutes, averaging about 575 miles per hour. The 306th Air Refueling Squadron's KC-97s, crammed with support personnel and equipment, deployed on the same dates as the B-47s. They stopped overnight at Ernest Harmon Air Force Base, Newfoundland, and then flew on to Mildenhall RAF Station.

When the 90-day rotation was over, the 305th Bomb Wing, SAC's second B-47 wing, was ready to begin rotational training. As the 305th arrived in England—the bombers went to Brize Norton and the tankers to Mildenhall—

the 306th began returning home. The return flight was nonstop, with the 306th Air Refueling Squadron's tankers providing one inflight refueling for the bombers shortly after leaving England. By the time the 305th's tour was over the 22d Wing had completed the transition to B-47s and was ready to rotate. The policy of maintaining at least one B-47 wing in England at all times would continue until early 1958.

RB-45s to FEAF. On 1 December, SAC's last four RB-45s, which had been assigned to a detachment of the 91st Strategic Reconnaissance Wing at Yokota Air Base, Japan, were transferred to FEAF.

Operation Big Stick. In August and September, the 92d Bomb Wing made the first mass B-36 flight to the Far East, visiting bases in Japan, Okinawa, and Guam. Nicknamed Operation Big Stick this 30-day exercise came shortly after the termination of hostilities in Korea and demonstrated the U.S. determination to use every means possible to maintain peace in the Far East.

Bombing Competition

Seventeen bomb wings sent two crews each to the Fifth Bombing Competition, which was held between 25 and 31 October. For the first time in the competition's history spare aircraft were prohibited. This placed emphasis upon high quality maintenance. The B-47 made its first appearance in the competition, with seven participating wings staging out of Davis-Monthan Air Force Base, Arizona. Walker Air Force Base, New Mexico, was the staging base for ten wings, four B-36, four B-50, and two B-29.

Maintenance was extremely good as there was only one ground abort. Results of the competition for the Fairchild Trophy were extremely close, with the winner not being decided until the last mission was flown. The 92d Bomb Wing, a B-36 unit of the Fifteenth Air Force, won the trophy with 1,687 points, edging out its nearest competitor, a B-50D wing, by 20 points. The B-50D wings fared extremely well in the meet, with the other three units taking third, fourth, and fifth places. The B-47 fell below expectations in several aspects, particularly navigation, and of the seven wings competing, one placed ninth, one tenth, and the other five brought up the rear.

Reconnaissance Competition

Ellsworth Air Force Base, South Dakota, was the staging base for this second competition, which was held from 18 through 27 October. The fourteen competing crews represented seven wings (four RB-36, one RB-50, one RB-29, and one YRB-47). The 5th Strategic Reconnaissance Wing, an RB-36 unit of the Fifteenth Air Force, won the P. T. Cullen Award.

1954

Resources

Personnel	189,106 (23,447 officers, 151,466 airmen, 14,193 civilians)
Tactical Aircraft	2,640 (209 B-36, 133 RB-36, 795 B-47, 78 B-50, 12 RB-50, 411 F-84, 54 C-124, 91 KB-29, 592 KC-97, 265 YRB/RB-47)
Tactical Units	Six Heavy Bomb Wings (30 UE) with B-36s
	Four Heavy Strategic Reconnaissance Wings (30 UE) with RB-36s
	24 Medium Bomb Wings (45 UE), 17 with B-47s, two with YRB-47s, two with B/RB-50s, and three equipping with B-47s
	Four Medium Reconnaissance Wings (45 UE) with RB-47s
	Six Strategic Fighter Wings (75 UE), four with F-84Fs, one with F-84Gs, and one converting from F-84Gs to F-84Fs, (the F-84F, a swept-wing fighter, was produced *after* the F-84G, a straight-wing model)
	32 Medium Air Refueling Squadrons (20 UE), 28 with KC-97s and four with KB-29s
	Four Strategic Support Squadrons (12 UE) with C-124s
Active Bases	30 in the CONUS and 11 overseas (Puerto Rico, North Africa, and United Kingdom)

Organization

Activation of 3d Air Division on Guam. In early 1954, Headquarters USAF directed that the FEAF Bomber Command be discontinued and that its three B-29 wings be returned to the United States and equipped with B-47s. On 18 June, concurrent with the inactivation of the FEAF Bomber Command at Yokota Air Base, Japan, Headquarters 3d Air Division was activated at Anderson Air Force Base, Guam, and assigned to SAC. The new division was manned largely with people from the FEAF Bomber Command. Brigadier General Joseph D. Caldara, the last commander of FEAF Bomber Command, became the first 3d Air Division commander. The 3d Air Division's primary responsibility was to control all SAC units operating in the Far East and to monitor the construction of bases and facilities to support these operations. Throughout 1954, the 3d Air Division operated as a tenant at Anderson, with logistical support being provided by FEAF's 6319th Air Base Wing. It was not until April 1955 that Anderson was transferred from FEAF to SAC.

Operations

With the acquisition of additional B-47s and KC-97s, SAC operations increased tremendously. Approximately 142,000 air refueling hookups were effected during the year. Operational training flights were conducted throughout the world, with more than 3,400 individual transatlantic and transpacific crossings being made by various types of aircraft.

Nonstop B-47 Flight to Japan. On 21 June, Major General Walter C. Sweeney, Jr., Fifteenth Air Force Commander, led a flight of three 22d Bomb Wing B-47s on a nonstop flight from March Air Force Base, California, to Yokota Air Base, Japan, a distance of 6,700 miles in less than fifteen hours. This flight, supported by two inflight refuelings by KC-97s, was the longest point-to-point, nonstop B-47 flight to that date. It marked the first appearance of the B-47 in the Far East.

Operation Leap Frog and fifth Mackay Trophy. On 6 and 7 August, two B-47s of the 308th Bomb Wing flew a 10,000-mile nonstop flight from Hunter Air Force Base, Georgia, to French Morocco and back to Hunter. Each aircraft was refueled four times by KC-97s. One made the flight in 24 hours and four minutes, while the other took 25 hours and 23 minutes.

This flight was conducted in conjunction with Operation Leap Frog, in which the two B-47 wings of the 38th Air Division tested a new concept of intercontinental bombing operations. In this test, the B-47s took off from Hunter, flew a simulated bombing mission, and then recovered at a base in North Africa. Prior to this time, SAC's concept of war operations was based on deployment of its bombers to forward bases where they would land, refuel, and subsequently take off for bombing. The Mackay Trophy was awarded to the 308th Bomb Wing for this flight.

B-47 record flight. On 17 November, Colonel David A. Burchinal, Commander of the 43d Bomb Wing, took off from Sidi Slimane, French Morocco, in a B-47 and directed his course toward Fairford RAF Station, England, where his wing was on 90-day rotational training. Bad weather prevented him from landing at Fairford, and he returned to French Morocco only to find bad weather at Sidi Slimane. With the assistance of nine inflight refuelings, Colonel Burchinal kept flying until the weather finally cleared at Fairford on 19 November. In the meantime, he had established a distance and endurance jet flying record of 21,163 miles in 47 hours and 35 minutes.

First B-36 wing rotation to Guam. On 15 and 16 October, the 92d Bomb Wing, A B-36 unit stationed at Fairchild Air Force Base, Washington, deployed to Anderson Air Force Base, Guam, for a 90-day rotational training assignment. This was the first time an entire B-36 wing had been deployed to an oversea base.

RB-36 Wings Given Bombardment Mission. Effective 16 June, SAC's four RB-36 equipped heavy strategic reconnaissance wings were given a primary mission of bombing. They retained limited reconnaissance as a secondary mission.

Bombing Competition

The sixth competition was held from 23 through 29 August. Competition ground rules were essentially the same as in 1953, with each wing being represented by two crews. Fifteen B-47 wings staged out of Barksdale Air Force Base, Louisiana, while six B-36 and two B-50 wings staged out of Walker Air Force Base, New Mexico. One RB-36 crew of the 28th Strategic Reconnaissance Wing was allowed to compete on the basis of its outstanding bombing performance in the 1954 SAC Reconnaissance Navigation Competition. The B-36 wings continued to dominate the meet as they finished "one-two-three" in both bombing and navigation. The 11th Wing, an Eighth Air Force B-36 unit, won the Fairchild Trophy. While the B-47 wings showed remarkable improvement in navigation, their bombing was still below that of the B-36 wings. The 305th Bomb Wing made the best showing of any B-47 wing by placing fourth in the Fairchild Trophy competition. The 28th Wing's lone entry tied for first place in crew navigation and placed 11th in crew bombing.

Reconnaissance and Navigation Competition

The 1954 (third) competition was held at Fairchild Air Force Base, Washington, from 9 through 14 August, and included two crews from each participating wing. In addition to the photo and navigation requirements, which were common to all participants, the four RB-36 wings also conducted radar bombing in recognition of their newly-acquired bombing mission. The RB-36 units monopolized the competition by capturing first place in the six events in which they competed against the two RB-47 wings. The 28th Strategic Reconnaissance Wing, the Eighth Air Force's lone entry, won the P. T. Cullen Award for the best combined score in photo and navigation.

1955

Resources

Personnel 195,997 (26,180 officers, 151,595 airmen, 18,222 civilians)

Tactical Aircraft 3,068 (205 B-36, 133 RB-36, 1,086 B-47, 234 RB-47, 12 RB-50, 18 B-52, 679 KC-97, 82 KB-29, 51 C-124, 568 RF/F-84)

Tactical Units 11 Heavy Bomb Wings, nine (30 UE) with B/RB-36s, and two (45 UE), one equipped and one equipping with B-52s

27 Medium Bombardment Wings (45 UE), 22 with B-47s and five equipping with B-47s

Five Medium Reconnaissance Wings (45 UE) with RB-47s

39 Medium Air Refueling Squadrons (20 UE), 33 with KC-97s, two equipping with KC-97s, four with KB-29s

Six Strategic Fighter Wings (75 UE) with F-84Fs

One Strategic Reconnaissance Wing, Fighter (75 UE), equipping with RF-84Fs and RF-84Ks

One Light Strategic Reconnaissance Squadron without aircraft assigned

Four Strategic Support Squadrons (12 UE) with C-124s

Active Bases 37 CONUS and 14 oversea bases (in Puerto Rico, North Africa, United Kingdom, and Guam)

Organization

Numbered Air Force realignment and move of Eighth Air Force. By 1955, the New York-New England area was becoming increasingly important to SAC operations. Dow and Loring Air Force Bases, Maine, had been supporting F-84 and B-36 wings, respectively, for some time; Westover Air Force Base, Massachusetts, which became a SAC installation on 1 April, was being groomed to support tankers and bombers; and new B-47/KC-97 bases were being built in Portsmouth, New Hampshire, and Plattsburgh, New York. In line with this expansion, SAC realigned its three numbered air forces and, effective 13 June, moved Headquarters Eighth Air Force from Carswell Air

A B-47B at altitude. The sleek lines, high speed, and minimal defensive armament of the Stratojet marked a radical change in strategic bomber design. Note the lack of unit markings; the SAC markings of a shield with a blue field, star-studded, had not yet been introduced. (Boeing photo)

Force Base, Texas, to Westover. Following this realignment, SAC's numbered air forces were generally responsible for units and bases in the following geographical sections of the country: Second—Southeast (including Texas); Eighth—Northeast and Central; Fifteenth—Southwest and West.

Organization of air refueling wings. Prior to 1955, the majority of air refueling squadrons were collocated with and assigned to bomber and fighter wings. A few squadrons were physically separated from their parent wings and located on non-SAC bases. In 1955, SAC departed from these practices and organized two air refueling wings, the 4060th at Dow and the 4050th at Westover, and assigned two KC-97 squadrons to each of them. Establishment of these two wings signaled the beginning of a program to concentrate air refueling strength in the Northeast. The buildup would continue well into the 1960s and would provide SAC with increased B-47 deployment mobility over the North Atlantic.

Redesignation of RB-36 strategic reconnaissance wings. Effective 1 October, SAC's four heavy strategic reconnaissance wings were redesignated heavy bombardment wings in recognition of the conversion of the RB-36 from a reconnaissance to a bomber aircraft. They retained "latent" reconnaissance capability.

The B-47—like other U.S. strategic bombers—had to be forward based or have multiple in-flight refuelings to reach the Soviet Union. This is a tanker's eye view of a B-47 being refueled at the rate of 600 gallons per minute. (Boeing photo)

Operations

Rotational training. SAC's mobility and flexibility were demonstrated by the rotation of entire combat wings, air refueling squadrons, and smaller units to various overseas bases for periods of time ranging from a few days to three months. Entire B-47 wings and KC-97 air refueling squadrons were periodically rotated to the North African bases of Benguerir and Sidi Slimane. Other B-47 wings, some with and others without air refueling squadrons were rotated to England, using such bases as Lakenheath, Upper Heyford, Fairford, Mildenhall, and Brize Norton. In early May, the 27th Strategic Fighter Wing deployed to Sturgate for a 90-day tour, marking the first time since 1951 that a fighter wing had been deployed to Great Britain.

To support these mass flights of B-47s and F-84s across the Atlantic, KC-97 squadrons were maintained on a rotational basis at such places as Goose Air Base, Labrador, Ernest Harmon Air Force Base, Newfoundland, and Thule Air Base, Greenland. At the same time, B-36 wings were deploying to Nouasseur Air Base, French Morocco; Burtonwood and Upper Heyford RAF Stations in the United Kingdom; and Anderson Air Force Base, Guam. The

Alaskan bases, Elmendorf and Eielson, were also busy supporting KC-97, B-47, and F-84 aircraft.

First B-52 delivered. The 93d Bomb Wing, located at Castle Air Force Base, California, was the first wing to be equipped with the B-52 Stratofortress. On 29 June, Brigadier General William E. Eubank, Jr., the wing commander, flew the first aircraft (a "B" model, serial number 52-8711) from the Boeing factory at Seattle, Washington, to Castle. Powered by eight turbojet engines, the B-52B had a gross takeoff weight of around 420,000 pounds and a maximum speed of 650 mph. It could fly above 50,000 feet. While it had an unrefueled range of 6,000 miles (substantially less than later models), its actual range was unlimited since it could be refueled in the air. Most of the B-52Bs produced were assigned to the 93d Bomb Wing during the period from June 1955 to March 1956.

Last B-50. On 20 October, the last B-50 ("D" model serial number 49-330) assigned to the 97th Bomb Wing, Biggs Air Force Base, Texas, was phased out of the SAC force.

Bombing Competition

With the B-50 phase out almost completed, there were only two types of aircraft, B-47s and B-36s, entered in the seventh bombing competition, held from 24 through 30 August. March Air Force Base, California, was the staging base for 23 B-47 wings. The ten B/RB-36 wings (RB-36s were no

More B-47s were produced than any other jet-propelled "strategic" bomber except for its Soviet counterpart, the TU-16 Badger. Some 2000 Badgers were built; almost half that number remain in Soviet service, but all the B-47s are long gone. This was a scene at the Boeing plant in Wichita, Kansas, in 1950.

The B-47 had a tandem landing gear with outriggers extending from the twin engine nacelles. A braking parachute was "popped" to help slow the aircraft for landing. This view shows the first of two XB-47s. (Boeing photo)

The Martin RB-57D provided the Strategic Air Command with a high-altitude, multi-sensor aircraft before the U-2 became available. The -D and later -F reconnaissance variants of the Canberra could easily be identified by their oversize wings and engine nacelles. The Canberra was the only foreign aircraft design to be adopted by the USAF after World War II.

longer classified as reconnaissance aircraft) staged out of Fairchild Air Force Base, Washington. Each wing was again represented by two crews.

The most significant factor in this competition was the tremendous improvement made by B-47s in both bombing and navigation. For the first time, a B-47 unit, Fifteenth Air Force's 320th Bomb Wing, won the Fairchild Trophy.

Reconnaissance Competition

With the conversion of all RB-36s to bombers, the fourth reconnaissance competition became an all RB-47 affair, with five strategic reconnaissance wings sending 15 crews. It was held at Lockbourne Air Force Base, Ohio, from 24 through 30 September. Eighth Air Force's 91st Strategic Reconnaissance Wing won the P. T. Cullen Award.

Missiles

Throughout the early 1950s, the Strategic Air Command became more and more involved in the development of missiles as a means of increasing its long-range striking power. The actual development and testing of missiles remained in the hands of contractors and the Air Research and Development Command, but SAC maintained close liaison with the various programs by presenting its requirements, offering technical assistance, and attending various meetings, conferences, and field tests.

By 1955, the Snark, a subsonic intercontinental missile (ICM), and the Rascal, an air-to-ground missile designed to be launched from a bomber, had undergone tests.

After President Dwight D. Eisenhower had placed the highest national priority on the development of missiles, Headquarters USAF accelerated the development of the Snark as well as the Navaho, another intercontinental missile, and the Atlas, an intercontinental ballistic missile (ICBM). Furthermore, in November, Headquarters USAF directed SAC to work closely with the Air Research and Development Command in establishing an "initial operational capability" for ICBMs, after which they would be turned over to SAC for operational use.

1956

Resources

Personnel	217,279 (27,871 officers, 169,170 airmen, 20,238 civilians)
Tactical Aircraft	3,188 (247 B/RB-36, 97 B-52, 254 RB-47, 1,306 B-47, 16 RB-57, 51 C-124, 750 KC-97, 74 KB-29, 366 F-84, 57 RF-84F)
Tactical Units	11 Heavy Bomb Wings, seven (30 UE) equipped with B/RB-36s, one (45 UE) with B-52s, and three (45 UE) in process of equipping with B-52s
	28 Medium Bomb Wings (45 UE), 27 with B-47s and one, the last wing to be equipped with B-47s, in the final stages of equipping
	Five Medium Strategic Reconnaissance Wings (45 UE) with RB-47s
	One Light Strategic Reconnaissance Wing being equipped with RB-57s
	Five Strategic Fighter Wings (75 UE) with F-84Fs
	One Strategic Reconnaissance Fighter Wing (75 UE) being equipped with RF-84s
	40 Medium Air Refueling Squadrons (20 UE), 36 with KC-97s and four with KB-29s
	Four Strategic Support Squadrons (12 UE) with C-124s
Active Bases	36 in the CONUS and 19 overseas (in Puerto Rico, North Africa, United Kingdom, and Guam)

Operations

B-52 conversion program. By the end of March, the 93d Bomb Wing, located at Castle Air Force Base, California, was fully equipped with 30 B-52s (it was later reorganized to operate 45 B-52s). Shortly thereafter, the 93d's 4017th Combat Crew Training Squadron, which had been activated on 8 January 1955, began training crews to man additional B-52 wings. The 42d Bomb Wing, Loring Air Force Base, Maine, was the second wing to be equipped with B-52s, with the first aircraft being delivered in June. The 42d was the first B-36 unit to convert to B-52s as the 93d had been a B-47 outfit prior to conversion. The 99th Wing, Westover Air Force Base, Massachusetts, the third B-52 wing, began receiving aircraft in December.

The Suez Crisis. In reacting to the Suez Crisis from mid-November to mid-December, KC-97 tankers were concentrated into tanker task forces at key bases in the northern part of the United States and overseas at Greenland, Newfoundland, and Labrador, on rotational training assignments. The oversea rotational training force consisted of one B-47 wing in England, one B-47 wing in North Africa, and one B-36 wing in Guam.

Quick Kick B-52 flight. On 24 and 25 November, in an operation called Quick Kick, four B-52s of the 93d Bomb Wing joined four B-52s of the 42d Bomb Wing for a nonstop flight around the perimeter of North America. The most publicized individual flight was that of a 93d Bomb Wing B-52 piloted by Lieutenant Colonel Marcus L. Hill, Jr. Colonel Hill's flight, which originated at Castle and terminated at Baltimore, Maryland, covered approximately 13,500 nautical miles in 31 hours and 30 minutes. The flight demonstrated both the value and the limitations of the KC-97 tanker. Without the four in-flight refuelings, the flight would have been impossible; but, according to Colonel Hill, flying time could have been reduced by at least three hours by using the KC-135, an all-jet tanker that was being developed by the Boeing Airplane Company.

Power House and Road Block. Within a two-week period ending on 11 December, SAC executed the largest and most complex B-47 and KC-97 exercise to date. In two related exercises, called Power House and Road Block, more than 1,000 B-47s and KC-97s flew gigantic simulated combat missions over North America and the Arctic. The KC-97s participating in these exercises were furnished by the strategically positioned tanker forces that had been formed in mid-November.

Last B-47 delivered. On 24 October, the last production-line B-47, an "E" model, serial number 53-6244, was delivered to the 40th Bomb Wing, Schilling Air Force Base, Kansas.

Last KC-97 delivered. On 16 November, the last production-line KC-97, a "G" model, serial number 53-3816, was delivered to the 98th Air Refueling Squadron, Lincoln Air Force Base, Nebraska.

First RB-57 delivered. On 31 May, the first RB-57 (a "D" model, serial number 53-3973), the reconnaissance version of the British-designed B-57 Canberra light bomber, was delivered to the 4080th Strategic Reconnaissance Wing at Turner Air Force Base, Georgia. The 4080th had received a B-57 ("C" model serial number 53-3842) for a trainer on 1 May.

Bombing and Reconnaissance Competition

The competition grew along with SAC, and in 1956, the largest one to date was held with 42 wings participating in a combined bombing, navigation, and reconnaissance meet. It was held from 24 through 30 August, with Lockbourne Air Force Base, Ohio, hosting 27 B-47 and five RB-47 wings and Loring Air Force Base, Maine, serving as the staging base for eight B/RB-36 and two B-52 wings. Each participant sent two crews. For the first time, jet reconnaissance aircraft (RB-47s) competed against bombers in bombing and

The KC-97 was the basic SAC tanker aircraft during the 1950s. From 1951 onward 888 C-97 and KC-97 aircraft were delivered to the USAF. Shown here is KC-97G number 53-3816, the last of the design to be delivered. Note the "chin" radar pod, underwing fuel tanks, B-29 type tail fin, and refueling boom in the stowed position. (Boeing photo)

navigation and, at the same time, competed against each other in the reconnaissance competition, the fifth in this series of meets. The B-36s of Second Air Force's 11th Bomb Wing won the Fairchild Trophy by beating out the B-47s, which had snared the trophy in 1955, and the newly-assigned B-52s that were competing in the event for the first time. Eighth Air Force's 91st Strategic Reconnaissance Wing won the P. T. Cullen Award.

First competition. Nicknamed Operation Left Hook, the first and only SAC fighter competition was held from 25 October to 14 November. Five strategic fighter wings competed, with each wing entering 36 F-84s. Although the requirement for all wings was the same, only one wing at a time flew in the competition, which was staged out of Offutt Air Force Base, Nebraska. The top wing in the competition, Second Air Force's 506th Strategic Fighter Wing, won the newly-established Auton Trophy. This trophy was named for Brigadier General Jesse Auton, a former SAC Deputy Director of Operations for fighters, who was killed in a B-25 crash at Offutt on 30 March 1952. Planned as an annual rotational trophy, such as the Fairchild and P. T. Cullen awards, the Auton Trophy was awarded only once because SAC disposed of its fighter wings in 1957.

Missiles

In March, Headquarters USAF gave SAC and the Air Research and Development Command responsibility for developing an initial operational capability with the Thor and assigned SAC the responsibility for deploying this missile to England and bringing it to a combat ready status after which it would be turned over to the Royal Air Force.

In July, Headquarters SAC announced that it was entering the planning phase of its missile program and that it was primarily interested in the Thor, Navaho, and Snark subsonic intercontinental missiles, and Titan and Atlas intercontinental ballistic missiles. Other missiles being developed for possible use by SAC included Goose, Rascal, and Quail. Carried aboard a B-47, the Rascal was a supersonic guided missile that was designed to penetrate enemy target defenses from a distance and make its carrier less vulnerable to the enemy defense system.

Through the early 1950s, all branches of service were involved in developing various types of missiles for military use. As these systems evolved through competition, there were changes in strategic concepts and different views on how the systems should be used and which branch of service should control them. On 26 November, Secretary of Defense Wilson issued a memo, which was designed to "improve the effectiveness of our overall military establishment, to avoid unnecessary duplication of activities and functions and to utilize most effectively the funds made available by the people through Congress."

The Air Force assigned intercontinental ballistic missiles. While Secretary Wilson treated several areas of responsibility in his directive, he was concerned primarily with clarifying the roles of the Army, Navy, and Air Force in regard to the development and use of various types of missiles. He gave USAF sole responsibility for operational employment of land-based intermediate range ballistic missiles and reconfirmed the earlier assignment to USAF of sole responsibility for operational employment of intercontinental ballistic missiles. Since the missiles being developed in these categories at that time were for strategic bombing purposes, SAC was assured a primary role in USAF's future missile program. At the same time, Secretary Wilson gave the Army responsibility for using land-based surface-to-air defensive missiles and surface-to-surface tactical missiles with ranges less than 200 miles. The Navy was given similar responsibility for ship-based intermediate range ballistic missiles.

1957

Resources

Personnel   224,014 (29,946 officers, 174,030 airmen, 20,038 civilians)

Tactical Aircraft   2,711 (127 B/RB-36, 243 B-52, 1,285 B-47, 216 RB-47, 24 RB-57, 50 C-124, 742 KC-97, 24 KC-135)

Aircraft Units   11 Heavy Bomb Wings, four (30 UE) with B/RB-36s, five (45 UE) with B-52s, and two (one 45 UE and one 30 UE) equipping with B-52s

One Heavy Strategic Wing (15 UE) without aircraft assigned

28 Medium Bomb Wings (45 UE) with B-47s

Four Medium Strategic Reconnaissance Wings (45 UE) with RB-47s

One Light Strategic Reconnaissance Wing with RB-57s and U-2s

35 Medium Air Refueling Squadrons (20 UE) with KC-97s

Five Heavy Air Refueling Squadrons (20 UE), one with and four equipping with KC-135s

Four Strategic Support Squadrons (12 UE) with C-124s

Missile Unit   One Strategic Missile Squadron (ICM-Snark) without missiles

Active Bases   38 CONUS and 30 overseas (Puerto Rico, United Kingdom, North Africa, Guam, Spain, Greenland, Newfoundland, and Labrador)

Organization

Sixteenth Air Force assigned to SAC. On 1 July, SAC assumed jurisdiction over the Sixteenth Air Force in Spain. Since its activation on 15 July 1956 at Torrejon Air Base, near Madrid, Headquarters Sixteenth Air Force had operated as a special organization under the direct control of Headquarters USAF. Its primary responsibility had been to monitor the construction of Spanish bases to be used by SAC bombers. In addition to Torrejon, the Sixteenth controlled three other bases in Spain. Concurrent with its assignment to SAC, the Sixteenth assumed command jurisdiction over the Fifth Air Division and its bases in French Morocco. It was not fully capable of taking over control of SAC operations in North Africa at this time. Second Air Force retained this responsibility throughout 1957.

First B-47s to Spain. On 23 and 24 July, the 40th Bomb Wing, which was on 90-day rotation in the United Kingdom, sent 15 B-47s to Zaragoza Air Base, Spain, for a short exercise.

Acquisition of NEAC Bases. The United States Air Force's base requirements in Newfoundland, Greenland, and Labrador were intensified in 1950 after the outbreak of the Korean war. The Joint Chiefs of Staff established the Northeast Air Command (NEAC), with headquarters at Pepperrell Air Force Base, Newfoundland, and gave it a twofold responsibility: to defend, in cooperation with ADC, the northeast approaches to the United States and to develop bases and support facilities to support SAC units deploying through or staging out of them. In the gigantic simulated combat mission associated with the Suez crisis in late 1956, four of these bases supported large tanker task forces. The success of the exercise strengthened Headquarters USAF's earlier decision that the bases no longer required close supervision by a major air command in the immediate area. Accordingly, NEAC was discontinued on 1 April, and its resources were reassigned to ADC and SAC. ADC received two bases and SAC received six. SAC, in turn, immediately placed its six bases under the jurisdiction of Eighth Air Force.

Relocation of headquarters SAC. In January, Headquarters SAC completed its move into the newly-built Control Center. This nine million dollar facility (subsequent additions raised the value far beyond this initial cost) actually consisted of two interconnected structures: an administration building, consisting of three stories above ground and a basement, and an underground three-story command post. Access from one facility to the other was provided by a tunnel. The underground facility, which was designed to be safe from anything but a direct hit by a high yield nuclear weapon, housed the Control Room and related communications equipment and computers designed to maintain close contact with SAC forces throughout the world. Giant panels of maps and boards were used to depict the exact disposition and operational status of the entire force. Prior to this move, which commenced in December 1956, Headquarters SAC had operated out of several buildings that had housed the Glenn L. Martin bomber plant in World War II.

Operations

One-Third ground alert. By 1957, the Soviet Union was showing progress in developing intercontinental ballistic missiles. In order to provide an effective and immediate retaliatory strike force, SAC devised the ground alert concept whereby it would maintain approximately one-third of its aircraft on ground alert, with weapons loaded and crews standing by for immediate takeoff. SAC's combat wings were neither manned nor organized to support this new concept. In order to determine what was needed to develop and maintain a one-third alert force, SAC conducted three extensive tests. The first test was conducted by the 38th Air Division (two B-47 wings and two KC-97 air refueling squadrons) at Hunter Air Force Base, Georgia, from November 1956 through March 1957. Nicknamed Operation Try Out, this test proved the concept to be feasible, but it pinpointed numerous areas where changes would be required to make it practical. In order to perfect these areas, SAC conducted two additional tests, Operation Watch Tower by the 825th Air Division (two B-47 wings, and one KC-97 air refueling squadron) at Little Rock Air Force Base, Arkansas, from April to November, and Operation Fresh Approach by the 9th Bomb Wing, a B-47 wing complete with one KC-97 air refueling squadron, at Mountain Home Air Force Base, Idaho, in September.

Convinced that the concept would work, although there still remained many organizational and operational details to be worked out, General Power directed that ground alert operations commence at several CONUS and overseas bases on 1 October.

Reflex Action. In July, Reflex Action commenced with four Second Air Force wings sending five B-47s each to Sidi Slimane Air Base, French Morocco. This new system of operation was based on the premise that a few crews and aircraft on ground alert at overseas bases would be more effective than maintaining entire wings at these bases on 90-day rotational training assignments. If successful, SAC planned to replace the 90-day wing rotational program at all overseas bases with Reflex Action, with aircraft and crews being frequently rotated from bases in the United States. On 1 October, the Reflex bombers at Sidi Slimane were placed on ground alert along with those aircraft at CONUS bases.

B-47 record flight from Guam to French Morocco. On 14 August, a 321st Bomb Wing B-47 under the command of Brigadier General James V. Edmundson, SAC Deputy Director of Operations, made a record nonstop flight from Anderson Air Force Base, Guam, to Sidi Slimane Air Base, French Morocco, a distance of 11,450 miles in 22 hours and 50 minutes. The flight required four refuelings by KC-97 tankers.

B-47 equipping program completed. In February, the 100th Bomb Wing, Pease Air Force Base, New Hampshire, was fully equipped with B-47s. The 100th Bomb Wing, the famous "Bloody Hundredth" of World War II, was the 29th and last SAC wing to be equipped with B-47s (one of these wings, the 93d, had converted to B-52s in 1955).

First KC-135. The first KC-135 (serial number 55-3127) all-jet tanker was delivered to the 93d Air Refueling Squadron, Castle Air Force Base, California, on 28 June. Jet tankers drastically reduced the time involved in air refueling operations. With a KC-97, the bomber had to slow down and descend to lower altitudes than normal to effect the hookup. With a KC-135, the refueling rendezvous could be conducted at the bomber's normal speed and altitude. It was estimated that the total flying time on the B-52 around-the-world flight, Operation Power Flite, could have been cut by five to six hours if KC-135s had been available.

By the end of the year, two additional air refueling squadrons, the 42d at Loring Air Force Base, Maine, and the 99th at Westover Air Force Base, Massachusetts, had commenced receiving KC-135s.

First U-2. On 11 June, the first U-2 (serial number 56-6696), was delivered to the 4080th Strategic Reconnaissance Wing, Laughlin Air Force Base, Texas.

Operation Power Flite, B-52 around-the-world flight and sixth Mackay Trophy. From 16 to 18 January, three B-52Bs of the 93d Bomb Wing made a nonstop, round-the-world flight. The flight was under the command of Major General Archie J. Old, Jr., Fifteenth Air Force Commander. General Old rode aboard the lead plane, Lucky Lady III, serial number 53-0394, which was commanded by Lieutenant Colonel James H. Morris. Colonel Morris had served as copilot on the Lucky Lady II flight in 1949.

Five aircraft, including two spares, started the trip from Castle Air Force Base, California. One bomber, unable to take on fuel at the first inflight refueling rendezvous with KC-97s, landed at Goose Air Base, Labrador; while the second spare continued on with the main flight until after receiving the second KC-97 inflight refueling over Casablanca, French Morocco, at which time it left the flight and landed at Brize Norton RAF Station, England, according to plan. With the aid of three more KC-97 inflight refuelings, the Lucky Lady III and its two companions completed the trip without incident.

The only deviation from the plan occurred at the end of the trip. The flight plan called for the lead aircraft to land at March Air Force Base, California, and the other two to land at their home base. Because of fog at Castle, however, all three bombers landed at March, after having completed the 24,325-mile flight in 45 hours and 19 minutes, less than one-half the time required on the Lucky Lady II flight.

General LeMay was on hand to personally congratulate the crews and to present each with the Distinguished Flying Cross. General LeMay said the flight was a "demonstration of SAC's capabilities to strike any target on the face of the earth."

Subsequently, the National Aeronautic Association recognized Operation Power Flite as the outstanding flight of 1957 and named the 93d Bomb Wing as recipient of the Mackay Trophy.

Beginning of B-47 Phase Out Program. On 14 October 1957, the first RB-47E type aircraft (serial number 51-5272), was sent to the storage facility at Davis-Monthan Air Force Base, Arizona. The aircraft was assigned to the 91st Strategic Reconnaissance Wing, Lockbourne Air Force Base, Ohio. It was inactivated on 8 November 1957. With inactivation of the 91st, the number of wings equipped with B-47 type aircraft was reduced to 32—28 bomb wings and four strategic reconnaissance wings.

Strategic Fighter Force. Because of technological advances, changes in tactics, and the programmed phase out of the slow-moving B-36, SAC's strategic fighter wings were no longer required for escort duty. One wing was transferred to TAC on 1 April, three were transferred to TAC on 1 July, and two were inactivated on 1 July.

Phase out of KB-29s. SAC also disposed of its KB-29 tankers, which had been used primarily to support F-84s. On 25 November, the last two KB-29Ps (serial numbers 44-83956 and 44-84075) assigned to the 27th Air Refueling Squadron, Bergstrom Air Force Base, Texas, were transferred to the USAF aircraft storage facility at Davis-Monthan Air Force Base, Arizona.

KC-135 world record flights by General LeMay. On 11 and 12 November, General Curtis E. LeMay, Vice of Chief of Staff, piloting a KC-135 (serial

A rare formation of strategic bombers: These are B-47s during a display of U.S. strategic air power over Washington, D.C. Once the most numerous aircraft in SAC, all were discarded by the end of 1967. Later, the Navy withdrew some from storage for electronic warfare development programs (designated EB-47E). (Boeing photo)

number 55-3126), established an official world record nonstop, nonrefueled flight of 6,322.85 miles from Westover Air Force Base, Massachusetts, to Buenos Aires, Argentina. Total flying time was 13 hours, 2 minutes and 51 seconds. By flying around the hump of Brazil, he added approximately 1,000 miles to the direct airline distance from Westover to Buenos Aires.

On the return flight of 13 November, General LeMay flew a more direct route, 5,204 miles, and established a world course speed record from Buenos Aires to Washington, D.C., averaging 471.451 mph in 11 hours, 3 minutes, 57.38 seconds. The LeMay flights were part of Operation Long Legs, the nickname for the U.S. Air Force's participation in Argentina's Annual Aeronautics Week.

B-52 nonstop flight. In another phase of Operation Long Legs that was conducted on 16 and 17 November, six B-52s of the 42d Bomb Wing flew a 10,600 mile nonstop, round-trip flight from Homestead Air Force Base, Florida, to Buenos Aires and back to Plattsburgh Air Force Base, New York. This flight was made possible by three inflight refuelings, two by KC-97s and one by a KC-135.

Bombing and Reconnaissance Competition

Once again, the bombing and reconnaissance competitions were combined and held from 30 October through 6 November. Pinecastle Air Force Base, Florida, was the staging base for 28 B-47 and five RB-47 wings, while Carswell Air Force Base, Texas, provided the same services for five B-36 and five B-52 wings. After an absence of several years, the Royal Air Force entered the competition with two Vulcan and two Valiant aircraft and crews.

With exception of the crew and wing navigation awards, which were won by a B-36 wing, the B-47 units won all the major events in which they were pitted against B-36 units. The Fairchild Trophy was won by the 321st Bomb Wing, a Second Air Force unit. The 321st also won the McCoy Trophy, a one-time award for the best B-47 wing. This trophy was named after Colonel Michael N. W. McCoy, who was serving as 321st Wing Commander at the time of his death in a B-47 aircraft accident on 9 October 1957. This accident also took the life of Group Captain John Woodroffe, commander of the Royal Air Force contingent that was in the United States for the SAC Bombing Competition.

Eighth Air Force's 26th Strategic Reconnaissance Wing won the P. T. Cullen Award.

Missiles

Snark program. In March, Headquarters USAF selected Presque Isle Air Force Base, Maine, as the first Snark base. In May, Headquarters USAF selected Patrick AFB, Florida, as the Snark training and testing site. Effective 15 December, SAC activated the 556th Strategic Missile Squadron at Patrick AFB. In July, Headquarters USAF cancelled the air-breathing Navaho missile in order to concentrate upon higher priority ballistic missiles.

1958

Resources

Personnel 258,703 (34,112 officers, 199,562 airmen, 25,029 civilians)

Tactical Aircraft 3,031 (22 B-36, 380 B-52, 1,367 B-47, 176 RB-47, 182 KC-135, 780 KC-97, 51 C-124, 54 F-86, 19 RB-57)

Aircraft Units 11 Heavy Bomb Wings, nine (six 45 UE and three 30 UE) equipped or equipping with B-52s, and two 30 UE) phasing out their B/RB-36s

Three Heavy Strategic Wings (15 UE), two equipped and one partially equipped with B-52s, and 11 without aircraft in various stages of development

28 Medium Bomb Wing (45 UE) with B-47s

Three Medium Strategic Reconnaissance Wings (45 UE) with RB-47s

One Combat Crew Training Wing (90 UE) with B/RB-47s

34 Medium Air Refueling Squadrons (20 UE) with KC-97s

One KC-97 Combat Crew Training Wing (40 UE)

14 Heavy Air Refueling Squadrons (eight 20 UE and six 10 UE), seven fully equipped and one partially equipped with KC-135s and six with no aircraft

Four Strategic Support Squadrons (12 UE), three with C-124s and one without aircraft

One Light Strategic Reconnaissance Wing with RB-57s and U-2s

Two Fighter Interceptor Squadrons (24 UE) with F-86s (these squadrons were located in Spain)

Missile Units Three Atlas D squadrons (one three UE, one six UE, and one nine UE), and one Snark squadron (no UE), none equipped with missiles

54

Budget and Financial Status
(FY 58, as of 30 June 1958)

Operations and Maintenance	$560,539,000, includes supplies, communications, civilian pay, minor equipment purchased, and aviation petroleum, oil and lubricants (POL)
Assets	$12,092,568,000, includes real property, inventories, equipment, and weapon systems
Operating Expenses	$1,316,350,000, includes O&M listed above, military pay, military family housing, troop subsistence, and procurement of equipment
Active Bases	39 in CONUS and 25 overseas (United Kingdom, Spain, French Morocco, Guam, Greenland, Labrador, Newfoundland, and Puerto Rico)

Organization

Reorganization to support the One-third Alert. The reorganization of tactical wings and air base groups to support the one-third ground alert concept was completed at 11 bases in the latter part of the year. The new organizational structure evolved out of the extensive service tests (Try Out, Watch Tower, and Fresh Approach) conducted in 1956 and 1957. It differed appreciably from the old structure that had been in effect since 1951. Since ground alert emphasized combat-ready aircraft and combat-ready crews, a deputy commander for maintenance and a deputy commander for operations were authorized to assist the wing commander, replacing the directorate system that had been in operation since 1951. Within each B-47 wing, a fourth bomb squadron was activated since alert operations logically fell into a four-cycle arrangement: ground alert duty, flight planning, flying, and a day off.

In order to bring similar functions under a single control, organizational maintenance squadrons were organized to replace periodic maintenance squadrons and to absorb all maintenance functions previously performed by the tactical squadrons. Air base groups were redesignated combat support groups in an attempt to more closely relate support functions to the ground alert requirement. Tactical hospitals were inactivated and USAF hospitals were discontinued. Medical functions were consolidated into medical groups, which were assigned directly to the wing commanders on single wing bases and to air division headquarters on double wing bases. Undoubtedly, the centralization of maintenance was the most important element of the reorganization. The 42d Bomb Wing's experience in Head Start I also substantiated the need for centralized maintenance in support of an airborne alert.

The reorganization started at two bases, Little Rock Air Force Base, Arkansas, and Lincoln Air Force Base, Nebraska, on 1 September. Beginning on 1 October, one base in each of the three numbered air forces would be reorganized on the first of each month.

The reorganization also applied to the B-52 wings, except for the activation of a fourth tactical squadron.

Organization of strategic wings. While the ground alert force was rapidly approaching its one-third objective, SAC was taking other actions to insure a survivable and responsive bomber force. During the expansion of the early and mid-1950s, bases had become overcrowded, with some of them supporting as many as 90 B-47s and 40 KC-97s. The first B-52 wings were also extremely large, composed of 45 bombers and 15 or 20 KC-135s, all situated on one base. As the Soviet missile threat became more pronounced and warning time became less, SAC bases presented increasingly attractive targets. Several KC-97 squadrons were separated from their parent B-47 wings and relocated to northern bases. The B-47 dispersal program was a long-range one and would be effected primarily through the phase out of wings in the late 1950s and early 1960s.

With the B-52 force, which was still growing, dispersal became an active program in 1958. Basically, the B-52 dispersal program called for the larger B-52 wings already in existence to be broken up into three equal-sized wings of 15 aircraft each, with two of them being relocated, normally to bases of other commands. In essence, each dispersed B-52 squadron became a strategic wing. This principle would also be followed in organizing and equipping the remainder of the B-52 force. The entire force was established at 42 squadrons by Headquarters USAF in 1958. Ideally, each B-52 wing would have one air refueling squadron of 10 or 15 aircraft.

By the end of 1958, SAC had activated 14 strategic wings, but only three had aircraft assigned. The others were in various stages of development, with some having only a headquarters and one officer and one airman authorized.

5th Air Division inactivated. On 15 January, Headquarters 5th Air Division was inactivated and the responsibility for directing operations in North Africa was transferred from Second Air Force to Sixteenth Air Force.

Fighter interceptor squadrons assigned to SAC. On 5 July and 1 September, SAC acquired the 497th and the 431st Fighter Interceptor Squadrons from the Air Defense Command and the US Air Forces in Europe, respectively. Located in Spain, these two squadrons were equipped with F-86 fighters.

Operations

The Lebanon Crisis. In mid-July, the President of Lebanon, fearful of Soviet-sponsored intervention, asked the United States for help. President Eisenhower took action by sending ground, naval, and air forces to the area. He also ordered SAC to place its bomber forces on alert. Generation of additional ground alert forces (SAC was already in the process of building up its ground alert forces to the one-third level) began immediately. Within a few hours, over 1,100 aircraft were poised and ready for takeoff. A full show-of-force was maintained for several days. When it became clear that the Russians did not intend to invade Lebanon, the alert forces were gradually phased down.

Taiwan Crisis. Inspired by Russia's actions in the Middle East, the Chinese Communists began a heavy artillery bombardment of the islands of Quemoy and Matsu, off the China coast. Again the U.S. took swift action by ordering the Seventh Fleet to the Formosa Strait. In support of the U.S. position of protecting Taiwan, SAC increased the strength of its ground alert forces at Anderson Air Force Base, Guam, and alerted several bomb wings for possible contingency operations in the Pacific. Since the Commander-in-Chief of Pacific Command did not anticipate having to use the SAC forces, they soon returned to their normal configuration.

One-Third Alert and expanded combat crew training. With adoption of the one-third alert concept, additional combat ready crews were required. On 15 May and 15 June, SAC converted the 70th and 90th Strategic Reconnaissance Wings' primary missions from reconnaissance to B-47 crew training to supplement the flow of crews from the Air Training Command's 3520th Combat Crew Training Wing, McConnell Air Force Base, Kansas.

On 1 July, SAC assumed responsibility for all B-47 and KC-97 combat crew training from the Air Training Command: the 3520th was transferred to SAC and redesignated the 4347th Combat Crew Training Wing and the 4397th Air Refueling Wing was organized at Randolph Air Force Base, Texas, assigned to SAC, and given the job of training KC-97 crews.

Termination of B-47 rotational training. The success of the ground alert program and Reflex Action prompted SAC to discontinue the 90-day rotational training program that had characterized B-47 operations since 1953. The 100th Bomb Wing, the last B-47 wing to become combat ready, was the last B-47 wing to perform the 90-day rotational assignment. This assignment was conducted at Brize Norton RAF Station, United Kingdom, from early January to early April. Upon departure of the 100th, B-47 Reflex operations began at Brize Norton. Reflex had already commenced in early January at Greenham Common and Fairford.

Airborne alert test. From 15 September through 15 December, the 42d Bomb Wing, Loring Air Force Base, Maine, successfully conducted a B-52 airborne alert test, nicknamed Head Start I.

Operation Top Sail KC-135 Record Flights. On 27 and 29 June, two KC-135s of the 99th Air Refueling Squadron broke the existing speed records in flights from New York to London and return. The actual official records were established by the lead aircraft, "Alfa" (serial number 56-3630), which was piloted by Major Burl B. Davenport, were as follows: New York to London—five hours, 29 minutes, and 14.64 seconds; London to New York—five hours, 53 minutes, and 12.77 seconds (the record-making flights originated at Westover Air Force Base, Massachusetts). A third KC-135, also scheduled to participate in the flight, crashed on takeoff at Westover. Among the fifteen casualties were Brigadier General Donald W. Saunders, 57th Air Division Commander, and Lieutenant Colonel George M. Broutsas, 99th Air Refueling Squadron Commander.

KC-135 weight lifting record. On 24 September, another KC-135 of the 99th Air Refueling Squadron, Westover Air Force Base, Massachusetts, piloted by Captain William H. Howell, captured the official world weight-lifting record by lifting a payload of 78,089.5 lbs. to an altitude of 2,000 meters (approximately one and one-quarter mile). This broke the old record of 44,214 lbs. airlifted by a Russian TU-104A jet transport on 6 September. The KC-135 carried a load of nails, concrete block, and steel plate.

KC-135 record flight Operation Jet Stream. On 7 and 8 April, a KC-135 (serial number 56-3601) of the 93d Air Refueling Squadron, Castle Air Force Base, California, established two official world records: distance in a straight line without refueling, 10,229.3 miles, Tokyo to Lajes, Azores; speed, 492.262 mph, Tokyo to Washington, D.C., in 13 hours, 45 minutes and 46.5 seconds. The KC-135 was piloted by Brigadier General William E. Eubank, Jr., 93d Bomb Wing Commander.

KC-135 world record flight. On 17 September, Captain Charles E. Gibbs, flying a KC-135 of the 92d Air Refueling Squadron, Fairchild Air Force Base, Washington, established four world records: distance in a closed circuit without refueling, 3,125.56 statute miles; speed for 2,000 kilometers, 589.278 mph, closed circuit with 2,204.6, 4,409.2, 11,023, and 22,046 lb. payloads; speed for 5,000 kilometers, 587.136 mph, closed circuit; and speed for 5,000 kilometers, 587.136 mph, closed circuit, with 2,204.6, 4,409.2, 11,023, and 22,046 lb. payloads.

B-52 world record flights. On 26 September, two B-52Ds of the 28th Bomb Wing, Ellsworth Air Force Base, South Dakota, established world speed records over two different routes: speed for 10,000 kilometers in a closed circuit without payloads, 560.705 mph, Lieutenant Colonel Victor L. Sandacz, pilot; speed for 5,000 kilometers in a closed circuit without payload, 597.675 mph, Captain Cholett Griswold, pilot.

Cheney Award. On 28 April, a 341st Bomb Wing B-47 took off from Dyess Air Force Base, Texas, on a training flight. The B-47 carried a three-man crew and a navigator-instructor. Approximately three hours out of Dyess, there was an explosion in one of the engines and the aircraft commander gave the proper order to bail out. He and the navigator parachuted to safety. As 1st Lieutenant James E. Obenauf, the copilot, prepared to leave the plane through the escape hatch (his ejection seat had failed to work), he noticed Major Joseph Maxwell, the instructor-navigator, was unconscious. Unable to revive Major Maxwell, Lieutenant Obenauf stayed with the crippled aircraft, which was in danger of burning. From the back-seat position, he flew the B-47 back to Dyess and successfully landed it. For this heroic act, Lieutenant Obenauf received the Cheney Award and Distinguished Flying Cross.

Bombing Competition

The tenth competition was held from 13 through 18 October, with RB/B-47s and the Royal Air Force's Valiants staging out of March Air Force Base, California, and the B-52s and the B-36s staging out of Castle Air Force Base, California. SAC participants included four crews from each of 38 bomb wings (two B-36, 26 B-47, and 10 B-52) and one RB-47 strategic reconnaissance wing. The Royal Air Force sent eight crews. Once again the competition was dominated by B-47 wings which won the first three places in combined bombing and navigation. The Fairchild Trophy went to Second Air Force's 306th Bomb Wing.

SAC participation in RAF competition. For the first time, SAC participated in the RAF Bombing Competition, held from 14 through 20 May. SAC's representative was the 92d Bomb Wing, which deployed six B-52s and crews, including two alternate aircraft and crews, to Brize Norton RAF Station. The 92d won five of the six awards for which it was eligible to compete.

Missiles

Missile launches. Total missiles and space systems launched during the year from Vandenberg Air Force Base, California: SAC—0; Other Agencies—1.

1st Missile Division assigned to SAC. Air Force's strategic missiles were developed to the point where they could start the transition from the research and development to the operational stage. As part of this transition, the 1st Missile Division, located at Cooke Air Force Base (renamed Vandenberg in October), California, was transferred from Air Research and Development Command to SAC. The transfer was effected on 1 January, and Major General David Wade assumed command of the division the following day. Included in the transfer was the 704th Strategic Missile Wing, which had been activated as USAF's first missile wing on 1 July 1957. The 704th had a dual mission of training missile crews for other units and attaining an operational capability with the Atlas ICBM. It had one Atlas D squadron, the 576th Strategic Missile Squadron assigned. Activated on 1 April, the 576th had a dual responsibility of maintaining an Atlas D alert force and providing training for other SAC Atlas units.

SAC MIKE established. On 1 January, the Office of Assistant CINCSAC (SAC MIKE) was organized at Inglewood, California. Designed to serve as an extension of Headquarters SAC, this office was responsible for working closely with the Air Force Ballistic Missile Division and providing SAC with the latest techniques and information on ballistic missiles and related programs.

Atlas and Titan Wings activated. The first Atlas wing was activated at Francis E. Warren Air Force Base, Wyoming, on 1 February under the designation of 4320th Strategic Missile Wing. In an inactivation and activation transaction on 23 February, the designation was changed to 706th Strategic Missile Wing (ICBM Atlas). Later in the year, two Atlas D squadrons were activated and assigned to the 706th. On 25 September, the first Titan unit, the 703d Strategic Missile Wing (ICBM-Titan) was activated at Lowry Air Force Base, Colorado. Both missile wings were assigned to the 1st Missile Division.

Thor program. Under an early 1958 agreement, the United States and the United Kingdom shared responsibility for the Thor missile program. The United Kingdom agreed to build four bases and to man four Thor squadrons, while the United States agreed to furnish the missiles and provide training for the RAF crews. Effective 20 February, the 705th Strategic Missile Wing (IRBM-Thor) was activated at Lakenheath RAF Station and assigned to the

7th Air Division. Shortly thereafter, the 705th moved to South Ruislip where it merged with Headquarters 7th Air Division. It was responsible for monitoring the Thor program and for providing technical assistance to the four RAF squadrons. Thor training for RAF crews began at Vandenberg in August. This training was provided by the 392d Missile Training Squadron which was activated at Vandenberg on 15 September 1957.

First Snark launched. On 27 June, at Patrick Air Force Base, Florida, the 556th Strategic Missile Squadron launched its first Snark missile.

First missile launched from Vandenberg. On 16 December, the first missile, a Thor, was launched from Vandenberg by a crew of the 1st Missile Division backed up by contractor personnel. This was officially credited as an Air Research and Development Command launch.

Jupiter program. SAC was also responsible for training Italian and Turkish crews in the operation of the U.S. Army-developed Jupiter, another intermediate range ballistic missile. In 1958, three SAC Jupiter squadrons were activated at Redstone Arsenal, Alabama, to handle this responsibility.

Rascal cancelled. On 29 November, Headquarters USAF cancelled the Rascal air-to-surface missile which was designed to be carried aboard modified B-47s (designated DB-47s). The entire SAC program was to have been concentrated in one squadron of the 321st Bomb Wing, McCoy Air Force Base, Florida. The Rascal was cancelled in deference to the Hound Dog and Quail, which were showing more promise of being effective weapon systems.

Goose cancelled. On 12 December, the Goose missile development program was terminated. Designed to simulate a B-52 or a B-47 on radar screens, the Goose was a turbojet subsonic decoy missile that was programmed to be launched from the United States. It was dropped in favor of the Snark, which carried a nuclear weapon.

"Peace Is Our Profession" adopted as SAC slogan. In late 1957, as part of a reenlistment program, a 50-foot Christmas tree was erected in front of the Headquarters SAC administration building. Unit commanders could light one of the bulbs by reenlisting a given number of first-team airmen. A status board was maintained nearby to reflect the names of those commanders who met the quota. A painter was called upon to affix a sign to the board reflecting the theme of the reenlistment drive—Maintaining Peace is Our Profession—but he found insufficient room to accommodate all these words. Lieutenant Colonel Edward Martin and Chief Warrant Officer Ben Kohot, project officers for the Tree of Peace program, decided to omit the word "Maintaining." While visiting Headquarters SAC, Colonel Charles T. Van Vliet, Eighth Air Force Director of Information, saw the sign, liked it, and took the idea back to Westover Air Force Base, Massachusetts. Subsequently, "Peace is Our Profession" appeared on a large sign at Westover's main entrance.

1959

Resources

Personnel 262,609 (36,435 officers, 199,970 airmen, 26,204 civilians)

Tactical Aircraft 3,207 (488 B-52, 1,366 B-47, 174 RB-47, 745 KC-97, 322 KC-135, 50 C-124, 6 RB-57, 56 F-86)*

Aircraft Units 12 Heavy Bomb Wings, six 45 UE, five with B-52s and one with no aircraft, two 30 UE with B-52s, and four 15 UE with B-52s

10 Heavy Strategic Wings (15 UE), nine equipped and one partially equipped with B-52s, and 12 without aircraft.

27 Medium Bomb Wings (26 45 UE and one 30 UE), 26 with B-47s, one reduced to one officer and one airman manning status and its aircraft used to equip two superstrength B-47 wings with 70 aircraft each

Three Medium Strategic Reconnaissance Wings (45 UE) with RB-47s

24 Heavy Air Refueling Squadrons, ten 20 UE, eight fully and two partially equipped with KC-135s, one 15 UE fully equipped, and 13 10 UE, 11 fully and one partially equipped with KC-135s, and one without aircraft

33 Medium Air Refueling Squadrons (20 UE) with KC-97s

One Light Strategic Reconnaissance Wing with RB-57s and U-2s

One B-47 Combat Crew Training Wing (90 UE)

One KC-97 Combat Crew Training Wing (45 UE)

Three Strategic Support Squadrons (16 UE) with C-124s

Two Fighter Interceptor Squadrons (24 UE) with F-86s and located in Spain

*Highest number in SAC history.

Budget and Financial Status
(FY 59, as of 30 June 1959)

Operations and Maintenance $650,652,000, includes supplies, communications, civilian pay, minor equipment purchased, and aviation petroleum, oil and lubricants (POL).

Assets $14,152,248,000, includes real property, inventories, equipment, and weapon systems.

Operating Expenses $1,617,130,000, includes O&M listed above, military pay, military family housing, troop subsistence, and procurement of equipment.

Missiles 6 Atlas D, 13 Snark, 5 Thor, 1 Hound Dog

Missile Units Four Atlas D Squadrons, two 6 UE, one with and one without missiles, and two 9 UE without missiles, and one Snark wing (30 UE), partially equipped

Active Bases 40 in CONUS; 25 overseas (United Kingdom, Spain, French Morocco, Guam, Greenland, Newfoundland, and Puerto Rico)

Organization

Numbered Air Force realignment. Effective 1 January, SAC realigned several bases and units between the Second and Eighth Air Forces. One base and its assigned units were transferred from the Eighth to the Fifteenth Air Force. Basically, this realignment placed the Eighth Air Force in control of forces in the Eastern section of the United States and Second Air Force in command of forces in the Central section. The Fifteenth's area of responsibility remained in the Western section of the country.

Dispersed air divisions. Prior to 1959, the air division headquarters was normally located on a double-wing base. In addition to the headquarters element, each air division consisted of two combat wings, a combat support group, and a medical facility. In a few cases, air division headquarters were located on single-wing bases, but in these cases, too, all elements of the air division were located on the same base.

With tremendous expansion accompanying the dispersal program, SAC found it necessary to expand the supervisory role of the air division headquarters, to increase the personnel assigned from approximately 17 to 25, and to activate new ones. Specifically, the air division's responsibility was extended to organizations that were located on bases other than the one that supported the headquarters element. As initiated on 1 January, the concept was first applied to those air divisions that were situated on single wing bases, but it was subsequently applied to those on double wing bases. In the last six months of 1959, six new air division headquarters were activated. The number of wings assigned to these air divisions varied from three to five.

Operations

Airborne alert. Based upon satisfactory results in 1958, SAC continued to test airborne alert in 1959. As General Power testified before Congress in

An RB-52B poses for its picture during a high altitude flight. The -B variant was convertible to the "recce" configuration with a bomb bay equipment-operator pod. Although two replacement aircraft were developed, the B-70 and then B-1, the B-52 will carry on as the mainstay of the SAC bomber force at least well into the 1980s.

February: "We in the Strategic Air Command have developed a system known as airborne alert where we maintain airplanes in the air 24 hours a day, loaded with bombs, on station, ready to go to the target. . . . I feel strongly that we must get on with this airborne alert. . . . We must impress Mr. Khrushchev that we have it, and that he cannot strike this country with impunity."

Low level training. In November, SAC and the Federal Aviation Agency jointly announced the establishment of seven special air routes over which SAC bombers would fly low-level training missions. Each corridor was to be approximately 20 miles wide and up to 500 miles long. Improved Soviet air defenses at high altitude had prompted SAC to concentrate on bombing at low altitudes, where detection was more difficult.

Last B-36 retired. On 12 February, SAC's last B-36 bomber, a "J" model (serial number 52-2827) which had been assigned to the 95th Bomb Wing at Biggs Air Force Base, Texas, was flown to Amon Carter Field, Fort Worth, Texas, to be placed on display as a permanent memorial. With the departure of this B-36, SAC had an all jet bomber force.

First B-52G. The first B-52G (serial number 57-6478) was delivered to the 5th Bomb Wing at Travis Air Force Base, California, on 13 February.

The B-52G, which would subsequently become the most widely used B-52 in SAC, contained several refined features over previous models. The addition of fuel tanks in the wings and permanently affixed fuel tanks under the wings increased the unrefueled range of this bomber to approximately 10,000 miles as compared to 6,000 miles for the earlier models. The bomber was also originally designed to carry two nuclear-armed Hound Dog air-to-surface missiles, thereby increasing its bombing capacity.

Delivery of first Hound Dog. Powered by a single turbojet engine, the 43-foot long Hound Dog could be launched from a B-52 when the bomber was over 500 miles away from the target. Two Hound Dogs could be carried under the wings of the B-52G and on modified earlier model Stratofortresses. The B-52H, which was scheduled for delivery to SAC in 1961, was also designed to carry two Hound Dogs.

On 21 December, the first Hound Dog was assigned to SAC. On 23 December, this missile was delivered to the 4135th Strategic Wing, Eglin Air Force Base, Florida, the unit responsible for supporting Category III Hound Dog tests in coordination with ARDC's Air Proving Ground Center.

The Daedalian Trophy. For its 1959 aircraft accident rate, the lowest in USAF, the Strategic Air Command was awarded the Daedalian Trophy.

Bombing Competition

The eleventh competition, which was held from 25 through 30 October, was unique in that air refueling squadrons participated for the first time in the history of the meet. Two crews represented each of the 47 bomb wings, 27 B-47 and 20 B-52, and each of the 47 air refueling squadrons, 27 KC-97 and 20 KC-135. This was the largest bombing competition ever held. All bombers staged out of McCoy Air Force Base, Florida, while all tankers operated out of Homestead Air Force Base, Florida. Second Air Force's 307th Bomb Wing, a B-47 unit, won the Fairchild Trophy and the Second's 55th Air Refueling Squadron, a KC-97 unit, won the award for the best air refueling squadron.

Missiles

Missile launches. Total missiles and space systems launched during the year from Vandenberg Air Force Base and the U.S. Naval Missile Facility, Point Arguello, California. All SAC launches were form Vandenberg: Launched by: SAC—1; Other Agencies—30

First missile wing to a numbered Air Force. The first missile wing was assigned to a numbered air force 1 January, when the 702d Strategic Missile Wing (ICM-Snark) was activated at Presque Isle Air Force Base, Maine, and assigned to the Eighth Air Force. On 27 May, the first Snark missile was delivered to the 702d, and on 16 July, the 556th Strategic Missile Squadron, which had been stationed at Patrick Air Force Base, Florida, conducting test launches, and under the direct control of SAC, was inactivated instead of moving to Presque Isle as planned. The 702d was unique because it had no subordinate squadrons. All operational and maintenance functions associated with the Snark were handled by the deputy commander for missiles.

Designated a surface-to-surface intercontinental missile, the Snark was a small, turbojet-powered pilotless aircraft. Unlike the Atlas and Titan, the Snark was non-ballistic with a subsonic cruising speed. It was designed to deliver a nuclear warhead on a target approximately 5,000 miles away from the launch site.

ICBM units assigned to Fifteenth Air Force. The assignment of ICBM units to numbered air forces continued on 15 January. At that time, the 703d Strategic Missile Wing (ICBM-Titan), located at Lowry Air Force Base, Colorado, and the 706th Strategic Missile Wing (ICBM-Atlas), located at Francis E. Warren Air Force Base, Wyoming, were transferred from the 1st Missile Division to Fifteenth Air Force. Francis E. Warren was also transferred to the Fifteenth. Lowry belonged to the Air Training Command and the 703d was a tenant there. On 1 February, the 395th Missile Training Squadron was activated at Vandenberg Air Force Base, California, to provide training for crews to man the other Titan units to be activated in SAC.

First Atlas launch. On 9 September, a crew of the 576th Strategic Missile Squadron, which was assigned to the 1st Missile Division, launched the first Atlas missile, a "D" model, from Vandenberg. The shot traveled approximately 4,300 miles at 16,000 mph. General Power declared the Atlas to be operational. Designed to deliver a nuclear warhead approximately 5,500 nautical miles, the Atlas D was powered by a cluster of liquid propellant rocket engines, burning liquid oxygen and RP-1, a kerosene-like fuel. It was approximately 75 feet long and 10 feet in diameter. The first Atlas D was placed on alert at Vandenberg on 31 October.

Last Atlas D Squadron activated; first missile unit assigned to Second Air Force. SAC's fourth and last Atlas D unit was activated at Offutt Air Force Base, Nebraska, and assigned to the Second Air Force on 15 August.

Thor program. On 16 April, an RAF crew launched its first Thor from Vandenberg as part of the training program. By the end of the year, three squadrons of Thor IRBMs had been turned over to the Royal Air Force and were operational in the United Kingdom.

1960

Resources

Personnel   266,788 (37,562 officers, 202,507 airmen, 26,719 civilians)

Tactical Aircraft   2,992 (538 B-52, 1,178 B-47, 113 RB-47, 405 KC-135, 689 KC-97, 19 B/TB-58, 50 C-124)

Aircraft Units   12 Heavy Bomb Wings, three 45 UE, two 30 UE, and seven 15 UE, with B-52s

22 Heavy Strategic Wings (15 UE), 16 with B-52s, six without aircraft

25 Medium Bomb Wings, 24 (23 45 UE and one 30 UE), with B-47s (includes two super strength wings with 70 aircraft each); one had been reduced to one officer and one airman manning status to provide resources for the two 70 aircraft wings, and one (36 UE), equipping with B-58s

Two Medium Strategic Reconnaissance Wings (45 UE) with RB-47s

30 Medium Air Refueling Squadrons (20 UE) with KC-97s

One B-47 Combat Crew Training Wing (90 UE)

One KC-97 Combat Crew Training Wing (40 UE)

29 Heavy Air Refueling Squadrons, 12 20 UE, one 15 UE, and 16 10 UE, with KC-135s

One Light Strategic Wing with U-2s

Three Strategic Support Squadrons (16 UE) with C-124s

Missiles   30 Snark, 12 Atlas, 93 Quail, 54 Hound Dog

Missile Units   Four Atlas D Squadrons, two 6 UE fully equipped and two 9 UE without missiles; three Atlas E Squadrons (9 UE) without missiles

Three Titan I Squadrons (9 UE) without missiles

One Strategic Missile Wing (30 UE) equipped with Snark missiles

Active Bases   46 in CONUS; 20 overseas (Puerto Rico, United Kingdom, Spain, French Morocco, Labrador, Newfoundland, Guam, and Canada)

Budget and Financial Status
(FY 60, as of 30 June 1960)

Operations and Maintenance $713,661,000, includes supplies, communications, civilian pay, minor equipment purchased, and aviation petroleum, oil and lubricants (POL)

Assets $15,738,327,000, includes real property, inventories, equipment, and weapon systems

Operating Expenses $1,742,225,000, includes O&M listed above, military pay, military family housing, troop subsistence, and procurement of equipment

Organization

JSTPS established. While SAC still controlled most of the country's nuclear strength in 1960, substantial additional striking power was being provided by ballistic missile submarines and nuclear-armed missile and air units of tactical forces deployed in forward areas. This proliferation of nuclear strength brought with it the need for closer coordination of target planning among the services. Consequently, on 16 August, Secretary of Defense Thomas S. Gates, Jr., publicly announced the creation of the Joint Strategic Target Planning Staff (JSTPS).

Composed of representatives of all services, the JSTPS was charged with the task of preparing and maintaining a National Strategic Target List and a Single Integrated Operational Plan (SIOP) which would commit specific weapon systems to the various targets to be attacked in the event of war. In order to fully use the strategic planning experience and facilities available in SAC, Secretary Gates directed the Commander in Chief of SAC to be the Director of JSTPS and that the staff be collocated with Headquarters SAC at Offutt. On 18 August, Secretary Gates named Rear Admiral (subsequently promoted to Vice Admiral) Edward N. Parker to become Deputy Director of JSTPS.

Fighter Interceptor Squadrons transferred. Effective 1 July, the 431st and the 497th Fighter Interceptor Squadrons, which were equipped with F-86s and located in Spain, were transferred to USAFE.

Operations

First B-58. On 1 August, General Power accepted the first operational B-58 medium bomber from Air Research and Development Command representatives in a ceremony at Carswell Air Force Base, Texas. This aircraft was one of 12 which were turned over to the 43d Bomb Wing, Carswell Air Force Base, Texas, on that date.

Built by the Convair Division of the General Dynamics Corporation, the B-58 "Hustler" was America's first supersonic bomber. This delta-wing bomber was capable of flying twice the speed of sound (Mach 2) and could be refueled by KC-135 tankers.

B-52 record flight. On 14 December, a B-52G of the 5th Bomb Wing,

A high-altitude U-2 employed in strategic reconnaissance from 1956 onward. Periodically, as in Cuba and the Middle East, the U-2s have been used for tactical reconnaissance of specific weapon installations and troop locations.

Travis Air Force Base, California, completed an official record-breaking flight of 10,078.84 miles without refueling in 19 hours and 44 minutes. The aircraft, commanded by Lieutenant Colonel T. R. Grissom, flew a closed-circuit course from Edwards Air Force Base, California, to El Paso, Texas, Andrews Air Force Base, Maryland, Ernest Harmon Air Force Base, Newfoundland, Eielson Air Force Base, Alaska, Philip, South Dakota, and back to Edwards.

Quail missile. On 27 February, the first Quail missile to be assigned to a SAC unit was delivered to the 4135th Strategic Wing, Eglin Air Force Base, Florida. The 4135th, working closely with Air Research and Development Command's Air Proving Ground Center at Eglin, was responsible for supporting Category III tests of the Quail.

Designated an air decoy missile, the Quail was carried in the bomb bay of a B-52 to be launched while en route to the target. Powered by a single turbojet engine, it could fly at approximately the same altitude and speed of a B-52. The "blip" it created on a radar screen was similar to the one produced by a B-52. The B-52G was built to carry four Quail missiles in addition to its normal bomb load.

First Hound Dog launch. On 29 February, as part of its Hound Dog Category III testing responsibilities, a B-52G crew of the 4135th Strategic Wing accomplished the first SAC launch of a Hound Dog missile.

In Operation Blue Nose, conducted on 12 April, a B-52G crew of the 4135th Strategic Wing successfully launched a "Hound Dog" missile as the climax of its 20 and one-half hour captive flight to the North Pole and back.

The crew completed extensive tests of both the B-52G and the Hound Dog's guidance system in temperatures as low as 75 degrees below zero.

First Quail launch. On 8 June, a B-52G crew of the 4135th Strategic Wing accomplished the first SAC launch of a Quail missile as part of the Category III Test Program.

Airborne command post test. On 1 July, SAC began testing an airborne command post at Offutt Air Force Base, Nebraska. Beginning that day and extending throughout the year, one of five specially modified KC-135s of the 34th Air Refueling Squadron was placed on ground alert and periodically tested to determine its ability to take off within 15 minutes. Once airborne, the KC-135's primary mission was to serve as an alternate command post, one that could assume control over the SAC combat force in the event an enemy attack destroyed the underground facility at Offutt and the other command posts collocated with the numbered air force headquarters. On each flight, the KC-135 was manned by a SAC general officer and a team of controllers and communications experts.

One-Third alert achieved. In May, SAC reached its goal of maintaining one-third of its bombers and tankers on 15-minute ground alert.

B-47 dispersal. On 9 June, SAC began testing a B-47 dispersal program, whereby B-47 aircraft could, in times of crises, be deployed to civilian air-fields and non-SAC military bases. This was another means of strengthening reaction capability and insuring a survivable force.

Transfer of last RB-57. On 22 April, SAC's last RB-57 ("C" model serial number 53-3839), which had been assigned to the 4080th Strategic Wing at Laughlin Air Force Base, Texas, was transferred to Headquarters Command, Bolling Air Force Base, Washington, D.C.

Short order. In March, a new single sideband HF radio communications system began operations. Called "Short Order," the new system consisted of four stations: one at Headquarters SAC and the others at the three numbered air force headquarters in the CONUS. Its primary function was to provide a means of exercising "Positive Control," over SAC bombers which had launched and were en route to their targets. Under "Positive Control" procedures, SAC could launch its bombers and have them fly to a designated point outside enemy territory. Upon reaching this point, the bombers would automatically return to their home bases unless they received orders, "the Go-Code," to proceed to their targets.

Bombing Competition

Twelfth Competition, first B-58 participation. Officially titled Combat Competition but still called the Bombing Competition, the 1960 meet was held from 12 through 15 September. It was a different kind of competition. Each numbered air force held a preliminary meet to determine the participants. Only one base, Bergstrom Air Force Base, Texas, was used for staging purposes because only 13 bomb wings and 13 air refueling squadrons were entered. Each numbered air force was represented by two B-52 wings, two

B-47 wings, two KC-135 squadrons, and two KC-97 squadrons. In addition, the 43d Bomb Wing was represented with the new B-58 and a seventh KC-135 was allowed to enter to provide refueling for the Hustler.

Saunders Trophy. The 11th Bomb Wing, a B-52 unit of the Second Air Force, won the Fairchild Trophy. The Saunders Trophy, which was first awarded in this competition, was won by the 310th Air Refueling Squadron, a KC-97 unit of the Fifteenth Air Force. Comparable to the Fairchild Trophy, the new air refueling trophy was named for Brigadier General Donald W. Saunders, who had formerly commanded the 57th Air Division at Westover Air Force Base, Massachusetts. General Saunders was killed in the KC-135 that crashed while taking off for a record flight attempt from Westover on 27 June 1958.

SAC participation in RAF bombing competition. Fifteenth Air Force's 6th Bomb Wing was selected to represent SAC in the 1960 RAF Bombing and Navigation Competition which was held from 1 through 3 May. Headquarters SAC selected the 6th Bomb Wing on the basis of it being the top B-52 unit in the 1959 SAC Bombing Competition. Flying out of Brize Norton RAF Station, the 6th Bomb Wing's six crews won the best unit award in the combined areas of bombing and navigation. Individual crews of the 6th also won top awards in bombing and in the combined areas of bombing and navigation.

With liquid oxygen bleeding off, an early Atlas missile is fired from the Air Force Missile Test Center at Cape Canaveral, Florida (now Cape Kennedy). There have been no test firings of deployed ICBMs from the interior of the United States because of the political problems of the missiles overflying American cities. The Soviet Union, without such political constraints, have long had a program of test firing missiles from operational silos.

Missiles

Missile launches. Total missiles and space systems launched during the year from Vandenberg Air Force Base and the U.S. Naval Missile Facility, Point Arguello, California. All SAC launches were from Vandenberg: Launched by: SAC—7; Other Agencies—36

Mobile Minuteman test. To determine the feasibility of deploying Minuteman ICBMs on mobile railroad car launchers, SAC conducted a series of tests from 20 June to 27 August. Operating out of Hill Air Force Base, Utah, the modified test train traveled across various railroad routes in the Western and Central sections of the United States to study such factors as the ability of the nation's railroads to support mobile missile trains, problems of communication and control, problems of vibration and their probable effect on sensitive missiles and launch equipment as well as the human factors involved in this operation. Six trial runs were projected, but only four were needed to realize all test objectives.

Thor deployment completed. On 22 April, the fourth and final Thor squadron, which had been trained at Vandenberg Air Force Base, California, was accepted by the Royal Air Force, thus completing the deployment of this intermediate range ballistic missile to the United Kingdom. On 1 April, the 705th Strategic Missile Wing, which had been located at South Ruislip in the United Kingdom, was discontinued.

First Snark on alert. On 18 March, the first Snark intercontinental missile was placed on alert at Presque Isle Air Force Base, Maine.

Titan I squadrons activated. Three Titan I squadrons were activated in 1960, with two being assigned to the 703d Strategic Missile Wing, Lowry Air Force Base, Colorado, and one to the 28th Bomb Wing, Ellsworth Air Force Base, South Dakota.

Atlas E squadrons activated. Three Atlas E squadrons were activated in 1960, with one being assigned to the 706th Strategic Missile Wing, Francis E. Warren Air Force Base, Wyoming, one to the 92d Bomb Wing, Fairchild Air Force Base, Washington, and one to the 21st Air Division, Forbes Air Force Base, Kansas.

Minuteman training squadron activated. On 1 July, the 394th Missile Training Squadron was activated at Vandenberg Air Force Base, California, to provide combat crew training for the Minuteman squadrons scheduled to be activated in SAC.

1961

Resources

Personnel	280,582 (37,555 officers, 216,148 airmen, and 26,879 civilians)
Tactical Aircraft	2,759 (571 B-52, 889 B-47, 138 EB/RB-47, 444 KC-135, 651 KC-97, 66 B/TB-58)
Aircraft Units	14 Heavy Bomb Wings (two 45 UE, three 30 UE, and nine 15 UE) all with B-52s except one 15 UE wing
	22 Heavy Strategic Wings (15 UE), 21 equipped with B-52s and one with no aircraft
	21 Medium Bomb Wings, 19 (45 UE) equipped with B-47s and two (40 UE), one equipped and one partially equipped with B-58s
	One B-47 Combat Crew Training Wing (90 UE)
	One Medium Strategic Reconnaissance Wing (45 UE) with RB-47s
	31 Heavy Air Refueling Squadrons (12 20 UE, two 15 UE, and 17 10 UE) all with KC-135s except two 10 UE units
	29 Medium Air Refueling Squadrons (20 UE) with KC-97s
	One KC-97 Combat Crew Training Wing (40 UE)
	One Light Strategic Reconnaissance Wing with U-2s
Missiles	230 Hound Dog, 397 Quail, 30 Atlas D, 32 Atlas E, 1 Titan I
Missile Units	Four Atlas D Squadrons (two 6 UE and two 9 UE), all equipped
	Three Atlas E Squadrons (9 UE each), all equipped
	Six Atlas F Squadrons (12 UE each) with no missiles assigned
	Six Titan I Squadrons (9 UE each) with no missiles assigned
	One Minuteman Squadron (50 UE) without missiles assigned
Active Bases	46 in CONUS; 16 overseas (Puerto Rico, United Kingdom, French Morocco, Spain, Newfoundland, Labrador, Canada, Guam)

Budget and Financial Status
(FY 61, as of 30 June 1961)

Operations and Maintenance
$716,489,000, includes supplies, communications, civilian pay, minor equipment purchased, and aviation petroleum, oil and lubricants (POL)

Assets
$15,830,227,000, includes real property, inventories, equipment, and weapon systems

Operating Expenses
$1,835,603,000, includes O&M listed above, military pay, military family housing, troop subsistence, and procurement of equipment

Organization

Redesignation of 1st Missile Division. Effective 21 July, Headquarters 1st Missile Division, located at Vandenberg Air Force Base, California, was redesignated Headquarters 1st Strategic Aerospace Division. Redesignation was in consonance with a Headquarters USAF policy that the term "aerospace" could be injected into or substituted for "air" in the names of those organizations significantly engaged in aerospace operations or support thereof. In order to qualify for the new designation, an organization was required to be involved in the operations or support of two or more of the following: air systems, ballistic missile systems, and space vehicle systems.

Strategic support squadrons discontinued. SAC's three strategic support squadrons transferred their C-124 aircraft and airlift functions to the Military Air Transport Service and the Air Force Logistics Command and were discontinued in March and June.

Operations

In a nationwide defense budget speech of 28 March, President John F. Kennedy requested an increase in funds to strengthen and protect the strategic deterrent force and to strengthen the ability to wage limited war.

Fifty percent ground alert. He called for one-half of SAC's B-52s and B-47s to be placed on 15-minute ground alert. He also directed an accelerated B-47 phase out program in order "to provide promptly the trained crews required for the expanded ground alert." The 50 percent ground alert posture by both bombers and tankers was attained in July.

Skybolt. President Kennedy further recommended additional funds for the Skybolt, an air-launched ballistic missile that was being developed to replace the Hound Dog. He observed that successful development and production of the Skybolt would extend the life of SAC's heavy bombers into the missile age. Congress subsequently approved the additional funds for Skybolt.

Death of the B-70. President Kennedy cancelled the B-70 Valkyrie, the Mach 3 bomber being developed as a replacement for the B-52. He cited several factors that prompted him to recommend reduction of the B-70 program. These included the high cost of developing the aircraft, its greater vulnerability in the air compared to missiles, and its late projected readiness date which coincided with the readiness date of intercontinental ballistic missiles. In his opinion, all these factors combined to make the B-70 "unnecessary and economically unjustifiable."

He recommended continuing a B-70 research and development program to explore the problems of flying three times the speed of sound. Following his recommendation, Congress reduced the funds for the B-70 and geared the program to one that involved the production of three XB-70 aircraft with no operational bomber production.

Thompson Trophy. On 14 January 1961, another 43d Bomb Wing B-58 broke three of the records made by the aircraft on 12 January. It established new records for a 1,000 kilometer course with payloads of 2,000 kilograms, 1,000 kilograms and no payload, all at 1,284.73 miles an hour. On 28 February, the crew was awarded the Thompson Trophy for 1961. This was the first time in its 31-year history that the trophy was awarded for a record set by a medium bomber. Sponsored by Thompson-Ramo-Wooldridge, Inc., and administered by the Air Foundation, the Thompson Trophy was awarded annually for supremacy in closed course speed flying. Recipients of the award were: Major Harold Confer, pilot; Major Richard Weir, navigator-bombardier; and Captain Howard Bialas, defensive systems operator. All were members of the 43d Bomb Wing, Carswell AFB, Texas.

Bleriot Cup. A new record for sustained speed was set by a 43d Bomb Wing B-58 Hustler on 10 May, flying 669.4 miles in 30 minutes and 45 seconds at an average speed of 1,302 miles per hour. The record flight won the

The delta-wing B-58 Hustler was the first supersonic bomber to enter production in the United States. The aircraft lacked sufficient range for SAC missions and was too expensive to maintain in the small numbers procured. The aircraft shown here was the first produced by the Convair Division of General Dynamics.

Aero Club of France's Bleriot Cup, for the pilot of the aircraft, Major Elmer E. Murphy. The trophy was named for Louis Bleriot, the first man to fly across the English Channel.

Another record, the seventh Mackay Trophy, and tragedy. The B-58 continued its record-setting pace on 26 May when it flew the 4,612 miles from New York to Paris in 3 hours, 19 minutes, and 41 seconds, thus setting another record. The time was almost one-tenth that taken by Charles Lindbergh in his famous solo flight of 1927. The crew consisted of Major William Payne, pilot; Captain William Polhemus, and Captain Raymond Wagener, all from the 43d Bomb Wing. The crew received the Mackay Trophy for this flight.

On 3 June, this B-58 crashed while participating in the Paris Air Show. All three crew members, those who had participated in the 10 May flight, were killed.

B-58 record flights. On 12 January, a SAC B-58 Hustler of the 43d Bomb Wing, piloted by Major Henry J. Deutschendorf, Jr., established six international speed and payload records on a single flight, thus breaking five previous records held by the Soviet Union. Staging out of Edwards AFB, California, the four-jet B-58 flew two laps around a course between Edwards AFB and a point east of Yuma, Arizona. The records were as follows: speed with no payload, 1,200.194 miles per hour; speed with one thousand kilogram payload, 1,200.194 miles per hour; and speed with two thousand kilograms, 1,200.194 miles per hour. The three additional records were set for a 2,000 kilometer run without payload, a 1,000 and a 2,000 kilogram payload—all at 1,061.808 miles per hour.

First B-52H. On 9 May, the first B-52H (serial number 60-001) was delivered to the 379th Bomb Wing, Wurtsmith Air Force Base, Michigan. Powered by eight turbofan engines, the B-52H had greater range and climbing power than earlier models. A Gatling gun, capable of firing 20 millimeter cannon rounds at the rate of 4,000 per minute, was a special feature of this aircraft.

Berlin Crisis and B-47 phase out. On 25 July, with the U.S. and Russia seemingly headed for a showdown on the Berlin question, President Kennedy delayed his previously directed accelerated B-47 phase out program in order to improve the national defense posture. Six bomb wings and six air refueling squadrons were affected.

Airborne command post began operations. Initiated on a trial basis in July 1960, the airborne command post, or Looking Glass as it was later called, began continuous operations on 3 February. "The results of six months of testing have proven conclusively the effectiveness of the airborne command post," declared General Power, SAC Commander.

Airborne command post headquarters were converted KC-135 tankers equipped with the latest and most advanced radio equipment. The command post could communicate with the Joint Chiefs of Staff, any SAC base or any SAC aircraft in the air or on the ground. General officers were to take turns in commanding the post. Each aircraft flew approximately 8 hours and was replaced by another identically equipped KC-135.

Airborne alert. On 18 January 1961, SAC publicly announced that B-52 heavy bombers were conducting airborne alert training. General Power declared that the indoctrination phase of airborne alert training had been completed and all combat ready B-52 bomber crews were participating in airborne alert training missions under realistic conditions. A number of B-52s would be in the air at all times. Approximately 24 bases were involved in the program because of the dispersal of heavy bomber units. More than 6,000 sorties during the previous two years had proved the feasibility of keeping a segment of the SAC bomber fleet in the air at all times.

SAC designated single manager for KC-135s. In November, Headquarters USAF established the SAC KC-135 program at 32 squadrons (each 20 UE) or a total authorized strength of 640 aircraft. At the same time, Headquarters USAF designated SAC as the single manager of all KC-135 air refueling operations and as such would provide support for all fighter aircraft assigned to the Tactical Air Command and other major commands.

BMEWS becomes operational. On 1 February, the Ballistic Missile Early

Looking like a strange bird with talons extended, a B-58 Hustler is about to touch down during an early test flight. Note the four podded engines mounted directly on the delta wing, and not on pylons as in the B-47 and B-52 designs. The 18-wheel, tricycle landing gear was required because the thin wing structure could not accommodate a conventional gear system with larger wheels. The proposed Martin B-68—cancelled in 1957—was also a delta-wing bomber.

Warning System (BMEWS) site at Thule Air Base, Greenland, became operational. Subsequently, BMEWS sites began operations at Clear, Alaska, and Fylingdales in the United Kingdom. Operated by the North American Air Defense Command (NORAD), BMEWS provided a means of detecting and warning SAC of an impending intercontinental ballistic missile attack in sufficient time to allow aircraft to be launched before the missiles reached U.S. bases. It also provided SAC with valuable time in which to prepare its own missile force for launch.

Bombing Competition

Following the basic ground rules established in 1960, each numbered air force held a preliminary contest to determine who would participate in the SAC-wide competition, which was held at Fairchild Air Force Base, Washington, from 16 through 22 September. Participants included 12 bomb wings (six B-52 and six B-47) and 12 air refueling squadrons (six KC-135s and six KC-97s). The two B-58 wings were too deeply in training to participate in the competition. Each KC-97 squadron sent four crews to team as pairs in accomplishing refueling (two tankers to one receiver) of both B-47s and B-52s; the other units entered two crews each. The 4137th Strategic Wing, a B-52 unit of the Eighth Air Force, received the Fairchild Trophy for having the highest score in the combined categories of alert exercise, bombing, navigation, electronic countermeasures, air refueling, pilot techniques, and munitions loading. The 915th Air Refueling Squadron, a KC-135 unit of the Eighth Air Force, won the Saunders Trophy.

Missiles

Missile launches. Total missiles and space systems launched during the year from Vandenberg Air Force Base and the U.S. Naval Missile Facility, Point Arguello, California. All SAC launches were from Vandenberg: Launched by: SAC—2: Other Agencies—38.

SAC MIKE discontinued. Effective 1 July 1961, the Office of Assistant CINCSAC (SAC MIKE) was discontinued. Replaced by a smaller office, SAC Representative (Aerospace), SAC MIKE had been gradually phased down and its duties appropriated by the Headquarters SAC staff. Functions of the new office included providing SAC representation to configuration control boards, advising respective BSD program offices and providing information to Headquarters SAC staff agencies on technical knowledge and understanding of the design and operational aspects of strategic missile systems.

Snark phased out. In his special defense budget message of 28 March, President Kennedy directed that the Snark missile be phased out as it was "obsolete and of marginal military value. . . ." On 25 June, less than four months after it had been declared operational, the 702d Strategic Missile Wing was inactivated at Presque Isle Air Force Base, Maine.

Mobile Minuteman cancelled. President Kennedy also deferred further action on the development of the Mobile Minuteman concept in favor of additional hardened Minuteman sites, and on 7 December, Secretary of Defense Robert S. McNamara cancelled the entire Mobile Minuteman program.

Titan II program cut. In his 28 March speech, President Kennedy also announced that two Titan II squadrons that had been programmed for SAC would be cancelled.

Atlas D program completed. On 30 March, the Atlas D program was completed when the fourth squadron, which was located at Offutt Air Force Base, Nebraska, was fully equipped and its last three sites at Arlington and Mead, Nebraska, and Missouri Valley, Iowa, were turned over to SAC.

First Minuteman wing activated. Effective 15 July, SAC's first Minuteman wing, the 341st Strategic Missile Wing, was activated at Malmstrom Air Force Base, Montana, and on 1 December, the 10th Strategic Missile Squadron was activated and assigned to this wing.

First Titan I launch from Vandenberg. On 3 May, an Air Force Systems Command crew launched the first Titan I from Vandenberg Air Force Base, California. Previous launches, some successful and others unsuccessful, had been made by Air Force Systems Command from Cape Canaveral, Florida.

Atlas E Program Completed. SAC accepted its entire Atlas E force, three squadrons, from the Air Force Systems Command in 1961. The 566th Strategic Missile Squadron, located at Francis E. Warren Air Force Base, Wyoming, was the last one to be accepted—on 20 November. The other Atlas E squadrons were located at Fairchild Air Force Base, Washington and Forbes Air Force Base, Kansas.

The Future of SAC Secretary McNamara. On 11 December, less than a year after he became Secretary of Defense, Robert S. McNamara issued a prophetic statement on the future of the Strategic Air Command:

> The introduction of ballistic missiles is already exerting a major impact on the size, composition, and deployment of the manned bomber force, and this impact will become greater in the years ahead. As the number of . . . ballistic missiles increases, requirements for strategic aircraft will be gradually reduced. Simultaneously, the growing enemy missile capability will make grounded aircraft more vulnerable to sudden attack, and further readiness measures will have to be taken to increase the survivability rate of the strategic bomber force.

1962

Resources

Personnel	282,723 (38,542 officers, 217,650 airmen, 26,531 civilians)*
Tactical Aircraft	2,759 (639 B-52, 880 B-47, 100 EB-47, 5 EB-47L, 41 RB-47, 76 B/TB-58, 515 KC-135, 503 KC-97)
Aircraft Units	11 Heavy Bomb Wings (one 45 UE, two 30 UE, and eight 15 UE) with B-52s
	22 Heavy Strategic Wings (15 UE) with B-52s
	Three Heavy Strategic Aerospace Wings (one 45 UE and two 15 UE) with B-52s
	17 Medium Bomb Wings, 15 (45 UE) with B-47s and two (40 UE) with B-58s
	Three Medium Strategic Aerospace Wings (45 UE) with B-47s
	One Medium Strategic Reconnaissance Wing (45 UE) with RB-47s
	One B-47 Combat Crew Training Wing (45 UE)
	Four Support Squadrons (9 UE) partially equipped with EB-47Ls
	33 Heavy Tanker Squadrons (12 20 UE, 13 15 UE, and eight 10 UE) with KC-135s
	24 Medium Tanker Squadrons (20 UE) with KC-97s
	One Light Strategic Reconnaissance Wing with U-2s
Missiles	30 Atlas D, 32 Atlas E, 80 Atlas F, 62 Titan I, 20 Minuteman, 547 Hound Dog, and 436 Quail
Missile Units	Four Atlas D Squadrons (two 9 UE and two six UE, including the Vandenberg squadron which had all three models of Atlas missiles assigned) fully equipped
	Three Atlas E Squadrons (9 UE) fully equipped
	Six Atlas F Squadrons (12 UE) fully equipped
	Six Titan I Squadrons (9 UE) fully equipped
	Six Titan II Squadrons (9 UE) with no missiles assigned
	Eight Minuteman Squadrons (50 UE) one of which was partially equipped

*Highest number of personnel in SAC history.

Active Bases	43 CONUS; 14 overseas (Puerto Rico, United Kingdom, French Morocco, Spain, Labrador, Newfoundland, Canada, Guam)

Budget and Financial Status
(FY 62, as of 30 June 1962)

Operations and Maintenance	$750,958,000, includes supplies, communications, civilian pay, minor equipment purchased, and aviation petroleum, oil and lubricants (POL)
Assets	$17,934,650,000, includes real property, inventories, equipment, and weapon systems
Operating Expenses	$1,949,864,000, includes O&M listed above, military pay, military family housing, troop subsistence, and procurement of equipment

Organization

In line with the Headquarters USAF policy to use the term "aerospace" in the official title of organizations employing two or more air, ballistic missile, or space systems, SAC began redesignating those air divisions and bomb wings that directed the operations of both aircraft and ballistic missile units. The first redesignations were effected on 15 February, at which time four air divisions (the 17th, 18th, 21st, and 821st) became "strategic aerospace divisions" and the 92d Bombardment Wing, Heavy, became the 92d Strategic Aerospace Wing. Subsequently, the term was applied to other air divisions and bomb wings.

Operations

Cuban Missile Crisis. The Russian buildup of offensive missiles in Cuba began influencing SAC operations several days before President Kennedy revealed the exact nature of the threat to the American people. In response to a Joint Chiefs of Staff directive, a SAC U-2 reconnaissance plane, piloted by Major Richard S. Heyser, flew over Cuba on 14 October and obtained the first photographs of Soviet intermediate range ballistic missiles being installed there. Further evidence of the missile buildup was gathered during the following days as the high altitude air surveillance mission assigned to the 4080th Strategic Wing, the U-2 unit, was greatly intensified by the President.

On 22 October, President Kennedy announced the arms quarantine against shipments destined for Cuba and demanded the removal of missiles already situated there. On the same day SAC further intensified its readiness posture: Battle staffs were placed on 24-hour alert duty, leaves were cancelled, and personnel recalled to duty. B-47s were dispersed to several widely separated and pre-selected civilian and military airfields, additional bombers and tankers were placed on ground alert, and the B-52 airborne alert indoctrination program was immediately expanded into an actual airborne alert involving 24-

hour flights and immediate replacement of every aircraft that landed. The ICBM force, numbering some 200 operational missiles, was brought into alert configuration.

On 25 October, with the arms quarantine in effect, SAC RB-47s and KC-97s joined other forces in the gigantic sea-search for Soviet ships bound for Cuba. On 27 October, an RB-47 of the 55th Strategic Reconnaissance Wing, which was engaged in this sea-search mission, crashed on takeoff at Kindley Air Force Base, Bermuda. All four crew members were killed. On the same day, Major Rudolph Anderson, Jr., a member of the 4080th Strategic Wing, was killed when his U-2 aircraft was shot down by an anti-aircraft missile while performing a reconnaissance mission over Cuba. The Distinguished Service Medal was awarded posthumously to Major Anderson.

The first major break in the crisis came on 28 October. The Soviet Union agreed to remove offensive missiles from Cuba, subject to verification by the United Nations. Throughout the next few days, SAC aircraft maintained close aerial surveillance while the missiles were dismantled, loaded on ships, and sent back through the quarantine to Russia.

On 20 November, when the Soviet leadership agreed to remove medium bombers from Cuba, the quarantine was lifted and SAC began shifting back to normal operations. Medium bombers returned to their home bases, the ground alert force dropped back to the normal 50 percent standard, and routine B-52 airborne alert indoctrination flights began once more.

While visiting Homestead Air Force Base, Florida, on 26 November, President Kennedy presented the Air Force Outstanding Unit Award to the 4080th Strategic Wing for its vital reconnaissance missions over Cuba.

On 7 December, President Kennedy visited Headquarters SAC, toured the underground command post and presented General Power with a unique plaque citing SAC's extraordinary role and safety record in the Cuban crisis. The citation read: "For outstanding record in flight safety during airborne alert in the Cuban emergency, 22 Oct—21 Nov 62."

Delivery of Last B-52. On 26 October, SAC received its last B-52, an "H" model serial number 61-040, which was assigned to the 4136th Strategic Wing, Minot Air Force Base, North Dakota.

Last B-58. On 26 October, SAC received its last three B-58s (serial numbers 61-2078, 61-2079, and 61-2080), which were assigned to the 305th Bomb Wing, Bunker Hill Air Force Base, Indiana.

SAC Bomber Production Ends. With the delivery of the last B-52 and the last B-58, for the first time since 1946 there was no bomber being produced or developed for the Strategic Air Command. The XB-70 was the only bomber-type aircraft under development and it had been excluded from consideration as a bomber. In September, an Air Force recommendation to expand the XB-70 program into a full-scale weapon system development was rejected by the Department of Defense.

Follow-on Bomber. On 30 October, Secretary of Defense McNamara requested the Air Force "consider an alternative bombing system" as a follow-on to the B-52, something that could serve as an airborne missile launching platform for the period beyond 1970.

Death of the Skybolt. On 7 December, President Kennedy confirmed reports that his Administration planned to curtail development of the Skybolt, an air-to-surface ballistic missile being developed to replace the Hound Dog on the B-52 and to be used on the Royal Air Force's Vulcan bombers. He further announced that the final decision would not be made until after he and British Prime Minister Macmillan met and discussed the matter in Nassau, Bahamas. On 21 December, upon completion of their discussions, President Kennedy and Prime Minister Macmillan issued a joint statement which confirmed the decision to cancel the Skybolt.

According to Secretary of Defense McNamara, the Skybolt ". . . turned out to be considerably more expensive to develop and produce than had been anticipated . . . it was overtaken by the successful development of other weapons that could carry out the task of suppressing enemy defenses at substantially lower cost . . . lost its status as a vital defense requirement . . ."

B-52 Record Flights, Operation Persian Rug. On 10-11 January, a B-52H (serial number 60-0040) of the 4136th Strategic Wing, Minot Air Force Base, North Dakota, completed a record-breaking 12,532.28-mile unrefueled flight from Kadena Air Base, Okinawa, to Torrejon Air Base, Spain. This flight broke the old "distance in a straight line" world record of 11,235.6 miles held by the U.S. Navy's propeller-driven "Truculent Turtle." The entire crew, commanded by Major Clyde P. Evely, received Distinguished Flying Crosses. The Stratofortress weighed exactly 488,000 pounds (244 tons) at takeoff. It flew at altitudes from 40,000 to 50,000 feet with a top speed of 662 miles per hour on the Kadena-Torrejon flight route.

A B-52H of the 19th Bomb Wing, Homestead Air Force Base, Florida, broke the world record for distance in a closed course without landing or refueling on 7 June. The closed course began and ended at Seymour Johnson Air Force Base, North Carolina, with a validated distance of 11,336.92 miles. The old record of 10,078.84 miles had been held by a B-52G of the 5th Bomb Wing since 1960.

B-58 Record Flight, the Eighth Mackay Trophy, and the First Bendix Trophy, Operation Heat Rise. On 5 March, a 43d Bomb Wing B-58 (serial number 59-2458), piloted by Captain Robert G. Sowers, broke three speed records in a round-trip flight between New York and Los Angeles. The Hustler made the trip in four hours, 41 minutes, and 14.98 seconds while averaging 1,044.46 miles per hour. Three inflight refuelings by KC-135s were required. On its New York to Los Angeles leg, which took two hours, 15 minutes, and 50.8 seconds, the B-58 beat the sun across the United States, averaging 1,081.8 miles per hour. The most impressive part of the flight was that from Los Angeles to New York: two hours and 58.71 seconds at an average speed of 1,214.65 miles per hour.

For this flight, the crew received the Mackay Trophy, the Bendix Trophy, Distinguished Flying Crosses, and congratulations from President Kennedy.

Expansion of the Post Attack Command Control System. SAC's Post Attack Command Control System (PACCS) was expanded to include three auxiliary airborne command posts and four support squadrons. In April, auxiliary airborne command posts were established at those three bases that supported numbered air force headquarters—Barksdale Air Force Base, Louisiana; Westover Air Force Base, Massachusetts; and March Air Force Base, California. These auxiliary airborne command posts were modified to carry communications equipment in much the same manner as the Looking Glass aircraft, the SAC airborne command post that had been in continuous operation since February 1961. On 20 July, as a further extension of PACCS, SAC organized support squadrons at four strategic locations—Mountain Home Air Force Base, Idaho; Lincoln Air Force Base, Nebraska; Lockbourne Air Force Base, Ohio; and Plattsburgh Air Force Base, New York. These units were later equipped with EB-47L aircraft, B-47s modified with communications equipment, and redesignated Post Attack Command Control Squadrons.

Bombing Competition

Not held due to Cuban Crisis and increased operational commitments.

Missiles

Missile Launches. Total missiles and space systems launched during the year from Vandenberg Air Force Base and the Naval Missile Facility, Point Arguello, California. All SAC launches were from Vandenberg: Launched by: SAC—15; Other Agencies—64.

Titan I Operational. On 20 January, the first Titan I launch to be conducted by a SAC crew was accomplished at Vandenberg. On 20 April and

A GAM-77 Hound Dog air-to-surface missile is shown in a test configuration under the wing of a B-29 bomber. Each B-52 could carry two of these stand-off missiles. The thrust of the missile's turbojet engine could be used to augment the bomber's engines during takeoff and in flight, with the missile being refueled from bomber fuel tanks before being released. Note the SAC markings on the Hound Dog's engine nacelle.

10 May, the first two Titan I squadrons became operational at Lowry Air Force Base, Colorado, both being assigned to the 703d Strategic Missile Wing.

Atlas F Operational. SAC's six Atlas F squadrons became operational between September and December 1962. The first squadron, the 550th Strategic Missile Squadron at Schilling Air Force Base, Kansas, became operational on 9 September. The last squadron to be accepted was the 556th Strategic Missile Squadron, located at Plattsburgh Air Force Base, New York, the only ICBM base east of the Mississippi River. It became operational on 20 December.

First Minuteman I Launch by SAC. On 28 September, the first Minuteman I to be launched by a SAC crew was accomplished at Vandenberg.

First Minuteman I Operational. The Minuteman program proceeded on schedule, with the first two Minuteman flights of 10 missiles each becoming operational at Malmstrom Air Force Base, Montana, in November. Addition of these 20 operational Minuteman missiles brought the total SAC ICBM force to 200.

Minuteman Educational Program. Under Minuteman alert conditions, combat crews were subjected to long hours of duty in remote, isolated underground launch control centers. The atmosphere was not conducive to developing and maintaining high morale. This was especially true since there was from four to eight hours in each 24 hour tour that was spare time, time during which individual crew members did not have to perform functions directly associated with maintaining the alert missiles.

In order to improve morale by detracting from the boredom associated with the inactivity of crew members and at the same time to attract and retain qualified officers for missile crews, SAC initiated a graduate college program for its Minuteman crews. The school began at Malmstrom Air Force Base, Montana, in November 1962. It was operated by the Air Force Institute of Technology.

Last Jupiter Squadron Deployed to Turkey. On 25 May, the 866th Technical Training Squadron was inactivated at Redstone Arsenal, Huntsville, Alabama. Inactivation of this Jupiter training squadron had been made possible by the deployment of the third Jupiter squadron to Turkey in late 1961.

1963

Resources

Personnel 271,672 (36,206 officers, 211,482 airmen, 23,984 civilians)

Tactical Aircraft 2,424 (636 B-52, 613 B-47, 94 EB-47, 40 RB-47, 36 EB-47L, 86 B/TB-58, 613 EC/KC-135, 306 KC-97)

Aircraft Units 32 Heavy Bomb Wings (29 15 UE and three 30 UE) with B-52s

Six Heavy Strategic Aerospace Wings (five 15 UE and one 30 UE) with B-52s

Ten Medium Bomb Wings (45 UE) and two Medium Strategic Aerospace Wings (45 UE) with B-47s

One Medium Strategic Reconnaissance Wing (30 UE) with RB-47s

Four Support Squadrons (three 10 UE and one 6 UE) with EB-47Ls

Two Medium Bomb Wings (40 UE) with B-58s

41 Heavy Air Refueling Squadrons (12 10 UE, 11 with KC-135s and one with no aircraft assigned; 23 15 UE, 21 with KC-135s, one partially equipped, and one with no aircraft assigned; and six 20 UE equipped with KC-135s)

Fourteen Medium Air Refueling Squadrons (20 UE) with KC-97s

One Light Strategic Reconnaissance Wing with U-2s

Missiles 28 Atlas D, 33 Atlas E, 79 Atlas F, 63 Titan I, 56 Titan II, 372 Minuteman, 593 Hound Dog, 492 Quail

Missile Units Four Atlas D Squadrons (two 9 UE and two 6 UE, including the Vandenberg squadron with all three types of Atlas missiles assigned) fully equipped

Three Atlas E Squadrons (9 UE) fully equipped

Six Atlas F Squadrons (12 UE) fully equipped

Six Titan I Squadrons (9 UE) fully equipped

Six Titan II Squadrons (9 UE) fully equipped

Thirteen Minuteman Squadrons (50 UE), six fully

	equipped, two partially equipped, and five with no missiles assigned
Active Bases	43 CONUS; 10 overseas (Puerto Rico, United Kingdom, Spain, Guam, Labrador, Newfoundland, and Canada).

Budget and Financial Status
(FY 63, as of 30 June 1963)

Operations and Maintenance	$723,017,000, includes supplies, communications, civilian pay, minor equipment purchased, and aviation petroleum, oil, and lubricants (POL)
Assets	$19,243,729,000, includes real property, inventories, equipment, and weapon systems
Operating Expenses	$2,020,428,000, includes O&M listed above, military pay, military family housing, troop subsistence, and procurement of equipment

Organization

When the B-52 dispersal began in the late 1950s, the new units created to support this program were named strategic wings and given four-digit designations (e.g., 4137th Strategic Wing). Under the USAF organization and lineage system, these four-digit units fell into the MAJCOM (major air command controlled) category and their lineage (histories, awards, and battle honors) ended with their discontinuation and could never be revived. By contrast, AFCON (Headquarters USAF controlled) units, which were readily distinguishable by having one, two, or three-digit designations, could go through a series of inactivations and activations and still retain their lineage.

In order to retain the lineage of the combat units and to perpetuate the lineage of many currently inactive units with World War II records, Headquarters SAC received authority from Headquarters USAF to discontinue its strategic wings that were equipped with combat aircraft and to activate AFCON units, most of which were inactive at the time.

The reorganization process, which extended from 1 January through 1 September, was applied to 22 B-52 strategic wings, three air refueling wings, and the 4321st Strategic Wing at Offutt Air Force Base, Nebraska. These units were discontinued and two and three-digit AFCON units were activated. In most cases, the bombardment squadrons that had been assigned to the strategic wings were inactivated and bombardment squadrons that had previously been assigned to the newly-activated wings were activated. While these actions were almost tantamount to redesignations, they were not official redesignations. Therefore, the records, awards and achievements of the strategic wings could not be inherited by the bomb wings.

Numbered air force realignment. On 1 July, SAC reorganized its three numbered air forces in the United States. This realignment was effected primarily to correct an imbalance in the assignment of missiles. Due to restrictive geological factors in the Eastern part of the United States, the Eighth Air

Force's role in the SAC ICBM program had been limited to one squadron of Atlas F missiles at Plattsburgh Air Force Base, New York. With additional B-47 and KC-97 units of the Eighth Air Force scheduled to be inactivated in the following years, the imbalance of forces among the three numbered air forces would be accentuated.

Completely disregarding whatever influence geographical factors may have had upon a numbered air force's area of responsibility, SAC directed that its three numbered air forces be realigned on 1 July, an action which overnight plunged the Eighth Air Force into an operational ICBM environment in the Midwestern and Rocky Mountain regions of the United States. From the Fifteenth, the Eighth acquired a tenant Titan I wing at Lowry Air Force Base, Colorado, and Francis E. Warren Air Force Base, Wyoming, with an operational Atlas wing. With the acquisition of F. E. Warren, a Minuteman wing was activated there. From the Second Air Force, the Eighth acquired a Titan II wing, which would begin receiving missiles shortly thereafter at McConnell Air Force Base, Kansas, and Whiteman Air Base, Missouri, together with its embryonic Minuteman wing.

Operations

B-58 Record Flight. On 16 October, in Operation Greased Lightning, a B-58 (serial number 61-2059) of the 305th Bomb Wing, Bunker Hill Air Force Base, Indiana, set an official world speed record in flying 8,028 miles from Tokyo to London in an elapsed time of eight hours, 35 minutes, and 20.4 seconds, averaging about 938 mph. This supersonic Hustler, piloted by Major Sidney J. Kubesch, took off from Kadena Air Base, Okinawa, and flew over Japan, Alaska, Northern Canada, Greenland, Iceland, and London before landing at Greenham Common RAF Station. Five inflight refuelings were provided by KC-135s. The aircraft also established speed records from Tokyo to Anchorage, Alaska—three hours, nine minutes, and 41.8 seconds, averaging 1,093.44 mph—and Anchorage to London—five hours, 24 minutes, and 54 seconds, averaging 826.91 mph.

SAC support of TAC. Operating under the single manager tanker concept, SAC KC-135s flew over 1,000 sorties in support of routine Tactical Air Command fighter training in 1963. In addition, more than 250 tankers were used to support various overseas deployments of TAC fighters. The largest movement of fighters was conducted as part of Operation Big Lift in October. Directed by Secretary of Defense McNamara, Operation Big Lift involved flying an entire armored division, some 15,000 men, from the United States to Europe and to have them ready to participate in NATO maneuvers within five days. A composite strike force of 115 aircraft accompanied this move to provide close air support for the exercise. Inflight refueling for 71 TAC fighter and reconnaissance aircraft assigned to this composite strike force was provided by approximately 50 KC-135s staging out of Loring and Dow Air Force Bases, Maine.

Medium aircraft phase out. During 1963, SAC continued to undergo transition from a manned aircraft force to a mixed aircraft and missile force. As intercontinental ballistic missiles became more numerous, the B-47s were phased out. By the end of December, only 12 B-47 wings, two of which were outfitted with highly sophisticated electronic countermeasures (ECM) equipment, remained in the combat inventory. Six B-47 wings were disposed of during the year. At the same time seven medium air refueling squadrons phased out their KC-97s and were either inactivated or equipped with KC-135s.

With the reduction of medium bombers, SAC began realigning its overseas Reflex forces. In July, B-47 Reflex operations ceased at the French Moroccan bases of Nouasseur, Benguerir, and Sidi Slimane and were thereafter concentrated at the three Spanish bases of Moron, Torrejon, and Zaragoza and in the United Kingdom at Brize Norton, Fairford, Greenham Common, and Upper Heyford. Medium bomber Reflex operations continued at Elmendorf Air Force Base, Alaska, while Air Mail operations, a variation of Reflex, continued at Anderson Air Force Base, Guam.

With the rapidly diminishing KC-97 force, fewer overseas support bases were required and SAC withdrew its tankers from Kindley Air Force Base, Bermuda, and Churchill, Cold Lake, and Frobisher Royal Canadian Air Force Stations, Canada. Ground alert forces of KC-97s remained at Namao Royal Canadian Air Force Station, Canada; Goose Air Base, Labrador; Ernest Harmon Air Force Base, Newfoundland; and Sondrestrom Air Base, Greenland.

Bombing Competition

Not held due to increased operational commitments and cost reduction programs.

Disposition of Fairchild and Saunders Trophies. General Power decided to award the Fairchild and Saunders Trophies to the bomb wing and air refueling squadron with the best overall combat capability record for Fiscal Year 1963. A special board of officers, composed of the deputy commanders of the Second, Eighth, and Fifteenth Air Forces, reviewed the records and selected the winners—Second Air Force's 2d Bomb Wing won the Fairchild Trophy and the Second's 46th Air Refueling Squadron won the Saunders Trophy.

Missiles

Missile launches. Total missiles and space systems launched during the year from Vandenberg Air Force Base and the U.S. Naval Missile Facility, Point Arguello, California. All SAC launches were from Vandenberg: Launched by: SAC—45; Other Agencies—71.

Titan II operational. On 23 September, for the first time, a SAC crew launched a Titan II from Vandenberg Air Force Base, California. The entire Titan II force of six squadrons began operating in 1963. The first was the 570th Strategic Missile Squadron at Davis-Monthan Air Force Base, Arizona. It was accepted by SAC on 8 June. The 374th Strategic Missile Squadron,

The need to refuel jet-propelled bombers at high speeds and high altitudes led to development of the KC-135 Stratotanker, shown here fueling a B-52D. The KC-135, derived from the commercial Boeing 707, is still in service and "tanks" fighter, attack, and transport aircraft as well as bombers.

A minuteman ICBM is checked out and readied for firing from a test silo at Cape Canaveral (later Cape Kennedy). Note the umbilical cables connected to the missile. Although SAC has had Minuteman missiles deployed since the early 1960s, the current weapons are several generations removed from the first ICBMs with that name.

located at Little Rock Air Force Base, Arkansas, was the last one to become operational. It was accepted on 31 December.

Weighing over 150 tons, the Titan II used storable propellants, could be launched directly from the silo, and employed an all-inertial guidance system. It could carry a heavier payload over a longer distance than any other SAC ICBM.

Minuteman Squadron operational. On 28 February, the first Minuteman squadron, the 10th Strategic Missile Squadron at Malmstrom Air Force Base, Montana, became operational. Five additional squadrons became operational by the end of the year.

On 1 February 1963, the 392d Missile Training Squadron, was inactivated at Vandenberg Air Force Base, California. Since 1958, it had served as a training and launch support squadron for the Royal Air Force and Thor missile force. The 392d had lost its primary mission in August 1962 when the United Kingdom discontinued its IRBM Thor force and, consequently, cancelled its combat training launches at Vandenberg.

Phase Out of the Thor. SAC responsibilities for the Thor program in the United Kingdom ended on 20 December, at which time the system was completely phased out by the Royal Air Force.

Minuteman Educational Program Expanded. Inaugurated at Malmstrom Air Force Base, Montana, in November 1962, the Minuteman Educational Program soon proved successful. In 1963, it was expanded to include the Minuteman crews at Ellsworth Air Force Base, South Dakota, and Minot Air Force Base, North Dakota. The schools at these bases were operated by state universities under contract with the Air Force Institute of Technology.

Organization of Combat Crew Training Squadron at Vandenberg. On 15 May, the 4315th Student Squadron was redesignated the 4315th Combat Crew Training Squadron at Vandenberg Air Force Base, California. Since its organization on 1 May 1958, the 4315th Student Squadron had served as a holding unit for personnel receiving operational readiness training at Vandenberg. Concurrently with this redesignation, the 4315th Combat Crew Training Squadron absorbed the crew training functions previously performed by Vandenberg's three ICBM squadrons—the 576th (Atlas), 394th (Minuteman) and 395th (Titan). These three squadrons then became primarily responsible for operating the launch facilities at Vandenberg and supporting the missiles launched from there.

1964

Resources

Personnel 259,871 (35,035 officers, 201,933 airmen, 22,903 civilians)

Tactical Aircraft 2,075 (626 B-52, 679 EC/KC-135, 391 B-47, 46 EB-47, 22 EB-47L, 27 RB-47, 190 KC-97, 94 B/TB-58)

Aircraft Units 32 Heavy Bomb Wings (29 15 UE and three 30 UE) and six Heavy Strategic Aerospace Wings (five 15 UE and one 30 UE) with B-52s

Four Medium Bomb Wings (45 UE) and four Medium Strategic Aerospace Wings (45 UE) with B-47s

Two Medium Bomb Wings (40 UE) with B-58s

One Medium Strategic Reconnaissance Wing (30 UE) with RB-47s

Two Post Attack Command Control Squadrons (one 10 UE and one 12 UE) with EB-47Ls

44 Heavy Air Refueling Squadrons (five 20 UE, 27 15 UE, 12 10 UE) with EC/KC-135s

Nine Medium Air Refueling Squadrons (20 UE) with KC-97s

One Light Strategic Reconnaissance Wing with U-2s

Missiles 13 Atlas D, 30 Atlas E, 75 Atlas F, 56 Titan I, 59 Titan II, 142 Minuteman A, 556 Minuteman B, 566 Hound Dog, 477 Quail

Missile Units Three Atlas E. Squadrons (9 UE) equipped

Six Atlas F Squadrons (12 UE) equipped

One Atlas D Squadron (the 576th at Vandenberg, which was no longer operational)

Six Titan I Squadrons (9 UE) equipped

Six Titan II Squadrons (9 UE) equipped

16 Minuteman Squadrons (50 UE), 14 equipped

The 341st SMW's three squadrons were equipped with 142 Minuteman A and eight Minuteman B. The other 11 squadrons were equipped with Minuteman B

Active Bases 43 CONUS; eight overseas (Puerto Rico, Spain, United Kingdom, Guam, Labrador, and Newfoundland)

Budget and Financial Status
(FY 64 as of 30 June 1964)

Operations and Maintenance	$737,370,000, includes supplies, communications, civilian pay, minor equipment purchased, and aviation petroleum, oil and lubricants (POL)
Assets	$21,084,000,000, includes real property, inventories, equipment, and weapon systems
Operating Expenses	$2,033,000,000, includes O&M listed above, military pay, military family housing, troop subsistence, and procurement of equipment

Operations

Development of SR-71. On 24 July, President Johnson announced the successful development of a new manned aircraft, the SR-71, which would be produced for the Strategic Air Command shortly after flight testing in early 1965. According to the President, "the SR-71 aircraft reconnaissance system is the most advanced in the world."

B-47 phase out. In line with Secretary of Defense McNamara's objective to dispose of all B-47s and KC-97s by the end of Fiscal Year 1966, four medium bomb wings and five medium air refueling squadrons disposed of their aircraft in 1964.

Reflex operations declined along with the phase out of B-47s and KC-97s. In April and May B-47s stopped Reflexing to Fairford and Greenham Common RAF Stations in England, and Zaragoza Air Base in Spain. The composition of the ground alert force at Anderson Air Force Base, Guam, changed in April when B-47s were replaced by B-52s. At the end of the year, only five bases continued to support B-47 Reflex forces. They were Moron and Torrejon Air Bases, Spain, Brize Norton and Upper Heyford RAF Stations, United Kingdom, and Elmendorf Air Force Base, Alaska.

In June, Sondrestrom Air Base, Greenland, and Namao RCAF Station, Canada, ceased to support KC-97 operations. In October, the Reflex force at Goose Air Base, Labrador, was switched from KC-97s to KC-135s. At the end of the year, Ernest Harmon Air Force Base, Newfoundland, was the only overseas base still supporting KC-97s.

ICBM alert force equals bomber alert force. On 21 April, the number of ICBMs on alert equaled the number of bombers on ground alert. From that day on, the ICBM alert force would outnumber the bomber alert force.

Future of the manned bomber. In 1964, with the B-47 force gradually committed to the storage facility at Davis-Monthan Air Force Base, Arizona, and the B-52 production having been completed since 1962, there was still no firm plan for a replacement bomber. According to Secretary of Defense McNamara, "various options are open for replacing the B-52s in the seventies, if a replacement requirement exists at that time. In case supersonic speed and high altitude are needed for the future strategic bomber, the experience gained from three different Mach 3 planes, currently in the research and development stage, will be available—the XB-70, the A-11, and the SR-71."

"In case low-level penetration capabilities turn out to be the key to future bomber effectiveness, the lessons being learned from the F-111, for example, will be applicable. . . . the fiscal year 1965 budget includes funds for a special study on an Advanced Manned Strategic Aircraft (AMSA), a long-range, low altitude penetrator to serve as an airborne missile platform."

SAC tankers first used to support combat operations. On 9 June, SAC tankers were used for the first time to support combat operations in Southeast Asia. Four KC-135s, operating out of Clark Air Base in the Philippines and nicknamed Yankee Team Tanker Task Force, refueled eight F-100 fighters on their way to strike communist-backed Pathet Lao anti-aircraft emplacements on the Plain of Jars in northern Laos. The tankers loitered over southern Laos until the strike was over. They then refueled two of the fighters before returning to Clark. They remained at Clark until mid-June when the Joint Chiefs of Staff directed them to return to Anderson Air Force Base, Guam, where they rejoined the main body of a larger tanker task force supporting routine Tactical Air Command deployments.

On 5 August, the Joint Chiefs of Staff reestablished the Yankee Team Tanker Task Force at Clark. Consisting of eight KC-135s and renamed Foreign Legion on 3 September, this force began supporting Pacific Air Forces (PACAF) fighters engaged in combat on 28 September.

Alaska earthquake. On 28 March, Headquarters USAF directed SAC to undertake a special aerial reconnaissance mission of the Alaska earthquake which had occurred on the previous evening. Two B-58s of the 43d Bomb Wing, Carswell Air Force Base, Texas, were given a priority assignment to conduct low-level photography over the quake area. Within two hours after being notified, the two aircraft had their special camera pods loaded and were on their way. Approximately 14½ hours after receiving the assignment, these aircraft had completed it, having flown a round trip flight of 5,751 miles, and the processed photographs of the quake were available in Washington, D.C. On the same day, SAC sent three U-2s and two RB-47s to photograph the area from high altitudes; and on the following day, two more 43d Bomb Wing B-58s flew the low-level mission again.

The Daedalian Trophy. With its 1964 aircraft accident rate being the lowest in USAF, the Strategic Air Command was named recipient of the Daedalian Trophy.

Bombing Competition

Not held due to continued emphasis upon cost reduction and increased SAC tanker support for TAC activities in Southeast Asia.

Disposition of Fairchild and Saunders Trophies. Continuing the program established in 1963, the Fairchild Trophy was awarded to the Second Air Force's 70th Bomb Wing and the Saunders Trophy was awarded to the

Eighth Air Force's 42d Air Refueling Squadron on the basis of their overall operational records for FY 1964.

Missiles

Missile launches. Total missiles and space systems launched during the year from Vandenberg Air Force Base. Included for the first six months of the year are those launches emanating from the U.S. Naval Missile Facility, Point Arguello, California. Effective 1 July, this 19,000 acre facility was transferred to SAC and became part of Vandenberg Air Force Base: Launched by: SAC—69; Other Agencies—50.

Phase out of Atlas D missiles. In 1964, the SAC ICBM program reflected the Department of Defense's 1961 decision to place major reliance upon solid-fueled (Minuteman) rather than liquid-fueled or first generation missiles with the phasing out of first generation missiles beginning. The phase out of Atlas D missiles started on 1 May, with the removal of the first missile from alert status at Vandenberg; it was concluded on 1 October, when the last missile of the 549th Strategic Missile Squadron, Offutt Air Force Base, Nebraska, was removed from alert. Three Atlas D squadrons were inactivated, while the fourth, the one at Vandenberg, remained active to support the Atlas E and Atlas F programs.

Atlas E and F and Titan I phase out. On 19 November, Secretary of Defense McNamara announced that all remaining first generation missiles, Atlas E and F and Titan I, would be phased out by the end of June 1965. The decision to phase out these missiles, some of which had been operational for less than two years, was indicative of the rapid technological advances being made in the missile field, particularly in the Minuteman and Polaris programs.

Redesignation of Vandenberg units. On 1 February, the 394th and 395th Missile Training Squadrons, Minuteman and Titan, respectively, were redesignated Strategic Missile Squadrons.

Minuteman ripple launch. On 29 February, two Minuteman missiles were launched in the "ripple" fashion, that is, a single launch crew of the 10th Strategic Missile Squadron, Malmstrom Air Force Base, Montana, gave both commands to launch. These successful launches, which occurred within less than 20 minutes of each other, were conducted at Vandenberg Air Force Base, California.

1965

Resources

Personnel	216,681 (30,336 officers, 164,414 airmen, 21,931 civilians)
Tactical Aircraft	1,490 (600 B-52, 665 EC/KC-135, 114 B-47, 93 B/TB-58, 18 EB/RB-47)
Aircraft Units	32 Heavy Bomb Wings (29 15 UE and three 30 UE) and six Heavy Strategic Aerospace Wings (five 15 UE and one 30 UE) with B-52s; this included two 15 UE Heavy Bomb Wings that were in early stages of phasing out their B-52B aircraft
	Two Medium Bomb Wings (45 UE), one with B-47s, and three Medium Strategic Aerospace Wings, one with B-47s; the other units, one Medium Bomb Wing and two Strategic Aerospace Wings, had retired their aircraft as part of the accelerated B-47 phase out program
	Two Medium Bomb Wings (40 UE) with B-58s
	44 Heavy Air Refueling Squadrons (three 20 UE, 29 15 UE, 12 10 UE) with EC/KC-135s
	Five Medium Air Refueling Squadrons (20 UE) without aircraft assigned
	Four Reconnaissance Wings, one equipped with RB-47s, one with U-2s, one with RC-135s, and one without aircraft assigned
Missiles	59 Titan II, 821 Minuteman, 542 Hound Dogs, and 465 Quail
Missile Units	Six Titan II Squadrons (9 UE) fully equipped
	19 Minuteman Squadrons (50 UE), 16 fully equipped and three partially equipped
Active Bases	40 CONUS; seven overseas (Puerto Rico, Spain, Newfoundland, Labrador, and Guam)

Budget and Financial Status
(FY 65, as of 30 June 1965)

Operations and Maintenance	$740,594,000, includes supplies, communications, civilian pay, minor equipment purchased, and aviation petroleum, oil, and lubricants (POL)

Assets	$20,578,200,000, includes real property, inventories, equipment, and weapon systems
Operating Expenses	$1,987,124,000, includes O&M listed above, military pay, military family housing, troop subsistence, and procurement of equipment

Organization

Inactivation of 7th Air Division. Effective 30 June, Headquarters 7th Air Division, located at High Wycombe Air Station, was discontinued. Inactivation was effected approximately 90 days after B-47 Reflex operations had ceased at Brize Norton and Upper Heyford RAF Stations, the last two United Kingdom bases to support B-47s.

Operations

KC-135 and B-52 operations in Vietnam War. In January, the 4252d Strategic Wing was activated at Kadena Air Base, Okinawa. Its mission at first was to provide KC-135 air refueling for the Pacific Air Forces' fighter-bombers engaged in air operations over South and North Vietnam. Later in the year, the 4252d began refueling B-52s that were carrying out bombing missions against Viet Cong bases in South Vietnam.

First B-52 Arc Light bombing mission. The first B-52 bombing mission was carried out on 18 June. On this mission, 27 B-52F bombers of the 7th and 320th Bomb Wings based at Guam were used to attack a Viet Cong jungle redoubt with conventional 750- and 1,000-pound bombs. In some circles, this first raid was regarded as a fiasco. Few, if any, Viet Cong were killed. Furthermore, two B-52s were lost in a mid-air collision on way to the target. The press, well indoctrinated in the nuclear bombing role of the B-52 and in the SAC strategic deterrence theory, regarded the use of B-52s against the Viet Cong as something closely akin to "swatting flies with a sledgehammer."

From June through December, the 7th, 320th, and 454th Bomb Wings, rotating crews and aircraft to the Pacific area, completed over 100 missions to South Vietnam. These B-52Fs were used primarily in saturation bombing of Viet Cong base areas, but later in the year, they were used in direct tactical support of the Marine Corps' Operation Harvest Moon and the First Cavalry Division's fight in the Ia Drang Valley.

"Big Belly" modification program. Throughout 1965, the SAC bombers committed to the Vietnam conflict were B-52F models. Each bomber's maximum bomb load was 51 750-pound bombs (27 internal and 24 external). In December, a "Big Belly" modification program was started to increase the B-52D's internal capacity to carry 500-pound bombs from 27 to 84 or its capacity to carry 750-pounders from 27 to 42. In addition, the B-52D could still carry 24 500-pound or 750-pound bombs externally. The maximum bomb load would be about 30 tons.

During the last six months of 1965, SAC KC-135s flew over 4,000 sorties in direct support of PACAF operations.

B-47 and KC-97 phase out accelerated. In early October, Headquarters USAF initiated Project Fast Fly, which directed that SAC's remaining five B-47 wings and six KC-97 air refueling squadrons be phased out approximately six months ahead of the previously-established deadline of June 1966. By the end of the year, three wings had disposed of their aircraft. Two wings, the 9th and 100th, retained their aircraft and ground alert requirements until 31 December, after which they began disposing of their aircraft.

Phase out of last KC-97s. On 10 November, the last KC-97 was removed from ground alert. It belonged to the 9th Air Refueling Squadron at Mountain Home Air Force Base, Idaho. Disposition of all KC-97s was completed on 21 December, when the last two aircraft, serial number 53-0282 of the 100th Air Refueling Squadron, Pease Air Force Base, New Hampshire, and one, serial number unknown, of the 384th Air Refueling Squadron, Westover Air Force Base, Massachusetts, were flown to the storage facility at Davis-Monthan Air Force Base, Arizona.

B-52 phase out. SAC's two B-52B squadrons were also earmarked for accelerated phase out in early 1966. The B-52B phase out program had actually begun in March 1965 when SAC began retiring those aircraft that had reached the end of their service life; that is, they had reached a specific number of flying hours under certain conditions of structural stress.

On 8 March, the first B-52B (serial number 52-8714) to be retired under this program was transferred from the 22d Bomb Wing, March Air Force Base, California, to Chanute Air Force Base, Illinois, to be used for instruction purposes by the Air Training Command. On 29 September, the first B-52 to be assigned to SAC, ("B" model serial number 52-8711), was transferred from the 22d Bomb Wing (it had been transferred from the 93d Bomb Wing to the 22d in early 1956) to the Aerospace Museum, Offutt Air Force Base, Nebraska.

Last KC-135 delivered. On 12 January, the last KC-135 (serial number 64-14840) to be assigned to SAC was delivered to the 380th Air Refueling Squadron, Plattsburgh Air Force Base, New York.

B-47 Reflex terminated in Spain. On 31 March, B-47 Reflex operations ended at Moron and Torrejon Air Bases, Spain.

B-58 and B-52 phase out. On 8 December, Secretary of Defense McNamara announced another aircraft phase out program that would further reduce the Strategic Air Command's bomber force. Basically, this program called for the retirement of all B-58s and the older B-52s (C, D, E, and F models) by the end of June 1971. This reduction would be accompanied by additional base closures and unit relocations.

The FB-111 selected for assignment to SAC. On 10 December, Secretary of Defense McNamara somewhat softened the impact of his 8 December phase out announcement by announcing that 210 FB-111s would be purchased at a cost of $1.7 billion and assigned to SAC as replacements for the older model B-52s and the B-58s. The new bomber was a modified version of the F-111 fighter which was originally designated TFX.

PACCS force converted to all KC-135. On 25 March, SAC's Post Attack Command Control System (PACCS) force was reorganized. The 4363d and the 4364th Post Attack Command Control Squadrons, located at Lockbourne Air Force Base, Ohio, and Mountain Home Air Force Base, Idaho, respectively, were discontinued. Their radio-relay missions were absorbed by EC-135As that were assigned to air refueling squadrons at Lockbourne and Ellsworth Air Force Base, South Dakota. Thereafter, the PACCS force became an all KC-135 system with EC-135s performing the Looking Glass and auxiliary airborne command posts' missions.

SAC Automated Command Control System (SACCS). On 1 March, the Strategic Air Command accepted the SAC Automated Command Control System (SACCS) from the Air Force Systems Command. Refined under the direction of the SACCS Management Group, which was established in Headquarters SAC, SACCS, or 465L as it was often called, provided means of complementing the numerous systems of voice transmission in operation throughout SAC with printed messages, which could be transmitted to and printed out by any or all SAC command posts in North America. SACCS also embodied data processing and data display subsystems. The data processing subsystem was composed of computers which stored information on the status of the aircraft and missile forces, while the data display subsystem provided a means for visually displaying this force status information to commanders and key national officials.

Spot promotions terminated. On 28 December, General John P. McConnell, USAF Chief of Staff, terminated the SAC Spot Promotion Program, which had been started by General LeMay in December 1949. General McConnell directed that all crew members who held these spot promotions would revert to their normal grades on 30 June 1966.

Bombing Competition

After being cancelled for three years, the fourteenth SAC Bombing Competition was held from 12 through 18 September. New ground rules, more compatible with the ones for the original competition than with those for recent years, were issued to the participants, which included one aircraft and one crew from each of 44 bomb wings, two B-58, five B-47, and 37 B-52. This was the last competition for the B-47s. All aircraft staged out of Fairchild Air Force Base, Washington. The 454th Bomb Wing, a B-52F unit of the Second Air Force, won the Fairchild Trophy.

Air refueling squadrons did not participate in this competition, but the Saunders Trophy, which was normally awarded to the best tanker unit in the meet, was awarded to the 922d Air Refueling Squadron, Eighth Air Force. This award was based upon the past year's performance.

Missiles

Missile launches. Total missiles and space systems launched during the year from Vandenberg Air Force Base: Launched by: SAC—50; Other Agencies—51.

Atlas E and F and Titan I phase out completed. In line with Secretary of Defense McNamara's 19 November 1964 directive, all first generation missiles were removed from alert during the period from 4 January through 12 April. By 20 April, all missiles had been shipped to storage facilities for later use as launch vehicles in various research and development programs. With the phase out completed, the missile squadrons, three Atlas E, six Atlas F, and Six Titan I, were inactivated.

Minuteman I program completed. SAC completed its Minuteman I program on 15 June, when the sixteenth squadron, the 400th Strategic Missile Squadron, became operational at Francis E. Warren Air Force Base, Wyoming. The operational Minuteman I force actually consisted of two types of missiles, the "A" and "B" models. The slightly larger Minuteman B's second stage motor chamber was made of titanium while the Minuteman A's chamber was made of steel. The Minuteman A was assigned only to the three squadrons of the 341st Strategic Missile Wing, Malmstrom Air Force Base, Montana.

Minuteman II program started. Three Minuteman II squadrons were activated and assigned to the 321st Strategic Missile Wing, Grand Forks Air Force Base, North Dakota. These squadrons were partially equipped by the end of the year. The Minuteman II, appreciably longer than the Minuteman I models, was outfitted with a more powerful second-stage engine and possessed a greater range than the Minuteman I. It also possessed a more accurate reentry vehicle and penetration aids to protect it from antiballistic missiles.

Operational base launch. On 1 March, a crew of the 44th Strategic Missile Wing launched a Minuteman I from Ellsworth Air Force Base, South Dakota. To preclude overflight accidents, Headquarters SAC limited the missile's flight to about seven seconds or a range of only two miles. Nicknamed Project Long Life, this successful firing demonstrated that a SAC missile crew could launch a Minuteman from an operational site.

1966

Resources

Personnel	196,887 (26,588 officers, 147,197 airmen, 23,102 civilians)
Tactical Aircraft	1,355 (591 B-52, 83 B/TB-58, 665 EC/KC-135, 16 RB-47)
Aircraft Units	29 Heavy Bomb Wings (25 15 UE and four 30 UE) and six Heavy Strategic Aerospace Wings (five 15 UE and one 30 UE) with B-52s
	43 Heavy Air Refueling Squadrons (five 20 UE, 28 15 UE and ten 10 UE) with KC-135s
	Two Medium Bomb Wings (40 UE) with B-58s
	Four Reconnaissance Wings, one equipped with RB-47s, one with U-2s, one with RC-135s, and one partially equipped with SR-71s
Missiles	60 Titan II, 908 Minuteman, 548 Hound Dog, 457 Quail
Missile Units	Six Titan II Squadrons (9 UE) fully equipped and 20 Minuteman Squadrons, 19 fully equipped and one partially equipped
Active Bases	35 CONUS; three overseas (Puerto Rico, Guam, and Labrador)

Budget and Financial Status
(FY 66, as of 30 June 1966)

Operations and Maintenance	$392,912,000, includes supplies, communications, civilian pay, and minor equipment purchased
Assets	$18,477,079,000, includes real property, inventories, equipment, and weapon systems
Operating Expenses	$1,591,457,000, includes O&M listed above, military pay, family housing, troop subsistence, and aviation petroleum, oil, and lubricants (POL)

Organization

Sixteenth Air Force transferred. With B-47 Reflex operations having ceased there in late March 1965, the Spanish base complex became less important to SAC operations. On 15 April, Headquarters Sixteenth Air Force and Moron,

Torrejon, and Zaragoza Air Bases were transferred from SAC to USAFE. SAC remained as a tenant at Torrejon, with its support functions being carried out by the 3970th Strategic Wing. On 25 June, the 3970th was discontinued and its personnel and functions were absorbed by the 98th Strategic Wing, one of those units preserved through redesignation after the B-47 phase out was completed.

Operations

Southeast Asia. SAC continued conventional bombing missions in Southeast Asia with B-52 and KC-135 inflight refueling. As in 1965, the SAC bombers concentrated upon area bombing of Viet Cong base camps, with the primary objective being to keep the enemy from building up large forces in the jungle sanctuaries. At the same time, B-52s began to be used in direct support of ground troops who were in contact with the enemy.

Although the B-52s were used primarily against targets in South Vietnam, they were also used to bomb the approaches to the Mu Gia Pass in North Vietnam on 12 and 26 April. The objective here was to stop the infiltration of enemy troops who, after leaving the Mu Gia Pass, crossed over into Laos and made their way down the Ho Chi Minh Trail.

By late June, after one year of participating in the war, the B-52s were dropping approximately 8,000 tons of bombs each month. Missions were flown in all types of weather, night and day. In 1966, over 5,000 B-52 sorties released bombs over target. General William C. Westmoreland, Commander of the U.S. Forces in Vietnam, said, ". . . we know, from talking to many prisoners and defectors, that the enemy troops fear B-52s, tactical air, artillery and armor, in that order."

Throughout 1966, the B-52s continued to operate from Anderson Air Force Base, Guam. Normally two B-52 wings with augmentee aircraft and crews from other wings were maintained there for that purpose. While committed to the conflict, these B-52 wings were assigned to the 3d Air Division's 4133d Bomb Wing, Provisional, which was organized on 1 February. Normally each wing remained in combat for about six months. After being replaced by a wing from the CONUS, it returned home.

With the deployment of the 28th and 484th Bomb Wings to Guam in April, the B-52D bomber, modified with the Big Belly to carry more bombs, replaced the B-52F as the SAC bomber in the Vietnam conflict.

In June, SAC activated the 4258th Strategic Wing at U Tapao Airfield, Thailand, and gave it responsibility for satisfying some of the growing demand for inflight refueling. The majority of the KC-135s assigned to the 4258th and the 4252d Strategic Wings came from air refueling squadrons that were deployed to the area at the same time their parent B-52 wings deployed to Guam. These tanker forces were also augmented with aircraft and crews from other air refueling squadrons.

Retirement of Last B-47s. In the first half of 1966, Project Fast Fly, the accelerated phase out of all SAC B-47, KC-97, and B-52B aircraft, was com-

During the lengthy Vietnam War, the Air Force again used strategic bombers in "tactical" strikes. Here a B-52D based on Guam unloads "iron bombs" over a suspected Viet Cong concentration during a 1966 bombing run.

pleted. On 11 February, SAC's last two B-47 bombers (B-47E serial number 53-2286, assigned to the 100th Bomb Wing, Pease Air Force Base, New Hampshire, and B-47E serial number 53-6235, assigned to the 9th Strategic Aerospace Wing, Mountain Home Air Force Base, Idaho) were transferred to the storage facility at Davis-Monthan Air Force Base, Arizona. There were still RB-47s assigned to the 55th Strategic Reconnaissance Wing.)

Disposition of Units. All Fast Fly units were either redesignated and reorganized to support other type aircraft or inactivated before the end of June. Because of their illustrious records, the five medium bomb wings were retained in SAC: two became B-52 units, two became strategic reconnaissance wings, and one was moved to Spain. SAC's last five KC-97 air refueling squadrons were inactivated. Of the two B-52B wings that were phased out (all B-52B aircraft had been sent to storage by the end of June), one was inactivated and the other was equipped with B-52D aircraft from a less illustrious wing that was inactivated.

First SR-71. On 7 January, SAC's reconnaissance force received the first SR-71, a "B" model trainer (serial number 61-7957), assigned to the 4200th Strategic Wing at Beale Air Force Base, California. Capable of flying three times the speed of sound (Mach 3) at altitudes over 80,000 feet, the SR-71 could carry a variety of photographic, radar, and infrared sensors. Manned

102

by a pilot and reconnaissance systems officer, the SR-71 could survey an area of 60,000 square miles in one hour.

B-52 Crash Palomares, Spain. On 17 January, a B-52 collided with a KC-135 tanker during a high altitude refueling operation and both aircraft crashed near Palomares, Spain. There were four survivors and seven fatalities. Some radioactive material was released when two weapons underwent non-nuclear TNT-type explosions on impact. Cleanup work began immediately and involved removing approximately 1,400 tons of slightly contaminated soil and vegetation to the U.S. for disposal. Simultaneously, an exhaustive land and sea search was started to locate a nuclear weapon that had been lost. It was finally located on 15 March by a submersible about five miles from the shore and approximately 2,500 feet under water. Following several unsuccessful attempts to retrieve the weapon, during which time it became dislodged and slipped deeper and deeper into the water, it was recovered intact by a U.S. Navy recovery force on 7 April.

Bombing Competition

Fifteenth Competition. SAC's fifteenth bombing competition was held from 2 through 8 October, Fairchild Air Force Base, Washington. Participants included one crew from each of 35 B-52 wings and two B-58 wings and three RAF crews flying Vulcan bombers.

Armed with the motto "Not to Win is a Very Bad Thing," which was provided by their commander, Lieutenant General David Wade, Eighth Air

In late 1965, Secretary of Defense McNamara ordered development of the controversial "swing-wing" TFX tactical strike fighter into a strategic attack configuration to help increase the size of the program. The first strategic FB-111 was delivered to SAC in October 1969. This FB-111A is flying high and slow, with variable-sweep wings fully extended and four SRAM attack missiles on underwing pylons. The wings sweep back for high-speed, low-level flight. Note the side-by-side crew seating. (General Dynamics photo)

Force wings completely dominated the competition. They captured the first four places in the overall competition for the Fairchild Trophy. The 19th Bomb Wing, a B-52 unit, won the trophy.

Saunders Trophy. In line with the procedure followed in previous years when air refueling squadrons did not participate in the competition, the Saunders Trophy was awarded to the unit with the best record in the previous fiscal year. The 1966 winner was Second Air Force's 906th Air Refueling Squadron.

Missiles

Missile Launches. Total missiles and space systems launched during the year from Vandenberg Air Force Base: Launched by: SAC—55; Other Agencies—68.

Minuteman Salvo Launch. On 24 February, combat crews of the 341st Strategic Missile Wing launched simultaneously two Minuteman "A" missiles from test silos at Vandenberg Air Force Base, California. This salvo launch successfully demonstrated the multiple countdown and launch techniques that might be used at operational sites under actual combat conditions.

Activation of Final Minuteman Squadron. On 1 April, the 564th Strategic Missile Squadron, SAC's 20th and last Minuteman squadron was activated at Malmstrom Air Force Base, Montana, and assigned to the 341st Strategic Missile Wing. The 341st already operated three squadrons of Minuteman I missiles. The fourth squadron was scheduled to become operational with Mintueman II missiles in early 1967.

Force Modernization Program. Force Modernization entailed the replacement of Minuteman I, "A" and "B" series, missiles with Minuteman II or "F" series missiles. Scheduled to apply to the entire Minuteman I force, the modernization program began at Whiteman Air Force Base, Missouri, on 7 May, when the first flight of ten Minuteman I, "B" series, missiles were removed from their silos.

In order to prepare for the emplacement of Minuteman II missiles, it was necessary to completely retrofit the original missile launchers, control facilities, and other ground equipment. The Modernized Minuteman missile systems were not identical to the Minuteman II systems installed at Grand Forks and in the fourth squadron at Malmstrom. The force modernization program included modifying the missile's underground launching site to accept the advanced Minuteman II and renovation of the launch control center and related ground support equipment to accommodate the more sophisticated missile.

Minuteman II Operational. On 25 April, the first Minuteman II squadron, the 447th Strategic Missile Squadron, became operational at Grand Forks Air Force Base, North Dakota. Two additional 321st Wing squadrons had become operational at Grand Forks by 22 November.

Inactivation of Last Atlas Squadron. On 2 April, the 576th Strategic Missile Squadron (ICBM Atlas) which had been located at Vandenberg Air Force Base, California, since 1 April 1958, was inactivated.

1967

Resources

Personnel	191,305 (25,745 officers, 143,412 airmen, 22,148 civilians)
Tactical Aircraft	1,327 (588 B-52, 81 B/TB-58, 658 KC-135)
Aircraft Units	28 Heavy Bomb Wings (24 15 UE and four 30 UE) and five 15 UE Heavy Strategic Aerospace Wings with B-52s
	Two Medium Bomb Wings (39 UE) with B-58
	42 Heavy Air Refueling Squadrons (four 20 UE, 31 15 UE, and seven 10 UE) with KC-135s
	Three Strategic Reconnaissance Wings (one equipped with U-2s, one with RC-135s, and one partially equipped with SR-71s); two Strategic Reconnaissance Squadrons with RC-135s
Missiles	63 Titan II, 973 Minuteman, 477 Hound Dog, and 448 Quail
Missile Units	Six Titan II Squadrons (9 UE) fully equipped and 20 Minuteman Squadrons (50 UE), 19 fully equipped and one converting from Minuteman I to Minuteman II missiles
Active Bases	32 CONUS; three overseas (Puerto Rico, Guam, and Labrador)

Budget and Financial Status (FY 67, as of 30 June 1967)

Operations and Maintenance	$397,952,000, includes supplies, communications, civilian pay, and minor equipment purchased
Assets	$16,942,453,000, includes real property, inventories, equipment, and weapon systems
Operating Expenses	$1,556,355,000, includes O&M listed above, military pay, family housing, troop subsistence, and aviation petroleum, oil, and lubricants (POL)

Operations

During 1967 B-52s flew approximately 9,700 effective bombing sorties in Vietnam, almost twice the number flown in 1966. Most of this bombing effort was to support U.S. ground troops in contact with the enemy. A great deal of attention was also devoted to enemy troop concentrations and supply lines in the Ashau Valley, around Dak To near the Cambodian border, and in and around the Demilitarized Zone. In September, the majority of the targets struck by the B-52s was in the Demilitarized Zone. On 6 May, SAC flew its 10,000th B-52 sortie in Southeast Asia. Until that time, more than 190,000 tons of bombs had been dropped in less than two years of combat operations.

"Big Belly" modifications completed. Throughout the year, only B-52D bombers outfitted with the "Big Belly" modification were used in SEA (on 13 September, the last B-52D was modified to carry the increased bomb load). During the year, the following wings served as cadre units and, augmented by bombers and crews from other wings, were responsible for carrying out the conventional bombing effort: 306th, 91st, 22d, 454th, 461st, and 99th.

B-52 operations from Thailand. In early April, part of this B-52 force began operating out of U Tapao Airfield, Thailand. Staging out of this base, the bombers could complete their missions without KC-135 inflight refueling which was required when operating from Guam. This saved both time and money. The 4258th Strategic Wing, which had been functioning strictly as a tanker organization since June 1966, assumed control of the bomber operations from U Tapao.

B-52 accidents in Southeast Asia. In July SAC lost three B-52Ds as the result of accidents in Southeast Asia. On 7 July, two B-52s collided in the air and crashed in the South China Sea. Among the six casualties was Major General William J. Crumm, Commander of the 3d Air Division. On 8 July, another bomber crashed and was destroyed while attempting an emergency landing at Da Nang Air Base, South Vietnam. Five of the six crew members were killed.

KC-135 Operations in Southeast Asia. During 1967, SAC KC-135s operating out of Kadena, U Tapao, and other Western Pacific bases flew over 22,000 sorties while dispensing over 1.1 million pounds of fuel in support of B-52s and fighters of the Pacific Air Forces.

KC-135 Refueling and Ninth Mackay Trophy. On 31 May, a KC-135 crew of the 902d Air Refueling Squadron (Clinton-Sherman Air Force Base, Oklahoma) was involved in a complex and spectacular air refueling operation over the Gulf of Tonkin. This mission started out as a routine inflight refueling to two F-104s, but before it was over it involved saving six fuel-starved, carrier-based U.S. Navy aircraft (two KA-3 tankers, two F-8 fighters, and two F-4 fighters). At one point in this intricate operation, the KC-135 was refueling a KA-3 tanker which in turn was refueling an F-8. While the KA-3 was partially loaded with fuel that could be dispensed to other aircraft, it could not transfer this fuel to its own tanks. After satisfying everybody's fuel requirements, the KC-135's own fuel supply was so low that it had to land at an alternate base.

The Mackay Trophy for 1967, symbolic of the most meritorious flight of the year, was awarded to Major John H. Casteel and his three-man crew for this life-saving mission. This marked the ninth time SAC personnel received this award.

SR-71 and the sonic boom. In July, SAC began making supersonic SR-71 training flights across the United States, after having warned residents of the corridors over which these flights were scheduled to expect sonic booms. Because the SR-71 normally operated at about 80,000 feet altitude, its sonic boom at that level resembled distant thunder and the impact was far less than that generated by the lower-flying supersonic B-58. However, when the SR-71 descended to around 30,000 feet for a refueling rendezvous with the KC-135, its sonic boom became more pronounced, particularly during descent and climb back to higher altitude. It was for this reason that refueling patterns were established over sparsely populated areas.

Last RB-47. On 29 December, SAC's last B-47 type aircraft was flown to the storage facility at Davis-Monthan Air Force Base, Arizona. This was an RB-47H reconnaissance aircraft (serial number 53-4296) of the 55th Strategic Reconnaissance Wing, Offutt Air Force Base, Nebraska. The last B-47 bomber aircraft had been retired on 11 February 1966.

B-52 phase out. In pursuance of Secretary of Defense McNamara's 1964 and 1965 decisions to eliminate a major part of the SAC bomber force by the end of FY 1971, three B-52 squadrons were inactivated in the first half of the year. However, the inactivation of these squadrons did not result in the immediate retirement of their "D" and "E" model aircraft. The "D" aircraft, which had been modified for conventional bombing, were used to bolster the resources of those SAC wings committed to the Southeast Asia conflict. Excess "E" model aircraft were designated nonoperational active (NOA) aircraft, that is, actively stored with operational units, maintained in a serviceable condition, and periodically flown. No additional crews or maintenance personnel were authorized for these aircraft. The only aircraft retired were a few "E" and "F" models that had reached the end of operational life by accumulating a specified number of flying hours under conditions of structural stress.

Maintaining a deterrent force. While the war in Southeast Asia was demanding more and more B-52 and KC-135 support, the primary mission of SAC remained one of deterring a nuclear attack upon the United States. Toward this objective, SAC continued to maintain about 40 percent of the bomber force and nearly 100 percent of the ICBM force on alert. A small number of bombers continued to fly daily alert indoctrination missions.

Bombing Competition

Scheduled to be held in October, the bombing competition was cancelled in August, because of "current operational commitments and overriding training requirements." Neither the Fairchild Trophy nor the Saunders Trophy was awarded in 1967.

RAF Bombing Competition. From 13 through 15 March, SAC participated in the RAF Bombing Competition. Each numbered air force sent one B-52 and crew to compete in this event at RAF Station Marham. Participants represented the 449th Bomb Wing, Second Air Force; 19th Bomb Wing, Eighth Air Force; and 93d Bomb Wing, Fifteenth Air Force. The overall SAC showing in this competition was disappointing; not one trophy was brought home.

Missiles

Missile launches. Total missiles and space systems launched during the year from Vandenberg Air Force Base: Launched by: SAC—38; Other Agencies—75.

First missile competition. With the ICBM force having become fairly stabilized, conditions were favorable to hold missile competitions similar to bombing competitions. Planning for the first missile competition began in mid-1966 and it was finally held from 3 through 7 April at Vandenberg Air Force Base, California. Participants included two combat crews and one target alignment team from each of the six Minuteman and three Titan wings. Crews were tested in missile procedure trainers, while the alignment crews were tested in the launch facilities.

The 351st Strategic Missile Wing, Eighth Air Force's lone Minuteman unit, made a clean sweep of the competition by winning all the Minuteman class awards and the Blanchard Trophy, which was awarded to the best wing in the competition. Established especially for the missile competition, this trophy was named in honor of General William H. Blanchard, who died on 31 May 1966 while serving as USAF Vice Chief of Staff. The recipient retained custody of the trophy until the next competition. The 381st Strategic Missile Wing, the Eighth Air Force's only Titan unit, won the Best Titan Wing award.

Minuteman force modernization. On 21 April, the 564th Strategic Missile Squadron, SAC's 20th Minuteman squadron, became operational at Malmstrom Air Force Base, Montana. It was equipped with Minuteman II or "F" series missiles, while its three sister squadrons, all assigned to the 341st Wing, were equipped with Minuteman I, "A" and "B" series, missiles. In December, the 341st entered the Force Modernization program, the conversion of its three older squadrons from Minuteman I to Minuteman II.

The Force Modernization program was completed at Whiteman Air Force Base, Missouri, where the 351st Strategic Missile Wing had become fully modernized and operational with Minuteman IIs on 3 October.

Resources

Personnel	168,500 (24,323 officers, 124,221 airmen, 19,956 civilians)
Tactical Aircraft	1,307 (579 B-52, 76 B/TB-58, 652 EC/KC-135)
Aircraft Units	23 Heavy Bomb Wings (19 15 UE and four 30 UE) and four 15 UE Heavy Strategic Aerospace Wings with B-52s
	Two Medium Bomb Wings (39 UE) with B-58s
	41 Heavy Air Refueling Squadrons (four 20 UE, 33 15 UE, and four 10 UE) with KC-135s
	Three Strategic Reconnaissance Wings (one with U-2s, one with RC-135s, and one with SR-71s)
	Two Strategic Reconnaissance Squadrons with RC-135s
Missiles	59 Titan II, 967 Minuteman, 312 Hound Dog, and 445 Quail
Missile Units	Six Titan II Squadrons (9 UE) fully equipped and 20 Minuteman Squadrons (50 UE), 19 fully equipped and one in process of converting from Minuteman I "A" and "B" series to Minuteman II or "F" series missiles
Active Bases	28 CONUS; three overseas (Puerto Rico, Guam, and Labrador)

Budget and Financial Status
(FY 68, as of 30 June 1968)

Operations and Maintenance	$365,730,000 includes supplies, communications, civilian pay, and minor equipment purchased
Assets	$16,436,434,000, includes real property, inventories, equipment, and weapon systems
Operating Expenses	$1,548,967,000, includes O&M listed above, military pay, family housing, troop subsistence, and aviation petroleum, oil, and lubricants (POL)

Organization

FB-111 Group Organized. Effective 2 July, the 340th Bombardment Group, Medium, was organized at Carswell Air Force Base, Texas. Assigned to the

19th Air Division of Second Air Force, the 340th was scheduled to be the first SAC unit to receive FB-111 aircraft. The 340th's primary mission was to train combat crews in the operation of the new bomber. Upon completion of their training, the crews would be assigned to an operational FB-111 wing.

Operations

Southeast Asia. In 1968, SAC B-52s were called upon to provide more bombing missions in support of the U.S. forces in the Vietnam conflict. An increase was already being carried out in the early part of the year when the enemy launched the Tet offensive and laid siege to the U.S. Marine base at Khe Sanh. Almost simultaneously, along with the overall buildup of U.S. forces in the area as a result of the seizure of the U.S. Navy intelligence ship *Pueblo*, additional SAC bombers were sent to the Western Pacific.

The defense of Khe Sanh developed into the largest and most significant air campaign to date. Around-the-clock strikes were made against enemy forces besieging the base, with SAC bombers accounting for approximately 60,000 tons of bombs dropped. With fighter-bomber support being limited by the monsoon season, which was at its height on 21 January when the base was surrounded, the B-52 was particularly valuable. In conducting this bombing, the B-52 crews relied upon ground-based radar to direct them to their targets, where they destroyed tons of North Vietnamese supplies that had been concentrated in the area. These air attacks helped break the siege on Khe Sanh and force the North Vietnamese to withdraw.

Although the siege of Khe Sanh ended in early April, the B-52 bombing operations continued at a high level throughout the year, with a variety of targets hit in South Vietnam. Special attention was directed toward enemy areas in the Ashau Valley, the Kontum-Dak To tri-border area, and especially the communist assault corridor running southeast from War Zone C and the Cambodian border to Saigon.

The following B-52D wings provided cadre forces in the Western Pacific during the year: 99th, 509th, 28th, 92d, 454th, and 70th.

Establishment of RTU at Castle. On 15 April, a Replacement Training Unit (RTU) was established within the 93d Bomb Wing's 4017th Combat Crew Training Squadron at Castle Air Force Base, California. The RTU's primary mission was to cross-train crews from B-52F through B-52H model wings in the operation of B-52D aircraft. Upon completing the two-week school, the crews were used to augment the cadre units in Southeast Asia, thereby more equitably spreading out the combat duties among the entire B-52 force and providing the resources needed to meet the increased bombing effort.

SAC's KC-135s, operating under the single manager tanker concept that had been in effect since 1961, continued to support a variety of operations in Southeast Asia in addition to those directly associated with aircraft engaged in combat. They made possible the rapid deployment of tactical fighters and interceptors to Korea following the seizure of the USS *Pueblo*. In rotating to and from Western Pacific bases under the operational nickname of Young

Tiger, the KC-135s also furnished priority airlift of support personnel and augmentation crews.

B-52 Crash at Thule. On 22 January, a B-52G with four nuclear weapons aboard crashed and burned on the ice of North Star Bay while attempting an emergency landing at nearby Thule Air Base, Greenland. In cooperation with the government of Denmark, the U.S. Air Force conducted an extensive cleanup operation to remove all possible traces of radioactive material. This gigantic operation was completed on 13 September.

B-52 Phase Out. Although six B-52 squadrons (accounting for an authorization of 90 bombers) were inactivated during the year, there was only a slight decrease in the number of B-52s assigned to SAC. The Department of Defense and Headquarters USAF continued to allow SAC to retain the serviceable "E" and "F" model aircraft from these inactivated units and to assign them to active units. Only those B-52s that had exceeded their service life criteria were retired.

Dispersal Program. The dispersal program, which had been effectively used by B-47s in the Cuban Missile Crisis of 1962, was revived and expanded in early 1968 to include B-52s and KC-135s. The objective of this program was to provide a means of dispersing the aircraft force over a large number of bases, both military installations and civilian airfields, during periods of increased tension or international crisis. By providing additional bases to which the aircraft could be dispersed, the enemy's targeting problem was compounded, and more bombers could become airborne within a given time period.

Missiles

Missile Launches. Total missiles and space systems launched during the year from Vandenberg Air Force Base: Launched by: SAC—24; Other Agencies—54.

Throughout 1968, the Force Modernization program continued within the 341st Strategic Missile Wing at Malmstrom Air Force Base, Montana. The 12th Strategic Missile Squadron was fully equipped with five flights of Minuteman IIs on 22 April. By the end of the year, the 10th Strategic Missile Squadron had almost completed the conversion, while the 490th Strategic Missile Squadron was still equipped with Minuteman I "A" and "B" series missiles.

1969

Resources

Personnel	164,328 (23,167 officers, 122,828 airmen, 18,333 civilians)
Tactical Aircraft	1,196 (505 B-52, 647 EC/KC-135, 41 B/TB-58, 3 FB-111A)
Aircraft Units	20 Heavy Bomb Wings (16 15 UE and four 30 UE) and four Heavy Strategic Aerospace Wings (15 UE) with B-52s
	Two 39 UE Medium Bomb Wings in process of phasing out their B-58s
	One 30 UE Medium Bomb Wing with no aircraft assigned and making preparations for equipping with FB-111As
	One Medium Bomb Group (15 UE), the FB-111 Training unit, with three FB-111As assigned
	39 Heavy Air Refueling Squadrons (31 15 UE, seven 20 UE, and one 10 UE) with KC-135s
	Three Strategic Reconnaissance Wings (one with SR-71s, one with RC-135s, one with U-2s)
	Two Strategic Reconnaissance Squadrons with RC-135s
Missiles	1,005 Minuteman, 60 Titan II, 349 Hound Dog, and 430 Quail
Missile Units	Six Titan II Squadrons (9 UE) fully equipped and 20 Minuteman Squadrons (50 UE), 10 equipped with Minuteman I "B" series missiles and 10 with Minuteman II "F" series missiles
Active Bases	25 CONUS; three overseas (Puerto Rico, Guam, and Labrador)

Budget and Financial Status
(FY 69, as of 30 June 1969)

Operations and Maintenance	$425,311,000, includes supplies, communications, civilian pay, and minor equipment purchased
Assets	$16,088,687,000, includes real property, inventories, equipment, and weapon systems

112

Operating	$1,878,666,000, includes O&M listed above, military
Expenses	pay, family housing, troop subsistence, and aviation
	petroleum, oil, and lubricants (POL)

Operations

Southeast Asia operations. SAC B-52 conventional bombing operations in Southeast Asia continued at a steady pace during the year. In early January, U Tapao Airfield in Thailand was converted from a forward operating base to a main operating base for B-52s on duty in Southeast Asia.

Greater emphasis was placed on harassment and disruption of enemy operations than in previous years. Potential and actual enemy forces were hampered in South Vietnam, particularly in the III Corps Area around Saigon. The communist assault corridor running southeast from War Zone C and the Cambodian border to Saigon was struck repeatedly throughout the year and received more B-52 strikes than any other area. SAC bombers also continued to hit enemy supply dumps, base areas, troop concentrations and the infiltration network that supplied the enemy forces in the south.

SAC KC-135 tanker operations also continued at a steady pace in Southeast Asia, with the total air refueling sorties flown being only slightly less than those of the previous year. SAC support of tactical fighters continued to account for the largest number of tanker missions.

Satellite basing. On 20 February, SAC began testing a new satellite basing program at Homestead Air Force Base, Florida, a Tactical Air Command installation. In this test, B-52s and KC-135s of the 72d Bomb Wing, Ramey Air Force Base, Puerto Rico, were relocated to Homestead and placed on ground alert. The test was successfully completed on 20 May, and on 1 July several additional bases were brought into the satellite program. The program was designed to help counter an increasing sea-launched ballistic missile threat.

By placing small cells of bombers and tankers on satellite bases, SAC was able to increase simultaneously the number of targets a potential enemy must reckon with and at the same time reduce the time required to get the entire alert force off the ground. Satellite basing was, in effect, a continuation of the dispersal program of the late 1950s and early 1960s, wherein large B-52 wings of 45 aircraft were divided up into small wings of 15 aircraft each and relocated to other bases. Other than the difference in the size of the force, the primary distinction between the two programs was that in the latter one the entire force was maintained on continuous ground alert. A small detachment of maintenance and support personnel was also relocated from the main operating base to the satellite base. Crews rotated to and from the site.

FB-111 program reduced. On 19 March, Secretary of Defense Laird, in presenting revised FY 69 and FY 70 military budgets to Congress, announced that the FB-111 program would be reduced to four operational squadrons of about 60 aircraft plus some replacement aircraft. Secretary Laird further declared that the FB-111 did not meet requirements for a true intercontinental bomber, but that purchase of four squadrons was necessary to "salvage what we can of work in progress."

First FB-111A delivered. On 8 October, in a formal ceremony at Carswell Air Force Base, Texas, SAC accepted the first operational FB-111A (serial number 67-7193). The aircraft was actually assigned to the 340th Bomb Group on 25 September; it was picked up by Colonel Winston E. Moore, the group commander, on 29 September. This FB-111A represented the first new type bomber the command had received since 1 August 1960, when SAC accepted the first B-58 in similar ceremonies at Carswell. Only two more FB-111As were delivered to the 340th before 24 December, at which time all F/FB-111 type aircraft were grounded following the 22 December crash of a F-111 fighter at Nellis Air Force Base, Nevada.

Advanced Manned Strategic Aircraft (AMSA). On 19 March, at the same time the FB-111 program was reduced, Secretary Laird announced that additional funds were being added to the defense budget to develop an entirely new, long-range manned bomber, the Advanced Manned Strategic Aircraft. He explained that these funds were not for purchasing the AMSA but rather for speeding up preliminary designs.

On 3 November, the Air Force requested proposal be submitted for full-scale engineering development of the AMSA or the B-1 as it had come to be called. The North American Rockwell Corporation, General Dynamics, and the Boeing Airplane Company were the three contractors interested in submitting proposals for the airframe and General Electric and Pratt and Whitney Division of United Aircraft for the engines.

Bombing Competition

Having been shelved for operational commitments since 1966, the Bombing Competition was renewed in 1969 and held from 5 through 15 October at Fairchild Air Force Base, Washington. Participants included one aircraft and crew from 22 B-52 wings and two B-58 wings. Three Royal Air Force crews flying Vulcan bombers also competed. The B-52D wings, those units being used for conventional bombing in Southeast Asia, were allowed to participate at the discretion of the numbered air force commanders. Eighth Air Force's 70th, 306th, and 509th Bomb Wings and Second Air Force's 7th Bomb Wing did not enter the competition.

As in previous competitions, the scoring was handled by the 1st Combat Evaluation Group through its fixed and mobile radar bomb scoring facilities. Second Air Force's 319th Bomb Wing, a B-52H unit, won the combined bombing and navigation award, the Fairchild Trophy.

Disposition of Saunders Trophy. Among the numerous awards presented during the closing ceremony was the Saunders Trophy. General Holloway presented it to Eighth Air Force's 919th Air Refueling Squadron, the unit which Headquarters SAC had previously judged to be the top air refueling squadron in SAC.

Missiles

Missile launches. Total missiles and space systems launched during the year from Vandenberg Air Force Base: Launched by: SAC—34; Other Agencies—61.

Phase out of Minuteman "A". As part of the force modernization program, the last Minuteman I series "A" missiles were removed from their launch facilities at Malmstrom Air Force Base, Montana, on 12 February. Immediately thereafter, contractors began refurbishing the facilities for Minuteman II or "F" missiles. On 27 May, the force modernization program was completed at Malmstrom, when Flight K was returned to the 341st Strategic Missile Wing.

Upon completion of the force modernization program at Malmstrom, the SAC Minuteman force was composed of three wings with ten squadrons of Minuteman I "B" series missiles, and three wings with ten squadrons of Minuteman II or "F" series missiles.

Missile Competition

SAC's second missile competition was held from 17 through 24 May at Vandenberg Air Force Base, California. Competitors included six Minuteman wings and three Titan II wings. Each wing was represented by two combat crews and one maintenance team. Each crew participated in three exercises which were conducted in a missile procedures trainer. The 4315th Combat Crew Training Squadron supplied the trainer facilities and the exercises were conceived and conducted by the 3901st Strategic Missile Evaluation Squadron. Maintenance teams participated in four exercises. They used the facilities of the 394th and 395th Strategic Missile Squadrons and the 51st Munitions Maintenance Squadron, all of which were located at Vandenberg.

Second Air Force's 321st Strategic Missile Wing, a Minuteman II unit, had the highest score in the combined areas of operations and maintenance and was awarded the Blanchard Trophy. The 321st also won the Best Minuteman Wing award, while Fifteenth Air Force's 390th Strategic Missile Wing won the Best Titan Wing award.

Inactivation of 395th Strategic Missile Squadron (Titan). Effective 31 December, the 395th Strategic Missile Squadron was inactivated. This inactivation was part of the Headquarters USAF directed manpower reduction program, Project 703. Since 1 February 1959, the 395th had been responsible for the maintenance and support of Titan facilities at Vandenberg Air Force Base, California. The 394th Strategic Missile Squadron, which had similar responsibilities for Minuteman missiles, absorbed some of the 395th's personnel and assumed responsibility for supporting Titan II activities at Vandenberg.

1970

Resources

Personnel 154,367 (23,244 officers, 112,401 airmen, 18,722 civilians)

Tactical Aircraft 1,159 (459 B-52, 658 EC/KC-135, 42 FB-111)

Aircraft Units 20 Heavy Bomb Wings (16 15 UE and four 30 UE) and four Heavy Strategic Aerospace Wings (15 UE), all with B-52s with exception of one strategic aerospace wing which was in the final stages of transferring its B-52s and making preparations to be equipped with FB-111As

One Medium Bomb Wing (30 UE) in early stages of equipping with FB-111As

One Medium Bomb Group (15 UE), the FB-111 training unit, with FB-111As

40 Heavy Air Refueling Squadrons (five 20 UE, 33 15 UE, and two 10 UE) with KC-135s

Three Strategic Reconnaissance Wings (one with U-2s, one with SR-71s, one with RC-135s)

Two Strategic Reconnaissance Squadrons with RC-135s

Three Airborne Command Control Squadrons with EC-135s

Missiles 982 Minuteman, 57 Titan II, 345 Hound Dog, and 430 Quail

Missile Units Six Titan II Squadrons (9 UE) fully equipped and 20 Minuteman Squadrons (50 UE), eight equipped with Minuteman I "B" series missiles, ten with Minuteman II "F" series missiles, one with Minuteman III "G" series missiles, and one in process of converting from Minuteman I "B" series to Minuteman III "G" series missiles

Active Bases 26 CONUS; three overseas (Puerto Rico, Guam, and Labrador)

Budget and Financial Status (FY 70, as of 30 June 1970)

Operations and Maintenance $401,594,000, includes supplies, communications, civilian pay, and minor equipment purchased

116

| Assets | $14,124,148,000, includes real property, inventories, equipment, and weapon systems |
| Operating Expenses | $1,676,454,000, includes O&M listed above, military pay, family housing, troop subsistence, and aviation petroleum, oil, and lubricants (POL) |

Organization

As part of a Headquarters USAF-directed manpower reduction program (Project 703), which was announced in August 1969, SAC reduced its numbered air forces in the CONUS from three to two and effected a major realignment of combat forces.

Closure of Headquarters Eighth Air Force. Headquarters Eighth Air Force ceased operations at Westover Air Force Base, Massachusetts, on 31 March. At that time, all Eighth Air Force Bases and units were transferred to SAC's two other numbered air forces, the Second and Fifteenth.

With the closure of Headquarters Eighth Air Force, SAC was left only two numbered air forces in the CONUS for the first time since late 1949 when the Second Air Force was assigned.

Numbered Air Force Realignment. Under the realignment, the Second Air Force became an all manned aircraft command, consisting of B-52, FB-111, and KC-135 units; while the Fifteenth Air Force became responsible for all combat ICBM units, the entire strategic reconnaissance force, and a few B-52 and KC-135 units.

Movement of Eighth Air Force. The Eighth Air Force was not inactivated as originally announced. It was preserved by transferring the numerical designation to Guam. Effective 1 April, Headquarters Eighth Air Force moved without personnel and equipment to Anderson Air Force Base, Guam. Concurrently, Headquarters 3d Air Division, which had been at Anderson since 1954, was inactivated and its personnel and functions were absorbed by Headquarters Eighth Air Force.

PACCS Reorganized. On 1 April, SAC reorganized its Post Attack Command Control System (PACCS) and moved some of its EC-135s out of Westover Air Force Base, Massachusetts, Barksdale Air Force Base, Louisiana, and March Air Force Base, California. In this reorganization, all EC-135s were assigned to the 2d, 3d, and 4th Airborne Command and Control Squadrons, which were activated at Offutt Air Force Base, Nebraska, Grissom Air Force Base, Indiana, and Ellsworth Air Force Base, South Dakota. The basic function of PACCS remained unchanged. Airborne command post aircraft (Looking Glass) continued to remain airborne at all times in the vicinity of Offutt. Auxiliary airborne command post and relay aircraft remained on round-the-clock ground alert.

Operations

Southeast Asia operations. Arc Light B-52 bombing operations in Southeast Asia declined during the year. Emphasis continued to be placed on harassment and disruption of enemy operations. SAC bombers continued to hit enemy supply dumps, base areas, and troop concentrations, as well as infiltration networks supplying the enemy forces. From November 1969 through April 1970, B-52s flew interdiction missions against targets in Laos in support of Commando Hunt III. In April and May, B-52 Arc Light missions were flown in support of ground operations in Cambodia.

SAC KC-135 tanker operations in Southeast Asia also continued at a steady pace, although the totals were under those of the previous years. SAC support of tactical aircraft continued to account for the largest part of this activity.

Retirement of last B-58. On 16 January, the B-58 retirement program was completed when the last two Hustlers (serial numbers 55-662 and 61-0278) were flown to the storage facility at Davis-Monthan Air Force Base, Arizona. Both aircraft had been assigned to the 305th Bomb Wing, Grissom Air Force

This high-angle front view of an **SR-71** strategic reconnaissance aircraft presents a menacing view of the Blackbird. The aircraft was designed to replace the **U-2** in overflights of the Soviet Union, but all such flights were halted after missiles downed a **U-2** flown by CIA pilot Francis Gary Powers on 1 May 1960.

118

Base, Indiana. At Davis-Monthan, these aircraft joined 82 other Hustlers, including eight TB-58s, that had been retired since 3 November 1969. The two aircraft that had been responsible for record-breaking flights in 1962 and 1963 escaped retirement to Davis-Monthan and were placed in museums: 59-2458, the aircraft flown in the 1962 round-trip flight from Los Angeles to New York to Los Angeles, went to the Air Force Museum, Wright-Patterson Air Force Base, Ohio; while 61-2059, the one flown in the 1963 flight from Tokyo to London, went to the SAC Aerospace Museum, Offutt Air Force Base, Nebraska.

Retention of units. Since both B-58 wings had histories extending back through World War II, they were retained in the Strategic Air Command. The 305th Bombardment Wing became the 305th Air Refueling Wing and remained at Grissom Air Force Base, Indiana. Effective 1 April, the 43d Bombardment Wing was redesignated the 43d Strategic Wing and replaced the 3960th Strategic Wing at Anderson Air Force Base, Guam. At the same time, two other illustrious units that had been inactive since 1965 were activated as strategic wings in the western Pacific. The 307th Strategic Wing replaced the 4258th Strategic Wing at U Tapao Airfield, Thailand, and the 376th Strategic Wing replaced the 4252d Strategic Wing at Kadena Air Base, Okinawa.

B-1 development contract. On 5 June, Secretary of the Air Force Robert C. Seamans, Jr., announced the two winners in the competition to receive the B-1 development contracts: North American Rockwell for the airframe and General Electric for the engines.

At that time, the B-1 was scheduled to be ready for flight testing in mid-1974, with production go-ahead, if authorized, to take place some time thereafter. The North American Rockwell contract called for the production of seven prototype airframes, five for flight tests, one for static tests, and one for fatigue tests. Subsequently, in February 1971, the number of aircraft scheduled to be built for flight tests was reduced to three in conjunction with a new concept to test more intensely and on an individual basis the airframe and engine before testing the completely developed aircraft.

P. T. Cullen Award. In 1970, Headquarters SAC revived the Brigadier General Paul T. Cullen Memorial Reconnaissance Trophy, which had been inactive since 1957 when it was given to the 26th Strategic Reconnaissance Wing for winning the SAC Reconnaissance Competition. It was revived as an annual rotating award to be presented to the reconnaissance unit that contributed most to the photographic and signal intelligence efforts of SAC. An *ad hoc* committee convened by the Headquarters SAC Deputy Chief of Staff for Operations selected the 82d Strategic Reconnaissance Squadron as the 1970 winner.

Benjamin D. Foulois Memorial Trophy (Daedalian Trophy). The 1970 Benjamin D. Foulois Memorial Trophy was awarded to SAC as the major air command with the most effective aircraft accident prevention program. After the death of Major General Benjamin D. Foulois in April 1967, the Order of the Daedalians renamed its annual rotating trophy to commemorate the many contributions that General Foulois had made to aviation and flight safety.

Bombing Competition

The 1970 Bombing Competition, which was held from 15 through 20 November, was unique in several aspects. For the first time since 1960, Fairchild Air Force Base, Washington, was not used as the staging base. Instead, McCoy Air Force Base, Florida, served as the host for all bombers. The tanker units staged out of their home bases. The second unique feature was that FB-111s participated for the first time. Also, tanker squadrons were included for the first time since 1961.

Competitors included one aircraft and crew from 23 B-52 wings and 28 KC-135 squadrons, two FB-111s and crews of the 340th Bomb Group, and three RAF crews with their Vulcan bombers. Nonparticipating SAC units included 12 KC-135 squadrons that were involved in Southeast Asia support or other assignments; the 96th Strategic Aerospace Wing, which was serving as a B-52 cadre unit in Southeast Asia; and the 509th Bomb Wing, which was in the process of equipping with FB-111s.

The Fairchild Trophy, which for many years had been awarded solely on the basis of bombing, was awarded to the B-52 wing and its assigned KC-135 air refueling squadron that had the highest combined points in the areas of bombing and navigation. It went to the 93d Bomb Wing, a B-52F unit of the Second Air Force.

The Saunders Trophy, previously given for air refueling and navigation, was given to the tanker crew with the most points for the navigation mission. Second Air Force's 11th Air Refueling Squadron was the recipient.

The Bombing Trophy, given for the best bomber crew in the area of bombing only, was awarded to one of the FB-111 crews of the 340th Bomb Group, also a Second Air Force unit.

The Navigation Trophy, denoting the best bomber or tanker crew in navigation, was won by the 5th Bomb Wing, a B-52H unit of the Fifteenth Air Force.

Mathis Trophy. The 5th Bomb Wing also won the Mathis Trophy, awarded to the bomber crew with the best score in the combined areas of bombing and navigation. Established by Headquarters SAC and given for the first time in the 1970 competition, this new trophy was named for 1st Lieutenant Jack W. Mathis, a World War II B-17 bombardier, who received the Medal of Honor posthumously for his bravery over Vegesack, Germany, on 18 March 1943. At the time of this action, Lieutenant Mathis was serving with the 303d Bomb Group of Eighth Air Force.

RAF bombing competition. In May 1970, four B-52 aircraft and crews from the 2d, 310th, 320th, and 379th Bomb Wings participated in the Royal Air Force Strike Command Bombing and Navigation Competition. These wings were selected to represent SAC on the basis of their standings in the 1969 SAC Bombing Competition. They were the two top B-52H and the two top B-52G wings in this meet.

Flying out of RAF Station Marham, a SAC team composed of crews and aircraft from the 319th, 320th, and 379th Bomb Wings won the Blue Steel Trophy, an inter-air force award for the best combined score in bombing and navigation.

Missiles

Missile launches. Total missiles and space systems launched during the year from Vandenberg Air Force Base: Launched by: SAC—44; Other Agencies—41.

Force modernization. On 12 January the Minuteman Force Modernization program was continued at Minot Air Force Base, North Dakota, when Flight H of the 741st Strategic Missile Squadron (91st Strategic Missile Wing) was turned over to the contractor to be modified.

In this phase of Force Modernization, Minuteman I "B" series missiles were replaced with Minuteman III "G" series missiles. As in the earlier conversion programs, the launch facilities, ground support systems, and the launch control facilities required modification in order to accommodate the Minuteman III.

Minuteman III employed an improved third stage booster, carried more penetration aids to counter antiballistic missile defense systems, and could carry the Mark 12 Multiple Independently targetable Reentry Vehicle (MIRV) with three separate nuclear warheads.

First Minuteman III accepted by SAC. On 19 June, SAC accepted the first flight of 10 Minuteman III missiles at Minot. These missiles were assigned to the 741st Strategic Missile Squadron.

On 30 December, the 741st Strategic Missile Squadron was fully equipped with 50 Minuteman IIIs. In the meantime, the second squadron of the 91st Strategic Missile Wing had entered the Force Modernization program.

Missile Competition

The Third Missile Combat Competition was held from 28 April to 5 May at Vandenberg Air Force Base, California. Three Titan II and six Minuteman wings competed, with each wing being represented by two missile combat crews and one maintenance team. Each combat crew participated in three individual exercises in a missile procedures trainer, and each maintenance team participated in four exercises.

The 44th Strategic Missile Wing, a Minuteman unit from Ellsworth Air Force Base, South Dakota, had the highest combined score in operations and maintenance and was awarded the Blanchard Trophy as well as the award for the Best Minuteman Wing. The 390th Strategic Missile Wing, Davis-Monthan Air Force Base, Arizona, won the award for the Best Titan Wing.

1971

Resources

Personnel	161,075 (23,043 officers, 118,300 airmen, 19,732 civilians)
Tactical Aircraft	1,126 (412 B-52, 648 EC/KC-135, and 66 FB-111)
Aircraft Units	19 Heavy Bomb Wings (15 15 UE, two 30 UE, one 25 UE, and one 22 UE) and three Strategic Aerospace Wings (two 15 UE and one 20 UE), one Strategic Wing (15 UE) with B-52s
	38 Heavy Air Refueling Squadrons (ten 20 UE, 27 15 UE, and one 10 UE) with KC-135s
	One Medium Bomb Wing (30 UE) and one Strategic Aerospace Wing (36 UE) with FB-111As
	Three Strategic Reconnaissance Wings (one with U-2s, one with SR-71s, one with RC-135s)
	Two Strategic Reconnaissance Squadrons with RC-135s
	Three Airborne Command and Control Squadrons with EC-135s
Missiles	990 Minuteman, 58 Titan, 340 Hound Dog, and 430 Quail
Missile Units	Six Titan II Squadrons (9 UE) fully equipped and 20 Minuteman Squadrons (50 UE), 10 equipped with Minuteman II "F" series missiles, six with Minuteman I "B" series missiles, three with Minuteman III "G" series missiles, and one in process of converting from Minuteman I "B" series to Minuteman III "G" series missiles
Active Bases	28 CONUS and two overseas (Guam and Labrador)

Budget and Financial Status
(FY 71, as of 30 June 1971)

Operations and Maintenance	$441,698,000, includes supplies, communications, civilian pay, and minor equipment purchased
Assets	$15,181,610,000, includes real property, inventories, equipment, and weapon systems
Operating Expenses	$1,717,122,000, includes O&M listed above, military pay, family housing, troop subsistence, and aviation petroleum, oil, and lubricants (POL)

Operations

Southeast Asia operations. On 18 June, SAC B-52s began their seventh year of conventional bombing in the Southeast Asia conflict. Throughout the year, the B-52s were used both in close bombing support of forces engaged in combat and in destroying roads and supply lines leading southward from North Vietnam along the Demilitarized Zone and the Laotian border. SAC's KC-135 tanker crews continued to provide inflight refueling for all types of tactical fighters engaged in the conflict. The KC-135s played an important airlift role by carrying men and equipment to and from Southeast Asia.

Delivery of last FB-111. On 30 June, SAC received its last FB-111 (serial number 68-291), which was assigned to the 340th Bomb Group, Carswell Air Force Base, Texas.

By early September, the 340th had transferred its FB-111s to the two operational wings—the 509th at Pease Air Force Base, New Hampshire, and the 380th at Plattsburgh Air Force Base, New York. Upon transfer of these aircraft the 340th's 4007th Combat Crew Training Squadron, which had been responsible for training FB-111 crews, ceased operations at Carswell and moved to Plattsburgh. Effective 31 December, the 340th Bomb Group was inactivated.

B-52 phase out. In 1971, SAC retired all "C" and several "F" model B-52s to the storage facility at Davis-Monthan Air Force Base, Arizona. SAC's last B-52C, serial number 53-402, which had been assigned to the 22d Bomb Wing, March Air Force Base, California, was retired on 29 September. The

All USAF tankers are managed by the Strategic Air Command, but support all Air Force operations. This KC-135A Stratotanker is refueling an A-10 Thunderbolt II, a light attack aircraft developed specifically for the ground attack/anti-tank role. On occasion, USAF tankers have refueled naval aircraft, although most of the latter are configured for the flexible hose, probe-and-drogue refueling technique. Some SAC tankers are rigged for both methods. (Fairchild Republic photo)

93d Bomb Wing, Castle Air Force Base, California, continued to operate B-52Fs.

Last C-47. On 7 July, SAC's last C-47 was transferred to the USS *Alabama* Monument Commission. This VC-47D had been assigned to the 97th Bomb Wing, Blytheville Air Force Base, Arkansas. Since its organization on 21 March 1946, SAC had continuously used C-47s, or "Gooney Birds" as they were usually called, for support and administrative purposes.

SR-71 record flight and Tenth Mackay Trophy. On 26 April, an SR-71 aircraft of the 9th Strategic Reconnaissance Wing, Beale Air Force Base, California, made a record-breaking 15,000-mile nonstop flight in ten and one-half hours, attaining speeds at times in excess of Mach 3 and at altitudes of over 80,000 feet. The flight, which began and ended at Beale, was made possible by several inflight refuelings by KC-135s. For this outstanding flight, Lieutenant Colonel Thomas B. Estes, aircraft commander, and Major Dewain C. Vick, reconnaissance systems officer, were named recipient of the Mackay Trophy for 1971.

P. T. Cullen Award. The P. T. Cullen Award, given annually to the unit that contributed most to the SAC photographic and signal reconnaissance mission, was awarded to the 55th Strategic Reconnaissance Wing for 1971.

Bombing Competition

The eighteenth Bombing Competition was held from 12 through 17 December at McCoy Air Force Base, Florida. SAC participants included one aircraft and crew from each of 54 units: 22 B-52, 30 KC-135, and two FB-111. Three RAF crews and their Vulcan aircraft also participated. All major awards went to Second Air Force units. These awards and their recipients were as follows:

Fairchild Trophy, for the bomb wing and collocated tanker squadron with the best combined score in bombing and navigation, awarded to the 449th Bomb Wing, a B-52H unit.

Mathis Trophy, awarded to the best bomber crew in the combined areas of bombing and navigation, 17th Bomb Wing, a B-52H unit, and the Saunders Trophy, awarded to the best tanker crew, 11th Air Refueling Squadron.

Bombing Trophy, awarded to the best bomber crew in the area of bombing, 17th Bomb Wing. The Navigation Trophy, awarded to the best bomber or tanker crew in navigation, 93d Bomb Wing, a B-52F unit.

RAF Bombing Competition. From 17 to 24 April, SAC again participated in the Royal Air Force Strike Command's Bombing and Navigation Competition. SAC participants included one aircraft and crew from four B-52 units (2d, 320th, 379th, and 410th Bomb Wings), one KC-135 unit (11th Air Refueling Squadron) and one RC-135 unit (55th Strategic Reconnaissance Wing). The 340th Bomb Group and the 509th Bomb Wing each sent one FB-111 and crew to participate in a demonstration capacity. The 410th Bomb Wing, a B-52H unit, won the Blue Steel Trophy, an inter-air force award that was given this year to the crew with the best combined score in bombing and navigation.

Missiles

Total missile and Space Systems launched during the year from Vandenberg Air Force Base: Launched by: SAC—43; Other agencies—41.

SAC's Minuteman Force Modernization Program continued throughout 1971. On 13 December, SAC accepted the last flight (Flight 0 of the 742d Strategic Missile Squadron) of Minuteman III "G" series missiles at Minot Air Force Base, North Dakota. With acceptance of this flight, the 91st Strategic Missile Wing became the first wing to be equipped with the new MIRV-carrying missile.

The 321st Strategic Missile Wing, Grand Forks Air Force Base, North Dakota, became the second wing to enter the Minuteman III force modernization program. Its first Minuteman III "G" series missile was postured on 24 December. In another phase of Force Modernization, Minuteman II "F" series missiles were replacing Minuteman I "B" series missiles in the 44th Strategic Missile Wing, Ellsworth Air Force Base, South Dakota.

First Minuteman III operational launch. On 24 March, a missile crew of the 91st Strategic Missile Wing conducted the first operational test of Minuteman III by successfully launching a missile from Vandenberg Air Force Base, California.

Missile Competition

The fourth Missile Combat Competition was held from 20 to 28 April at Vandenberg Air Force Base. Competitors included two combat crews and one maintenance team from each of the nine strategic missile wings. The 351st Strategic Missile Wing, a Minuteman unit from Whiteman Air Force Base, Missouri, had the highest combined score in operations and maintenance and was awarded the Blanchard Trophy as well as the Best Minuteman Wing award. The 308th Strategic Missile Wing, Little Rock Air Force Base, Arkansas, was named Best Titan Wing.

1972

Resources

Personnel	162,701 (24,040 officers, 119,777 airmen, 18,884 civilians)
Tactical Aircraft	1,105 (402 B-52, 643 EC/KC-135, 60 FB-111)
Aircraft Units	22 Heavy Bomb Wings (17 15 UE, two 30 UE, one 25 UE, one 22 UE, and 20 UE) and one Strategic Wing (15 UE) with B-52s
	38 Heavy Air Refueling Squadrons (ten 20 UE, 27 15 UE, and one 10 UE) with KC-135s
	Two Medium Bomb Wings (one 30 UE and one 36 UE) with FB-111As
	Three Strategic Reconnaissance Wings (one with U-2s, one with SR-71s, one with RC-135s)
	Two Strategic Reconnaissance Squadrons with RC-135s
	Three Airborne Command and Control Squadrons with EC-135s
Missiles	955 Minuteman, 57 Titan, 338 Hound Dog, 417 Quail, and 227 SRAM
Missile Units	Six Titan II Squadrons (9 UE) fully equipped and 20 Minuteman Squadrons (50 UE), nine equipped with Minuteman II "F" series missiles, five with Minuteman III "G" series missiles, three with Minuteman I "B" series missiles, one converting from Minuteman I "B" series to Minuteman III "G" series missiles, one converting from Minuteman I "B" series to Minuteman II "F" series missiles, and one converting from Minuteman II "F" series to Minuteman III "G" series missiles
Active Bases	30 CONUS and two overseas (Guam and Labrador)

Budget and Financial Status
(FY 72, as of 30 June 1972)

Operations and Maintenance	$468,972,000, includes supplies, communications, civilian pay, and minor equipment purchased
Assets	$15,324,145,260, includes real property, inventories, equipment, and weapon systems

Operating Expenses	$1,946,362,000, includes O&M listed above, military pay, family housing, troop subsistence, and aviation petroleum, oil, and lubricants (POL)

Organization

In order to control effectively the additional B-52 and KC-135 aircraft and crews deployed to counteract the North Vietnamese offensive of early 1972, SAC created several new Eighth Air Force units. Completed on 1 July 1972, this expansion included activating provisional units (air divisions, air refueling squadrons, bomb squadrons, and consolidated maintenance wings) at seven Western Pacific and Southeast Asia bases.

Operations

Southeast Asia operations. By early April, the North Vietnamese had launched a strong three-pronged attack against the South Vietnamese, striking specifically at Quang Tri, Kontum, and An Loc. As the offensive intensified, SAC sent additional B-52s and KC-135s to several Western Pacific and Southeast Asia bases. Anderson Air Force Base, Guam, which had not supported the B-52 bombing mission since late 1970, rejoined U Tapao Airfield, Thailand, as a B-52 launch base. U Tapao and Kadena Air Base, Okinawa, continued to support KC-135s engaged in refueling B-52s and tactical aircraft. By mid-year, as the demand for tactical aircraft support grew, tankers were also operating out of Clark Air Base, Philippines, and the three Thailand bases of Don Muang, Korat, and Takhli. Although successful in the early months, the North Vietnamese offensive was soon repelled as the B-52 incessantly bombed enemy troop positions and supply concentrations in all three areas of the attack.

Linebacker II. In mid-December, after the North Vietnamese had terminated peace negotiations in Paris, President Nixon ordered the bombing of military targets in the Hanoi and Haiphong areas of North Vietnam in an effort to bring the North Vietnamese back to the peace table. Nicknamed Linebacker II and covering an 11-day period from 18 through 29 December—there was a 24-hour pause in the bombing on Christmas—the B-52s flew over 700 sorties against 24 target complexes, including rail yards, shipyards, communications facilities, power plants, railway bridges, MIG aircraft bases, air defense radars, and missile sites. All together, U.S. bombers, including tactical and Navy aircraft as well as B-52s, dropped 20,370 tons of bombs in this 11-day attack, with the B-52s accounting for over 15,000 tons.

In this attack on Haiphong and Hanoi, the B-52s encountered what has been described as one of the most heavily defended areas of the world, characterized by heavy concentrations of surface-to-air missiles (SAMs), MIG fighter aircraft, and anti-aircraft gun emplacements. The anti-aircraft and MIG fighters did not pose a formidable threat to the penetrating B-52s, but the SAMs did. In this 11-day war, over 1,000 missiles were fired at the B-52s and fifteen B-52s were shot down by SAMs.

Of the 92 crew members aboard these bombers, 26 were recovered by rescue teams, 33 bailed out over North Vietnam and were captured, 29 were listed as missing, and four perished in a bomber that crash landed. By 28 December, the North Vietnamese air defenses had been practically neutralized, and on the last two days of Linebacker II, the B-52s were able to fly over Hanoi and Haiphong without suffering any damage. On 30 December, North Vietnam announced that it was ready to resume peace negotiations.

While the bombing against North Vietnam was carried out by B-52s and tactical and Navy aircraft, the campaign would surely have been less effective, more costly, and appreciably prolonged without KC-135 tankers. From 18 through 29 December, the SAC tankers flew more than 1,300 sorties and provided inflight refueling for B-52s as well as tactical fighter and attack aircraft.

The Collier Trophy. The Collier Trophy, presented annually by the National Aeronautic Association for the greatest achievement in aeronautics or astronautics in America, was awarded jointly to the Eighth Air Force, the Pacific Air Force's Seventh Air Force, and the Navy's Task Force 77 for their combined efforts in the 11-day air campaign against North Vietnam.

First SRAM. On 4 March, the first operational Short Range Attack Missile (SRAM) was delivered to a SAC unit—the 42d Bomb Wing, Loring Air Force Base, Maine.

Designated the AGM-69A, the SRAM measures 14 feet in length and 18 inches in diameter and weighs approximately 2,230 pounds. Powered by a solid-propellant rocket motor and armed with a nuclear warhead, it can be launched from a bomber prior to reaching the target to increase the bomber's ability to attack heavily defended targets.

Each B-52G and H model aircraft could carry up to 20 of these missiles on wing pylons and on a rotary launcher in the bomb bay, while the FB-111 could carry as many as six missiles, two internally and four externally on wing pylons. All B-52G and H units and two FB-111 wings were to be equipped with the new missile.

On 15 June, a B-52G crew of the 42d Bomb Wing successfully launched the first operational SRAM over the White Sands Missile Range, New Mexico.

P. T. Cullen Award. The 100th Strategic Reconnaissance Wing was selected as the unit that contributed most to the SAC photographic and signal intelligence mission in 1972. For this significant accomplishment, it received the P. T. Cullen Award.

Bombing Competition

Due to the heavy B-52 support of bombing operations in Southeast Asia, the 1972 SAC Bombing and Navigation Competition was cancelled.

RAF Bombing Competition. For the Royal Air Force Strike Command Bombing and Navigation Competition, conducted from 14 through 20 May, SAC entered four B-52 bombers and crews representing the 2d, 17th, 28th, and 449th Bomb Wings. The 28th Bomb Wing, a B-52G unit, won the Blue

Steel Trophy, which was given to the crew with the highest combined score in bombing and navigation.

Missiles

Missile launches. Total missile and space systems launched during the year from Vandenberg Air Force Base: Launched by: SAC—21; Other Agencies—44.

Force modernization. SAC's Minuteman Force Modernization Program, replacing older model missiles with new ones, continued at Grand Forks Air Force Base, North Dakota, and Ellsworth Air Force Base, South Dakota, throughout 1972. At Grand Forks, the 321st Strategic Missile Wing was converting from Minuteman II "F" series missiles to Minuteman III "G" series missiles, while at Ellsworth, the 44th Strategic Missile Wing was replacing its Minuteman I "B" series missiles with Minuteman II "F" series missiles.

Command data buffer. In November, the 90th Strategic Missile Wing, Francis E. Warren Air Force Base, Wyoming, entered the Force Modernization Program when it started removing its Minuteman I "B" series missiles and making the sites ready for the new MIRV-carrying Minuteman III "G" series missiles. As part of the 90th's conversion program, a new retargeting system was to be installed. Called Command Data Buffer, the new system would enable crews in launch control centers to retarget rapidly through electrical means the Minuteman III missiles. It would replace a time-consuming procedure that required maintenance personnel to physically insert a new target tape into each missile.

Missile Competition

SAC's fifth Missile Competition was held at Vandenberg Air Force Base from 6 through 14 April. In order to broaden participation and further increase interest in the meet, each wing sent four crews instead of two as in previous years. For the first time since the competition began in 1967, a Titan unit, the 381st Strategic Missile Wing, McConnell Air Force Base, Kansas, had the highest combined score in operations and maintenance and won the Blanchard Trophy. The 381st was also named the Best Titan Wing, while the 351st Strategic Missile Wing, Whiteman Air Force Base, Missouri, won the Best Minuteman Wing award.

1973

Resources

Personnel   163,754 (23,686 officers, 121,060 airmen, 19,008 civilians)

Tactical Aircraft 1,163 (422 B-52, 670 EC/KC-135, 71 FB-111), includes SAC aircraft undergoing maintenance and modification work at Air Force Logistics Command facilities; previously, these aircraft were not considered as being assigned to SAC

Aircraft Units   22 Heavy Bomb Wings (18 15 UE, two 30 UE, one 22 UE, one 20 UE) and one Strategic Wing (15 UE) all with B-52s except two 15 UE bomb wings which had transferred their aircraft to other SAC wings in preparation for inactivation as part of the programs to close McCoy Air Force Base, Florida, and to transfer Westover Air Force Base, Massachusetts, to the Air Force Reserve

38 Heavy Air Refueling Squadrons (Nine 20 UE and 29 15 UE) with KC-135s

Two Medium Bomb Wings (one 30 UE and one 36 UE) with FB-111As

Three Strategic Reconnaissance Wings (one U-2, one SR-71, one RC-135)

Two Strategic Reconnaissance Squadrons with RC-135s

Three Airborne Command and Control Squadrons with EC-135s

Missiles   970 Minuteman, 57 Titan, 329 Hound Dog, 417 Quail, and 651 SRAM

Missile Units   Six Titan II Squadrons (9 UE) fully equipped and 20 Minuteman Squadrons (50 UE), ten equipped with Minuteman II "F" series missiles, seven with Minuteman III "G" series missiles, two with Minuteman I "B" series missiles, and one converting from Minuteman I "B" series to Minuteman III "G" series missiles

Active Bases   30 CONUS and one overseas (Guam).

130

Budget and Financial Status
(FY 73, as of 30 June 1973)

Operations and Maintenance	$509,873,000, includes supplies, communications, civilian pay, and minor equipment purchased
Assets	$16,088,315,000, includes real property, inventories, equipment, and weapon systems
Operating Expenses	$2,194,824,000, includes O&M listed above, military pay, family housing, troop subsistence, and aviation petroleum, oil, and lubricants (POL)

Organization

Air Force and Air Division Realignments. By 1 July, the Second and Fifteenth Air Forces had completed a major unit realignment program. This program entailed giving the air divisions diversified missions with a variety of weapon systems rather than allowing them to specialize in one weapon system. It also included placing some ICBM units—one Minuteman and two Titan wings—under the Second Air Force rather than having all missile units concentrated in the Fifteenth Air Force as had been the case since the numbered air force realignment of early 1970. The numbered air force realignment was effected in a series of reassignment actions extending from 15 February through 1 July.

Operations

Southeast Asia Operations. Following the B-52 Linebacker II bombing of targets in North Vietnam during December 1972, North Vietnam resumed the stalled Paris peace negotiations on 8 January. While the talks continued, B-52s pounded logistics targets in North Vietnam south of the 20 degree parallel. The B-52 bombing over North Vietnam ended on 15 January, and on 27 January, an agreement ending the war in Vietnam was signed in Paris. On that same day, B-52s flew their final mission of the war over targets in South Vietnam. Bombing of targets in Laos continued with a halt scheduled for 22 February as part of a peace agreement reached by the Laotian government. Because of enemy cease-fire violations, however, B-52s struck again on 23 February at the request of the Laotian government. Similar violations brought the bombers back briefly on 15, 16, and 17 April. Following the February halt to bombing in Laos, the B-52s struck only targets in Cambodia. Rebel Cambodians and North Vietnamese/Viet Cong forces advancing on Phnom Penh were repeatedly bombed by B-52s. Logistics targets located throughout Cambodia were also hit heavily in an effort to stem the enemy's drive. The bombers also struck gun positions and troop emplacements along road and river supply routes to enable needed supplies to reach the defenders of Phnom Penh.

End of SAC bombing in Southeast Asia. On 15 August, when all U.S. bombing of targets in Cambodia ceased, SAC B-52s terminated more than eight years of conventional bombing operations in Southeast Asia.

Benjamin D. Foulois Memorial Trophy (Daedalian Trophy). The 1973 Benjamin D. Foulois Memorial Trophy, also known as the Daedalian Trophy, was awarded to SAC as the major air command with the most effective aircraft accident prevention program.

P. T. Cullen Award. The P. T. Cullen Award, presented annually to the Strategic reconnaissance unit contributing most to the SAC photographic and signal intelligence effort, was won by the 6th Strategic Wing.

Bombing Competition

In the spring of 1973, preliminary plans were made to renew the SAC Bombing and Navigation Competition. It was to be held at Carswell Air Force Base, Texas. In early June, however, Major General George H. McKee, SAC Chief of Staff, announced that the competition would not be held. Once again, as in 1972, operational commitments in Southeast Asia forced cancellation of the meet.

RAF Bombing Competition. In the 1973 Royal Air Force Strike Command Bombing and Navigation Competition, held from 29 April through 5 May, SAC's entries were from the 5th, 17th, 319th, and 410th Bomb Wings. In the competition for the Blue Steel Trophy, awarded to the top crew in the meet, the SAC wings placed second, seventh, eighth, and ninth. For SAC, it was the poorest showing since the 1967 meet.

Missiles

Total missiles and space systems launched during the year from Vandenberg Air Force Base: Launched by: SAC—13; Other Agencies—31.

Force modernization. The force modernization program continued throughout 1973 in the 90th Strategic Missile Wing, Francis E. Warren Air Force Base, Wyoming. On 20 June, SAC accepted the first flight (Flight P of the 400th Strategic Missile Squadron) of Minuteman III missiles, and on 21 November, the entire squadron became operational when the last flight (Flight S) was accepted. In the meantime, the second squadron of the 90th Wing had entered the force modernization program.

The 1973 SAC Missile Competition was the sixth to be held. Six Minuteman wings and three Titan wings each entered four combat crews and a composite maintenance team. The main competition took place during the period from 26 April to 4 May at Vandenberg Air Force Base, California. However, since Vandenberg no longer had Minuteman I launch facilities in operation, a portion of the competition was held at Francis E. Warren Air Force Base, Wyoming, from 9 through 13 April. This action was taken to accommodate the 90th Strategic Missile Wing, which was still operating Minuteman Is.

The 90th Strategic Missile Wing won the Blanchard Trophy, the award given to the best wing in the combined areas of operations and maintenance. The 90th also won the best Minuteman Wing award, while the 381st Strategic Missile Wing, the 1972 winner of the Blanchard Trophy, won the Best Titan Wing award.

1974

Resources

Personnel	152,321 (22,873 officers, 109,778 airmen, 19,670 civilians)
Tactical Aircraft	1,165 (422 B-52, 671 EC/KC-135, 72 FB-111)
Aircraft Units	20 Heavy Bomb Wings (17 14 UE, one 17 UE, one 28 UE, one 33 UE) and one Strategic Wing (14 UE) with B-52s
	38 Heavy Air Refueling Squadrons (nine 20 UE and 29 15 UE) with KC-135s
	Two Medium Bomb Wings (one 30 UE and one 36 UE) with FB-111As
	Three Strategic Reconnaissance Wings (one U-2, one SR-71, one RC-135)
	Two Strategic Reconnaissance Squadrons with RC-135s
	Three Airborne Command and Control Squadrons with EC-135s
Missiles	999 Minuteman, 57 Titan II, 327 Hound Dogs, 415 Quail, 1,149 SRAM
Missile Units	Six Titan II Squadrons (9 UE) fully equipped and 20 Minuteman Squadrons (50 UE), ten equipped with Minuteman II "F" series missiles, nine equipped with Minuteman III "G" series missiles, and one in final stages of converting from Minuteman I "B" series to Minuteman III "G" series missiles
Active Bases	28 CONUS and one overseas (Guam)

Budget and Financial Status
(FY 74, as of 30 June 1974)

Operation and Maintenance	$534,010,000, includes supplies, communications, civilian pay, and minor equipment purchased
Assets	$17,715,494,760, includes real property, inventories, equipment, and weapon systems
Operating Expenses	$2,338,711,000, includes O&M listed above, military pay, family housing, troop subsistence, and aviation petroleum, oil, and lubricants (POL)

Operations

SR-71 record flights. In September, an SR-71 aircraft of the 9th Strategic Reconnaissance Wing, Beale Air Force Base, California, made two world record speed flights. On 1 September, the aircraft flew from New York to London in one hour, 55 minutes, and 32 seconds, averaging 1,810.9 miles per hour. The old record, set by an RAF Phantom F-4K in 1969, was four hours, 46 minutes, and 57.6 seconds. The SR-71 was flown by Major James B. Sullivan, pilot, and Major Noel F. Widdifield, reconnaissance systems officer.

On 13 September, the same SR-71 aircraft, flown by Captain Harold B. Adams, pilot, and Major William C. Machorek, Jr., reconnaissance systems officer, established a world speed record in a flight from London to Los Angeles. This flight took three hours, 47 minutes, and 39 seconds at an average speed of 1,487.81 miles per hour.

P. T. Cullen Award. The P. T. Cullen Award, presented each year to the reconnaissance unit that contributed most to the overall SAC photographic and signal intelligence effort, was won by the 9th Strategic Reconnaissance Wing.

First B-1 flight. The B-1 bomber, which was being developed by Rockwell International Corporation was flight tested on 23 December, when Charles C. Bock, Rockwell's chief test pilot, flew the new aircraft for the first time. It took off from the B-1 assembly facility at Palmdale, California, and landed almost one and one-half hours later at Edwards Air Force Base, California.

Bombing Competition

Having been canceled since 1971 due to operational commitments in Southeast Asia, the SAC Bombing Competition was renewed in 1974. Conducted from 10 through 16 November, the 1974 meet was the first one ever held at Barksdale Air Force Base, Louisiana, and the first one in which the Tactical Air Command participated. SAC participants included 20 B-52 wings, two FB-111 wings and 27 air refueling squadrons, with each participant entering one aircraft and crew. Tactical Air Command entered two F-111s and the Royal Air Force sent four Vulcan bombers. The major unit awards and their recipients were:

Fairchild Trophy, for the bomb wing and assigned tanker unit with the best combined score in bomber and tanker activity, 380th Bomb Wing, FB-111/KC-135.

Mathis Trophy, best bomber crew in bombing and celestial navigation, RAF, Vulcan.

Saunders Trophy, best tanker crew, 911th Air Refueling Squadron of the 68th Bomb Wing.

Bombing Trophy, best bomber unit in high and low bombing, 380th Bomb Wing, FB-111.

Navigation Trophy, best unit in navigation (FB-111s, and F-111s, did not compete), RAF Vulcan.

The swing-wing B-1 was planned to replace the venerable B-52 as a strategic bomber. However, President Carter cancelled the B-1 program on 30 June 1977. This photograph shows the three flying prototypes; the fourth, a ground test aircraft, was also built by Rockwell International, formerly North American Aviation. (Rockwell International photo)

A closeup of one of the three flying protoype B-1s. The aircraft has the SAC shield and band around the nose, as do two sister planes behind her. The B-1 has a length over the nose probe of 150.2 feet; the probe is 6.9-feet long. Note the forward-retracting landing gear and the downward opening crew hatch with retractable ladder. In addition to a four-man crew, there are folding seats for two additional personnel for test or training flights. (Rockwell International photo)

William J. Crumm Linebacker Memorial Trophy Awarded for First Time.
William J. Crumm Linebacker Memorial Trophy, best B-52 crew in high
bombing, 92d Bomb Wing. This trophy was named in honor of Major General
William J. Crumm, former Commander of the 3d Air Division, who was killed
while on a combat mission in a 1967 B-52 crash in the South China Sea.
Donated to SAC by Boeing Aerospace Company, the trophy was first presented in the 1974 meet in memory of the B-52 crew members killed in action
during Linebacker II, the December 1972 bombing of Hanoi and Haiphong,
North Vietnam.

Missiles

Total missiles and space systems launched during the year from Vandenberg
Air Force Base: Launched by: SAC—14; Other Agencies—35.

Force modernization program. The force modernization program continued
throughout 1974 in the 90th Strategic Missile Wing, Francis E. Warren Air
Force Base, Wyoming. On 3 September, the last Minuteman I was taken off
alert, and by the end of December 1974, only two flights of the 320th Strategic Missile Squadron remained to be converted to Minuteman III.

Missile Competition

Conducted at Vandenberg Air Force Base, California, from 25 April
through 3 May, the 1974 Missile Competition was an exacting and hard-
fought contest. The 321st Strategic Missile Wing, Grand Forks Air Force
Base, North Dakota, competing under the slogan "Eat 'Em Up," came from
eighth place on 26 April to first place on the final day to win the Blanchard
Perpetual Trophy as the best missile wing in SAC. The 321st also won the
award for Best Minuteman Wing, while the 390th Strategic Missile Wing,
Davis-Monthan Air Force Base, Arizona, a close second for the Blanchard
Trophy, won the award for the Best Titan II Wing.

1975

Resources

Personnel	140,735 (21,788 officers, 98,890 airmen, 20,057 civilians)
Tactical Aircraft	1,145 (420 B-52, 653 EC/KC-135, 69 FB-111, 3 E-4)
Aircraft Units	19 Heavy Bomb Wings (one 33 UE, one 28 UE, two 18 UE, one 17 UE, three 16 UE, 11 14 UE) and one Strategic Wing (14 UE) with B-52s
	36 Heavy Air Refueling Squadron (one 22 UE, eight 20 UE, one 19 UE, three 18 UE, two 16 UE, 19 15 UE, one 14 UE, one 13 UE) with KC-135s
	Two Medium Bomb Wings (one 36 UE and one 30 (UE) with FB-111As
	Three Strategic Reconnaissance Wings (one U-2, one SR-71, one RC-135)
	Two Strategic Reconnaissance Squadrons with RC-135s
	Three Airborne Command and Control Squadrons, two with EC-135s and one with E-4s
Missiles	1,010 Minuteman, 57 Titan II, 308 Hound Dog, 355 Quail, and 1,451 SRAM
Missile Units	Six Titan II squadrons (9 UE) fully equipped and 20 Minuteman Squadrons (50 UE), nine equipped with Minuteman II "F" series missiles and 11 with Minuteman III "G" series
Active Bases	28 CONUS and one overseas (Guam)

Budget and Financial Status
(FY 75 as of 30 June 1975)

Operation and Maintenance	$582,050,000, includes supplies, communications, civilian pay, and minor equipment purchased
Assets	$18,234,032,783, includes real property, inventories, equipment, and weapon systems
Operating Expenses	$2,558,099,158, includes O&M listed above, military pay, family housing, troop subsistence, and aviation petroleum, oil, and lubricants (POL)

Personnel

First Navigator to Command Flying Unit. On 16 February, Brigadier General Eugene D. Scott became the first navigator in the USAF to command an operational flying unit, assuming command of the 47th Air Division, Fairchild Air Force Base, Washington. Only pilots were authorized to command flying units prior to 18 December 1974, when President Ford signed a law removing Congressional restrictions on command.

Organization

Movement of Headquarters Eighth Air Force, inactivation of Headquarters Second Air Force. Effective 1 January 1975, Headquarters Eighth Air Force moved without personnel and equipment from Anderson Air Force Base, Guam, to Barksdale Air Force Base, Louisiana, where it absorbed the functions and personnel of Headquarters Second Air Force, which was inactivated. Headquarters Eighth Air Force had been located at Anderson since 1 April 1970, when it moved there from Westover Air Force Base, Massachusetts, in order to direct SAC combat operations in Southeast Asia.

At the time of this action, Headquarters USAF planned to move Headquarters Eighth Air Force to Barksdale and to inactivate Headquarters Second Air Force as soon as SAC operations in Southeast Asia had subsided.

Activation of Headquarters 3d Air Division. Concurrent with the above actions, Headquarters 3d Air Division, which had been inactivated at Anderson on 1 April 1970, was activated at that base and absorbed the personnel and functions of Headquarters Eighth Air Force.

Transfer of KC-135s to air reserve forces. In July 1974, Secretary of Defense Schlesinger directed SAC to transfer 128 KC-135 tankers to the air reserve forces in order to equip 16 eight UE units. Three units of the Air Force Reserve and 13 units of the Air National Guard would be involved in this program, which would extend over a four-year period. In the event of wartime mobilization, SAC would have control of these squadrons.

Tanker aircraft transferred. The transfer of aircraft actually began on 18 April 1975, when the 301st Air Refueling Squadron, Rickenbacker Air Force Base, Ohio, transferred the first KC-135, serial number 57-1507, to the 160th Air Refueling Group, also located at Rickenbacker. The 160th began operating on an eight UE basis on 1 July 1975. The second unit, the 157th Air Refueling Group, Pease Air Force Base, New Hampshire, entered the program on 1 October. Thus, by the end of December, a 16 UE element had been withdrawn from SAC to support these two units.

While these actions were taking place, SAC had inactivated two 15 UE air refueling squadrons: the 922d at Wright-Patterson Air Force Base, Ohio, on 30 September as part of the phase out of SAC activities at that base, and the 301st at Rickenbacker on 31 December as part of the Air Reserve Forces program. Redistribution of the 14 UE element remaining after these squadrons were inactivated was scattered among several units. This action along with other aircraft authorization realignments created eight different categories of squadrons, each with a distinct UE.

ACCS transferred to SAC. Effective 1 November 1975, Headquarters USAF transferred the 1st Airborne Command and Control Squadron (ACCS) located at Andrews Air Force Base, Maryland, from Headquarters Command to SAC. Concurrent with this action, SAC acquired the E-4, a modified Boeing 747. The 1st ACCS had three E-4s, outfitted with EC-135 type communications equipment, to serve as the National Emergency Airborne Command Post. A fourth E-4 was at the Boeing plant in Seattle, where it was being outfitted with advanced type communications equipment.

PACCS reorganization. In a separate action to consolidate resources, SAC reorganized its Post Attack Command Control System (PACCS). Effective 31 December, the 3d Airborne Command and Control Squadron was inactivated at Grissom Air Force Base, Indiana, after its functions had been assumed by the 70th Air Refueling Squadron at Grissom and the 2d Airborne Command and Control Squadron at Offutt.

Operations

Operation New Life. During the final evacuations from Cambodia and Vietnam, SAC flew tanker and reconnaissance sorties in support of the American withdrawal. Accompanying the final Americans were thousands of refugees fleeing the communist takeover of their homeland. From 23 April to 16 August, Anderson Air Force Base, Guam, became a temporary haven for the refugees. Practically everyone on Anderson assisted in Operation New Life, which processed about 110,000 refugees on their way to the U.S. and other countries.

Spaatz Trophy awarded. In appreciation of the outstanding support given its fighters over the years by SAC tankers, the Tactical Air Command donated a new trophy to SAC on 4 September 1975. Named "The General Carl 'Tooey' Spaatz Award" in memory of the first USAF Chief of Staff and a pioneer in the development of inflight refueling, the award would go on an annual rotating basis to the best air refueling unit. On 4 October, the trophy was presented for the first time to the 11th Air Refueling Squadron, Altus Air Force Base, Oklahoma.

First SAC refueling of B-1. On 21 April, SAC conducted its first inflight refueling of the B-1. The crew, under command of Lieutenant Colonel Fred C. Hartstein, came from the 1st Combat Evaluation Group, Barksdale Air Force Base, Louisiana, while the KC-135 tanker was furnished by the 22d Air Refueling Squadron, March Air Force Base, California. Previously, on 10 April, an Air Force Systems Command KC-135 and crew had conducted the first inflight refueling of the new bomber.

First SAC pilot flies B-1. On 19 September, Major George W. Larson, who was assigned to the 4200th Test and Evaluation Squadron, Edwards Air Force Base, California, became the first SAC pilot to fly the B-1. Accompanied by Charles C. Boch and Richard Abrams of Rockwell International Corporation,

Major Larson handled the aircraft controls for approximately one-third of the 6½-hour flight.

P. T. Cullen Award. The P. T. Cullen Award, presented annually to the reconnaissance unit contributing most to the overall SAC photographic and signal intelligence effort, was won by the 55th Strategic Reconnaissance Wing.

Missiles

Total missiles and space systems launched during the year from Vandenberg Air Force Base: Launched by: SAC—14; Other Agencies—33.

Force modernization program completed. The force modernization program, a nine-year effort to replace all Minuteman Is with either Minuteman IIs or Minuteman IIIs was completed in 1975. The program within the 90th Strategic Missile Wing, Francis E. Warren Air Force Base, Wyoming, was completed on 21 January, about three weeks ahead of schedule. On that date, the Boeing Aerospace Company, the contractor responsible for remodeling the launch facilities, turned over to SAC the last flight of ten Minuteman III missiles (Flight Juliet of the 320th Strategic Missile Squadron).

A related program involved replacing 50 Minuteman II missiles of the 341st Strategic Missile Wing, Malmstrom Air Force Base, Montana, with a like number of Minuteman IIIs. This conversion began on 20 January, with Ogden Air Logistics Center handling the missile swap on an individual site basis, and was completed on 11 July when the 50th site of the 564th Strategic Missile Squadron was returned to SAC. This action brought the SAC Minuteman force up to a 450-Minuteman II/550-Minuteman III configuration.

As with previous meets, the 1975 SAC Missile Competition was held at Vandenberg Air Force Base, California, from 24 April through 2 May.

In addition to entering combat crews and maintenance teams, each wing sent a security police team. These security police teams competed in exercises to evaluate their reaction to normal and emergency situations endemic to their bases, written tests, and ability with the M-16 rifle.

The 1975 competition was also significant in that women participated for the first time. Sergeant Jo A. Williamson served on the 321st Strategic Missile Wing's electronics laboratory maintenance team, while Airman First Class Jeanine A. Sousley was a member of the 308th Strategic Missile Wing's reentry vehicle maintenance team.

The 381st Strategic Missile Wing, McConnell Air Force Base, Kansas, compiling the highest score in operations, maintenance, and security police exercises, received the Blanchard Perpetual Trophy. In duplicating its 1972 performance, the 381st became the first Titan II unit to win the top award for the second time. The 381st also won awards for Best Titan Wing and Best Missile Operations. Other major unit awards and their recipients were: Best Minuteman Wing, 44th Strategic Missile Wing, Ellsworth Air Force Base, South Dakota; Best Missile Maintenance, 308th Strategic Missile Wing, Little Rock Air Force Base, Arkansas; and Best Missile Security Police, 321st Strategic Missile Wing, Grand Forks Air Force Base, North Dakota.

1976

Resources

Personnel 127,599 (19,662 officers, 91,722 airmen, 16,175 civilians)

Tactical Aircraft 1,102 (419 B-52, 68 FB-111, 612 EC/KC-135, 3 E-4)

Aircraft Units 18 Heavy Bomb Wings (one 33 UE, one 28 UE, two 18 UE, one 17 UE, three 16 UE, ten 14 UE), one Strategic Wing (14 UE) with B-52s

2 Medium Bomb Wing (one 36 UE, one 30 UE) with FB-111As

35 Heavy Air Refueling Squadrons (four 20 UE, three 19 UE, three 18 UE, one 17 UE, two 16 UE, twelve 15 UE, nine 14 UE, one 13 UE) with KC-135s

2 Strategic Reconnaissance Wings (one with U-2s and SR-71s, one with RC-135s)

1 Strategic Reconnaissance Squadron with RC-135s

3 Airborne Command and Control Squadrons (two with EC-135s, one with E-4s)

Missiles 1,094 Minuteman (including missiles in depot modification), 58 Titan II, 288 Hound Dog, 355 Quail, 1,431 SRAM

Missile Units 6 Titan II Squadrons (9 UE) fully equipped, 20 Minuteman Squadrons (50 UE), 9 with Minuteman IIF series missiles, 11 with Minuteman IIIG series

Active Bases 26 CONUS and 1 on Guam

Budget and Financial Status
(FY 76 as of 30 June 1976)

Operations and Maintenance $670,545,354, includes supplies, communications, civilian pay, minor equipment purchased

Assets $18,262,117,573, includes real property, inventories, equipment, and weapon systems

Operating Expenses $2,541,093,542, includes O&M listed above, military pay, family housing, troop subsistence, and aviation petroleum, oil, and lubricants (POL)

| New Fiscal Year Procedure Began | In accordance with the Congressional Budget and Impoundment Act of 1974 (PL 93-44), a new fiscal year from 1 October through 30 September was established, replacing the 1 July through 30 June fiscal year. A three-month transitional period called FY 7T was provided in the act to bridge the gap between 1 July and 30 September 1976. |

(FY 7T as of 30 September 1976)

Operations and Maintenance	$171,254,080, includes supplies, communications, civilian pay, minor equipment purchased
Assets	$18,262,117,573, includes real property, inventories, equipment, and weapon systems
Operating Expenses	$612,906,264, includes O&M listed above, military pay, family housing, troop subsistence, and aviation petroleum, oil, and lubricants (POL)

Organization

SAC's 30th Anniversary. On 21 March, the Strategic Air Command observed its 30th anniversary. In connection with this event, Secretary of Defense Donald H. Rumsfeld flew in a B-52H from Offutt AFB, Nebraska, to Whiteman AFB, Missouri, where he toured Minuteman II missile facilities prior to returning to Washington, D.C.

Reorganization Under Tri-Deputy Concept. Effective 1 July, SAC reorganized its wing/base structure under the tri-deputy concept. In accordance with this reorganization, directed by Headquarters USAF, a deputy commander for resources was created and placed under the wing commander on a coequal status with the existing deputy commander for operations and deputy commander for maintenance. The newly organized deputy commander for resources received the functions of comptroller, procurement, supply, and transportation from the combat support group, thereby enabling the base commander to become more deeply involved in people programs. Concurrently, the supply and transportation squadrons were transferred from the combat support group to the wing.

Realignment of Communications Function. In accordance with Headquarters USAF policy of creating a single manager for all Air Force communications, the Air Force Communications Service (AFCS) assumed command and management responsibility for all SAC communications systems and functions. SAC retained operational control over its communications. The arrangement was facilitated by the creation of Headquarters Strategic Communications Area (SACCA), an Air Force Communications Service unit at Offutt AFB. The commander of SACCA also served as the director of communications-electronics of Headquarters SAC's deputy chief of staff/operations. Within the

142

command, SAC's communications groups and squadrons were transferred to the AFCS.

Operations

SR-71 Record Flights. In July, three crews of the 9th Strategic Reconnaissance Wing, Beale AFB, California, set seven speed and altitude records with the SR-71. On 27 July, Major Adolphus H. Bledsoe, Jr., pilot, and Major John T. Fuller, reconnaissance systems officer, flew the Blackbird at a speed of 2,092.29 miles per hour over a 621.4-mile (1,000-km) course in the vicinity of Edwards AFB, California. In this flight, they set three closed circuit records: 1) world absolute speed; 2) world jet speed with 2,200 lb (1,000 kg) payload; and 3) world jet speed without payload.

The record-breaking flights continued on 28 July with four additional records being established. Captain Eldon W. Joersz, pilot, and Major George T. Morgan, RSO, flew their SR-71 at a speed of 2,193.64 miles per hour, setting two records: world absolute and jet speed over a 9-to-15-mile (15-to-25-km) straight course. Finally, Captain Robert C. Helt, pilot, and Major Lang A. Elliot, RSO, flew a Blackbird to a height of 85,069 feet over the test range at Edwards AFB and established both world absolute and jet records for altitude in horizontal flight.

B-1 Development. On 2 December, Secretary of Defense Rumsfeld authorized the Air Force to proceed with production of the B-1 bomber. In September, however, Congress restricted funding of the B-1 to $87 million per month through February 1977. This action, in effect, left the B-1 production decision up to Jimmy Carter, who would become president on 20 January 1977.

Air Launched Cruise Missile Tested. On 5 March, the Air Launched Cruise Missile, which was being developed by Boeing for use by SAC, was successfully test launched from a B-52G at the White Sands Missile Range, New Mexico. The ALCM, as it was popularly referred to, was designed to carry a nuclear warhead into enemy defenses.

Last SAC Aircraft Left Southeast Asia. In February 1964, a U-2 had been the first SAC aircraft deployed to Southeast Asia. On 22 March 1976, a U-2 departed U-Tapao Airfield, Thailand, to become the last SAC aircraft to leave Southeast Asia.

SAC Participated in Red Flag. On 29 November 1975, the Tactical Air Command unveiled a complex of simulated enemy facilities on the Nellis AFB Nevada Desert Test Ranges to provide realistic combat training in exercises known as Red Flag. SAC was invited to participate in the April 1976 exercise, Red Flag IV. SAC flew numerous B-52 and FB-111 sorties, beginning with three 7th Bomb Wing B-52Ds on 12 April.

Spaatz Trophy. The 41st Air Refueling Squadron, Griffiss AFB, New York, was selected as the best air refueling unit in SAC for 1976.

A prototype B-1 flies low and slow, with wings fully extended and landing gear lowered. Her four General Electric F101-series engines were developed in the 1960s specifically for the planned advanced strategic bomber. The aircraft's aerodynamic shape provides high speed at low levels and a relatively small radar cross section. Cost-saving modifications to the engine inlets have reduced the aircraft's maximum speed. Several other cost reduction modifications have been made to the earlier B-1 designs. (Rockwell International photo)

P. T. Cullen Trophy. The 306th Strategic Wing, Ramstein AB, Germany, was selected for the 1976 award for being the reconnaissance unit contributing most to the photographic and signals intelligence efforts of SAC.

Omaha Trophy. The 449th Bomb Wing, Kincheloe AFB, Michigan, was selected the outstanding wing in SAC for 1976.

Drones Transferred to Tactical Air Command. On 1 July, the SAC drone reconnaissance program, which had been in the 100th Strategic Reconnaissance Wing at Davis-Monthan AFB, Arizona, was transferred to the Tactical Air Command (TAC). The drones, built by Teledyne Ryan Aeronautical Division of Teledyne, Inc., were small, unmanned, remotely piloted, jet-powered vehicles that were launched from DC-130 aircraft. After completing their reconnaissance missions, they were retrieved in mid-air by CH-3 helicopters. All SAC drone assets, including several AQM-34 remotely piloted vehicles (RPV), six DC-130 launch aircraft, and seven CH-3 recovery helicopters, were transferred.

Bombing Competition

Twentieth Competition. The 1976 SAC Bombing Competition was revised, being divided into three phases. The first phase, held in July and August, was an in-unit competition with participants including all mission-ready bomber and tanker crews except B-52 crews of the 43d Strategic Wing, Andersen AFB, Guam, and KC-135 crews of the 376th Strategic Wing, Kadena AB, Japan. The top three bomber and/or tanker crews plus one "wild card" crew from each unit then progressed to the semifinal round that was held from 27 through 30

September. The Royal Air Force also entered four Vulcan crews and aircraft in the semifinal phase. In the final round, held on 4–5 October, each SAC and RAF unit entered its two top crews.

Throughout the competition, SAC units operated out of their home bases, while the RAF contingent staged out of Barksdale AFB, Louisiana. Barksdale also served as the competition headquarters for giving awards. The major awards and their recipients were: Fairchild Trophy, 380th Bomb Wing, FB-111/KC-135; Mathis Trophy, 7th Bomb Wing, B-52; Saunders Trophy, 92d Bomb Wing, KC-135; Crumm Trophy, 7th Bomb Wing, B-52; and the Bombing Trophy, 7th Bomb Wing, B-52.

RAF Bombing Competition. In the 1976 RAF Bombing Competition, held from 5–14 April at RAF Station Marham, SAC participants included one B-52G crew and aircraft from the 2d, 92d, 97th, and 320th Bomb Wings. The 320th Bomb Wing won the Blue Steel Trophy, awarded to the crew with the highest combined score in bombing and navigation, and the Camrose Trophy, for the crew with the best score in bombing. This marked the first time a SAC unit won the Camrose Trophy.

Barrentine Trophy Created. Ellsworth AFB, South Dakota, became the permanent home for the SAC Munitions Loading Competition for the next decade. SAC established the Chief Master Sergeant Wilbur R. Barrentine Memorial Munitions Loading Trophy for the wing with the best munitions competition team in SAC. In the competition, held from 27 September through 6 October, the 7th Bomb Wing, Carswell AFB, Texas, was the first winner of the trophy. The presentation of the trophy was made at Barksdale AFB, Louisiana, during the Bombing Competition awards ceremonies on 6–7 October. The other major awards given were: Best Munitions Load Crew, 7th Bomb Wing; Best Security Police Team, 97the Bomb Wing, Blytheville AFB, Arkansas; Best Crew Chief, 379th Bomb Wing, Wurtsmith AFB, Michigan; Best Combined Load Crew, 379th Bomb Wing.

Missiles

Missile Launches. Total missiles and space systems launched during the year from Vandenberg AFB: SAC—15; other agencies—26.

New Titan II Guidance System. A replacement for the Titan II ICBM Inertial Guidance System (IGS), the Universal Space Guidance System (USGS), proved its reliability by guiding the flight of a Titan IIIC space booster on 27 June 1976 at Vandenberg AFB, California.

Missile Competition

Ninth Competition. Following the precedent established in the 1975 meet in which security police teams were added as participants, the 1976 SAC Missile Competition was further expanded to include communications, engineering, and vehicle support teams. As in the past, Vandenberg AFB was the site of the meet, held 20–30 April. The 341st Strategic Missile Wing (Minuteman) at Malmstrom AFB, Montana, took the bulk of the major awards, including the Blanchard Perpetual Trophy for the highest combined score in all exercises, Best Minuteman Wing, Best Missile Operations, Best Missile Maintenance, Best Missile Communications, and Best Missile Civil Engineering. The 381st Strategic Missile Wing, McConnell AFB, Kansas, was judged the Best Titan Wing, while the 351st Strategic Missile Wing, Whiteman AFB, Missouri, won the Best Vehicle Support Team, and the Best Security Police Team award went to the 321st Strategic Missile Wing, Grand Forks AFB, North Dakota.

1977

Resources

Personnel 123,042 (18,726 officers, 89,440 airmen, 14,876 civilians)

Tactical Aircraft 1,110 (417 B-52, 66 FB-111, 574 EC/KC-135, 3 E-4)

Aircraft Units
- 17 Heavy Bomb Wings (one 33 UE, one 30 UE, one 28 UE, one 20 UE, three 17 UE, ten 14 UE), one Strategic Wing (14 UE) with B-52s
- 2 Medium Bomb Wing (one 36 UE, one 30 UE) with FB-111As
- 34 Heavy Air Refueling Squadrons (one 25 UE, one 20 UE, seven 19 UE, two 16 UE, nine 15 UE, six 14 UE, three 13 UE, three 12 UE, two 10 UE) with KC-135s
- 2 Strategic Reconnaissance Wings (one with U-2s and SR-71s, one with RC-135s)
- 1 Strategic Reconnaissance Squadron with RC-135s
- 3 Airborne Command and Control Squadrons (two with EC-135s, one with E-4s)

Missiles 1,162 Minuteman (including missiles in depot modification), 57 Titan II, 249 Hound Dog, 354 Quail, 1,415 SRAM

Missile Units 6 Titan II Squadrons (9 UE) fully equipped, 20 Minuteman Squadrons (50 UE), 9 with Minuteman IIF series missiles, 11 with Minuteman IIIG series

Active Bases 25 CONUS and 1 on Guam

Budget and Financial Status
(FY 77 as of 30 June 1977)

Operation and Maintenance $658,204,983, includes supplies, communications, civilian pay, minor equipment purchased

Assets $17,804,995,267, includes real property, inventories, equipment, and weapon systems

Operating Expenses $2,412,063,735, includes O&M listed above, military pay, troop subsistence, and aviation petroleum, oil, and lubricants (POL)

Military Family	$64,226,232, includes O&M expenses (Military Family
Housing	Housing Defense Appropriation) in support of housing
	units

Organization

Reorganization of Minuteman Security Police Functions. Effective 1 October, Headquarters SAC reorganized security police functions at the six Minuteman bases. The reorganization improved efficiency by dividing the existing squadrons into smaller and more manageable units. It was accomplished by activating eight new missile security squadrons—one each at four installations and two each at two installations that supported the largest Minuteman wings.

Operations

President Carter Flew on E-4A. On 11 February, President Jimmy Carter flew in an E-4A National Emergency Airborne Command Post (NEACP) of the 1st Airborne Command and Control Squadron from Andrews AFB, Maryland, to Robins AFB, Georgia. This marked the first time a U.S. president flew in an E-4A.

President Carter Stopped Action on Selecting a New Tanker. On 19 February, President Carter stopped action to select an Advanced Tanker/Cargo Aircraft (ATCA) being considered for use by SAC.

President Carter Dropped the B-1 in Favor of the Cruise Missile. On 30 June, President Carter announced in a nationwide television address that the B-1 bomber would not be produced. He stated:

> This has been one of the most difficult decisions that I have made since I have been in office. Within the last few months I've done my best to assess all the factors involved in production of the B-1 bomber. My decision is that we should not continue with deployment of the B-1, and I am directing that we discontinue plans for production of this weapons system. The secretary of defense agrees that this is a preferable decision. . . . The existing testing and development now underway on the B-1 should continue to provide us with the needed technical base in the unlikely event that more cost-effective alternative systems should run into difficulty. . . . In the meantime, we should begin development of cruise missiles using air-launched platforms such as our B-52s, modernized as necessary.

Cancellation of B-1 Explained by Secretary of Defense Brown. On 1 July, Secretary of Defense Harold Brown, at a Pentagon press conference, stated:

> My recommendation to the president, and his decision not to proceed with production of the B-1, were based on the conclusion that aircraft carrying modern cruise missiles will better assure the effectiveness of the bomber component of U.S. strategic power in the 1980s. Both the B-1 and the cruise missile offer high assurance of survivability and penetration. But the president and I are convinced that the cruise missile will provide more certainty for our defense.

Advanced Tanker/Cargo Aircraft Development. In July, Secretary of Defense Brown approved acquisition of a force of between 12 and 20 Advanced Tanker Cargo Aircraft instead of 91 as approved by President Ford in January. On 19 December, the secretary selected McDonnell-Douglas to provide 20 DC-10-type aircraft for the ATCA role.

Spaatz Trophy. The 306th Strategic Wing, Ramstein AB, Germany, was selected as the best air refueling unit in SAC for 1977.

P. T. Cullen Trophy. The 9th Strategic Reconnaissance Wing, Beale AFB, California, was selected for the 1977 award for being the reconnaissance unit contributing most to SAC's photographic and signals intelligence efforts.

Omaha Trophy. The 42d Bomb Wing, Loring AFB, Maine, was selected the outstanding wing in SAC for 1977.

Bombing Competition

Twenty-first Competition. The 1977 SAC Bombing Competition resembled the competition in 1976. For SAC units, the competition again was divided into three phases, with the first phase an in-unit competition held from 1 June through 31 August. Four bomber crews and two tanker crews from each unit competed in the second phase held from 13 through 16 September. From this phase, 18 bomb wings (the 93d Bombardment Wing, Castle AFB, California, and the 43d Strategic Wing, Andersen AFB, Guam, did not participate) and 24 tanker units (909th Air Refueling Squadron, Kadena AB, Japan, did not compete) entered two crews each in the final meet, conducted from 21 through 23 September. Competing with the SAC bomber crews were two Royal Air Force Vulcan crews and two Tactical Air Command F-111 crews.

The major awards and their recipients were:

Fairchild Trophy, best combined bomber and tanker scores in bombing and navigation.

380th Bomb Wing, FB-111/KC-135. Mathis Trophy, best bombing unit, 509th Bomb Wing, FB-111.

Saunders Trophy, best tanker unit, 384th Air Refueling Wing, KC-135.

Crumm Trophy, best B-52 unit in high-altitude bombing, 7th Bomb Wing.

Meyer Trophy, top FB-111 unit in low-level bombing and electronic countermeasures activity, 509th Bomb Wing.

Navigation Trophy, best KC-135 unit in celestial navigation, 380th Bomb Wing.

Bombing Trophy, 380th Bomb Wing, FB-111.

The Doolittle Trophy Presented for the First Time. The Doolittle trophy, donated by Rockwell International Corporation, was named in honor of Lieutenant General James H. Doolittle, leader of the Army Air Forces' low-level bombing raid over Japan on 18 April 1942 and former commander of the 8th Air Force. The trophy was awarded to the numbered air force whose B-52 unit compiled the best overall results in low-level bombing during the competition. The Eighth Air Force was the first recipient of the Doolittle Trophy, with its 379th Bomb Wing compiling the best score.

RAF Bombing Competition. In sharp contrast to their performance in the 1976 RAF Bombing Competition, SAC crews did not fare well in the 1977 meet. The 5th, 319th, 410th, and 449th represented SAC, with each sending one B-52H aircraft and crew to RAF Station Marham for the 9–17 May competition.

In this meet, the ground equipment associated with the radar bomb scoring sites malfunctioned, and it was necessary to tabulate scoring by using vertical bombing photography from the aircraft. The B-52H bombers were not adequately equipped to conduct this type of photography, and they failed to retain the Blue Steel or the Camrose Trophy. The 449th Bomb Wing came in second for the former award, while a SAC team composed of crews from the 5th, 410th, and 449th Bomb Wings placed fifth in the Comrose competition.

Munitions Loading Competition. The annual competition was held at the same location as last year, Ellsworth AFB, South Dakota, from 13 through 20 September. The winner of the Barrentine Memorial Munitions Loading Trophy for the wing with the best munitions competition team in SAC was the 93d Bomb Wing, Castle AFB, California.

The other major awards given were:

Best Munitions Load Crew, 7th Bomb Wing, Carswell AFB, Texas
Best Security Police Team, 379th Bomb Wing, Wurtsmith AFB, Michigan
Best Crew Chief, 5th Bomb Wing, Minot AFB, North Dakota
Best Combined Load Crew, 319th Bomb Wing, Grand Forks AFB, North Dakota

Missiles

Missile Launches. Total missiles and space systems launched during the year from Vandenberg AFB: SAC—12; other agencies—20.

Minuteman Crew Reduction. Between 1 October 1977 and 31 March 1978, SAC reduced the Minuteman crew force by approximately 600, saving an estimated $14 million annually. The reduction was achieved by shortening the Minuteman alert tour from 36 to 24 hours and permitting one crew member to sleep while inside the Launch Control Center (LCC). Circuitry modifications to the LCC's launch enable control group panel eliminated the remote possibility of an unauthorized launch by a single crew member.

Missile Competition

Tenth Competition. Between 25 April and 6 May, the competition was held at Vandenberg AFB, California. The 351st Strategic Missile Wing, Whiteman AFB, Missouri, captured the Blanchard Perpetual Trophy, having compiled the highest combined score for all exercises as well as trophies for Best Minuteman Wing, Best Missile Operations, and Best Missile Civil Engineering.

Other major awards and their recipients were:

Best Titan Wing, 390th Strategic Missile Wing, Davis-Monthan AFB, Arizona
Best Missile Maintenance, 341st Strategic Missile Wing, Malmstrom AFB, Montana
Best Missile Security Police, 91st Strategic Missile Wing, Minot AFB, North Dakota
Best Missile Communications, 44th Strategic Missile Wing, Ellsworth AFB, South Dakota
Best Missile Vehicle Operator, Francis E. Warren AFB, Wyoming

1978

Resources

Personnel 122,500 (18,177 officers, 90,625 airmen, 13,698 civilians)

Tactical Aircraft 952 (344 B-52, 66 FB-111, 539 EC/KC-135, 3 E-4)

Aircraft Units 18 Heavy Bomb Wings (one 33 UE, one 30 UE, one 28 UE, one 20 UE, three 17 UE, eleven 14 UE) with B-52s

2 Medium Bomb Wing (one 34 UE, one 26 UE) with FB-111As

34 Heavy Air Refueling Squadrons (one 25 UE, five 19 UE, one 16 UE, nine 15 UE, six 14 UE, five 13 UE, one 12 UE, one 10 UE, five 9 UE) with KC-135s

2 Strategic Reconnaissance Wings (one with U-2s and SR-71s, one with RC-135s)

1 Strategic Reconnaissance Squadron with RC-135s

3 Airborne Command and Control Squadrons (two with EC-135s, one with E-4s)

Missiles 1,180 Minuteman (including missiles in depot modification), 57 Titan II, 1,408 SRAM

Missile Units 6 Titan II Squadrons (9 UE) fully equipped, 20 Minuteman Squadrons (50 UE), nine with Minuteman IIF series missiles, 11 with Minuteman IIIG series

Active Bases 25 CONUS and 1 on Guam

Budget and Financial Status
(FY 78 as of 30 September 1978)

Operation and Maintenance $645,985,086, includes supplies, communications, civilian pay, minor equipment purchased

Assets $17,522,065,313, includes real property, inventories, equipment, and weapon systems

Operating Expenses $2,397,381,283, includes O&M listed above, military pay, troop subsistence, and aviation petroleum, oil, and lubricants (POL)

Military Family Housing $82,416,277, includes O&M expenses (Military Family Housing Defense Appropriation) in support of housing units

Organization

Headquarters 7th Air Division Activated in Germany. Headquarters 7th Air Division was activated at Ramstein Air Base, Germany, on 1 July. This improved command and control of SAC's growing tanker, bomber, and reconnaissance activities in Europe and strengthened liaison with U.S. and allied commands in the area. Concurrently, the 306th Strategic Wing was assigned to 7th Air Division, moving without personnel and equipment from Ramstein to RAF Mildenhall, U.K., and the 922d Strategic Squadron was activated at Hellenikon AB, Greece. On 1 August, the 34th Strategic Squadron was activated at Zaragoza AB, Spain. The Hellenikon and Zaragoza squadrons, which replaced detachments of the 306th Strategic Wing, were assigned to the 306th. A final action in the 1978 expansion of SAC activities in the European area, was the activation of the 11th Strategic Group at RAF Fairford on 15 November and its assignment to the 7th Air Division.

Operations

Retirement of Older B-52 Bombers and Hound Dog and Quail Missiles. During 1978, SAC disposed of 68 older B-52 D/F bomber variants, with approximately 60 being sent to storage at Davis-Monthan AFB, Arizona, and the remainder being redistributed for various training and display purposes. All AGM-28 Hound Dog and ADM-20 Quail missiles also were retired.

Red Flag/Maple Flag. By the end of 1978, all SAC B-52 and FB-111 wings were participating in Tactical Air Command's Red Flag Exercises on the Nellis AFB, Nevada, ranges. The concept was so successful that it was expanded to include the use of Canadian ranges near Cold Lake. The first SAC B-52 sorties on the Canadian ranges — nicknamed Maple Flag — occurred on 27 April 1978.

Transfer of Last KC-135 to Air Reserve Forces. On 16 September, SAC completed the program to transfer 128 KC-135s to the Air Reserve Forces. On this date, the 128th tanker (KC-135A, Serial Number 57-1438) was transferred from the 7th Bomb Wing, Carswell AFB, Texas, to the 931st Air Refueling Group, an Air Force Reserve unit at Grissom AFB, Indiana.

First Female Officers On Aircraft Alert Duty. On 23 March, Captain Sandra M. Scott became the first female pilot to perform alert duty in SAC. She was assigned to the 904th Air Refueling Squadron, a KC-135 unit at Mather AFB, California. On 27 April, two KC-135 crew members shared the distinction of being the first female navigators to perform SAC alert duties, Captain Elizabeth A. Koch, 22d Air Refueling Squadron, March AFB, California, and First Lieutenant Ramona L. S. Roybal, 916th Air Refueling Squadron, Travis AFB, California.

Spaatz Trophy. The 912th Air Refueling Squadron, Robins AFB, Georgia, was selected as the best air refueling unit in SAC for the period January-to-September 1978. Beginning this year, the award will be presented on a fiscal-year basis.

P. T. Cullen Trophy. The 6th Strategic Wing, Eielson AFB, Alaska, was selected for the 1978 award for its contribution to SAC's photographic and signals intelligence efforts.

Omaha Trophy. The 319th Bomb Wing, Grand Forks AFB, Georgia, was selected the outstanding wing in SAC for 1978.

Bombing Competition

Twenty-second Competition. In the 30 years since its inception, the SAC bombing competition (officially called the SAC Bombing and Navigation Competition) had changed appreciably. For many years, the competitors gathered at one or two bases where all missions were flown. More recently, participants operated from their home bases and gathered at Barksdale AFB, Louisiana, for the awards ceremony. Barksdale was a logical site for the competition headquarters since it was the home of the 1st Combat Evaluation Group, the competition's official scoring unit. Also, Barksdale normally supported the Royal Air Force Vulcan bombers when they participated.

The Fairchild Trophy, first awarded in 1951, remained the top award in 1978, but nine additional major trophies were presented in recognition of unit and crew performances. In the final phase, held on 18 and 19 October, SAC participants included one aircraft and crew from 18 B-52/FB-111 wings (the 43d Strategic Wing, Andersen AFB, Guam, and the 93d Bomb Wing, Castle AFB, California, did not compete) and 25 KC-135 tanker units (909th Air Refueling Squadron, Kadena Air Base, Japan, did not compete, and on those bases where two air refueling squadrons were stationed, only one squadron was represented). Also, one RAF Vulcan crew, two Tactical Air Command F-111 crews, eight Air National Guard KC-135 crews, and two Air Force Reserve KC-135 crews competed. From 23 through 25 October, a competition symposium was held at Barksdale and attended by all crews participating in the final phase. Major awards presented at the symposium were as follows:

Fairchild Trophy, SAC wing compiling most points in bomber and tanker activity, 380th Bomb Wing, FB-111/KC-135

Mathis Trophy, top bomber unit in combined high- and low-level bombing, 509th Bomb Wing, FB-111

Saunders Trophy, top tanker unit, 28th Bomb Wing, KC-135

Crumm Trophy, B-52/Vulcan unit compiling most points in high altitude bombing, 28th Bomb Wing, B-52

Meyer Trophy, top F/FB-111 in low-level bombing and electronic countermeasures activity, 380th Bomb Wing, FB-111

Doolittle Trophy, numbered air force whose B-52 units achieved highest combined average score for low-level bombing, Eighth Air Force.

Navigation Trophy, tanker unit compiling most points in navigation, 924th Air Refueling Squadron, KC-135

Bombing Trophy, bomber crew with most points in high and low bombing, 509th Bomb Wing, FB-111

The General Russell E. Dougherty Short Range Attack Missile (SRAM) Awarded for First Time. The Dougherty trophy, donated by the Boeing Aerospace Company, was named for General Russell E. Dougherty, former commander-in-chief of SAC, and was given to the B-52/FB-111 unit with the best score

ICBM mobility and survivability have eluded U.S. defense planners. Shown here is a "breakout" test during the evaluation of the buried trench concept. With this technique, the MX would be shuttled through trenches covered by ten inches of concrete and five feet of dirt to provide protection from reconnaissance satellites and radiation. Photo courtesy of Martin-Marietta Corp.

in simulated SRAM launching. The 319th Bomb Wing, a B-52 unit, was the first winner.

The Major James F. Bartsch Electronic Warfare Trophy Awarded for First Time. This new trophy was donated by the Association of Old Crows, an independent, nonprofit organization dedicated to furthering the advancement of electronic warfare. It was named for Major James F. Bartsch, a 410th Bomb Wing electronic warfare officer, who was killed in a B-52 accident on 2 April 1977. The award is for the B-52 unit compiling the most points in electronic countermeasures activity. The first recipient was the 92d Bomb Wing.

Munitions Loading Competition. This year's Munitions Loading Competition was held at Ellsworth AFB, South Dakota, from 15 through 22 August. The 43d Strategic Wing, Andersen AFB, Guam, won the Barrentine Trophy for the Best Munitions Competition Team.

The other major award winners were:

Best Security Police Team, 44th Strategic Missile Wing, Ellsworth AFB, South Dakota

Best Munitions Load Crew, 43d Strategic Wing

Best Crew Chief, 416th Bomb Wing, Griffiss AFB, New York

Best Combined Load Crew, 43d Strategic Wing

RAF Bombing Competition. Three SAC B-52G units (the 2d, 92d, and 279th Bomb Wings) participated in the Royal Air Force Strike Command Bombing

Competition held at RAF Station, Marham, from 26 June through 3 July. SAC units did not win any major trophies.

Missiles

Missile Launches. Total missiles and space systems launched during the year from Vandenberg AFB: SAC—10; other agencies—22.

Titan II Mishap - McConnell AFB. On 24 August 1978, a nitrogen tetroxide oxidizer that leaked from a Stage I booster disabled Launch Complex 533-7 of the 381st Strategic Missile Wing, McConnell AFB, Kansas. The escaped oxidizer also severely damaged the ICBM housed within the complex and caused two fatalities. During the mishap SAC temporarily evacuated civilians residing nearby.

Minuteman Motor Maintenance. In July 1978, Ogden Air Logistics Center, Utah, began the phased depot maintenance of Minuteman motors. This step was to eliminate several age-related anomalies that afflicted Minuteman ICBM motors. During the first portion of phased maintenance, Aerojet Corporation, the program's contractor, reconditioned Minuteman II, Stage II motors at an estimated cost of $200 million. At a later date, Aerojet received other Minuteman motors for reconditioning, giving priority to the oldest.

Women on Titan II Crews. On 18 August 1978, Airman First Class Tina M. Ponzer, assigned to the 381st Strategic Missile Wing, McConnell AFB, Kansas, became the first enlisted female to perform a Titan II alert. On 16 September, First Lieutenant Patricia M. Fornes, also with the 381st Wing, was the first female officer to pull Titan II alert.

Universal Space Guidance System (USGS) Installations. In February 1978, the first operational Universal Space Guidance System was installed at Launch Complex 373-6 of the 308th Strategic Missile Wing, Little Rock AFB, Arkansas. Installation of operational USGS sets at Little Rock began at the end of March. In late 1978, SAC also was installing the USGS at the 390th Strategic Missile Wing, Davis-Monthan AFB, Arizona.

Missile Competition

Eleventh Competition - Participation Reduced. Held from 28 April through 4 May, the 1978 competition differed appreciably from 1977. While the entire previous year's competition had been held at Vandenberg AFB, California, Titan II maintenance evaluations in 1978 were conducted at McConnell AFB, Kansas, because Vandenberg's last Titan II launch facility had been closed. Then, due to budgetary constraints, vehicle operator teams were dropped from the event and the number of combat crews representing each wing was reduced from four to two. Trailing all other competitors at the end of the first day, the 91st Strategic Missile Wing, Minor AFB, North Dakota, made a remarkable recovery and won the competition, amassing 2,783 points out of a possible 3,000. In addition to winning the Blanchard Perpetual Trophy, the 91st Wing won top awards for the Best Minuteman Wing and Best Missile Operations. The 381st Strategic Missile Wing, McConnell AFB, Kansas, received trophies for the Best Titan Wing, Best Missile Maintenance Team, and Best Missile Security Police Team. The 308th Strategic Missile Wing, a Titan II unit at Little Rock AFB, won the Best Missile Communications Team Trophy, and the 90th Strategic Missile Wing, a Minuteman unit at Francis E. Warren AFB, Wyoming, won the Best Missile Civil Engineering Team Award.

A B-1B bomber high over the Pacific Ocean with wings extended for cruise flight.

1979

Resources

Personnel 118,967 (18,451 officers, 86,315 airmen, 14,201 civilians)

Tactical Aircraft 952 (343 B-52, 65 FB-111, 541 EC/KC-135, 3 E-4)

Aircraft Units 17 Heavy Bomb Wings (one 33 UE, one 30 UE, one 28 UE, three 17 UE, ten 14 UE), one Strategic Wing (14 UE) with B-52s

2 Medium Bomb Wing (one 34 UE, one 26 UE) with FB-111As

33 Heavy Air Refueling Squadrons (one 25 UE, six 19 UE, three 16 UE, eight 15 UE, four 14 UE, five 13 UE, one 12 UE, two 10 UE, three 9 UE) with KC-135s

2 Strategic Reconnaissance Wings (one with U-2s and SR-71s, one with RC-135s)

1 Strategic Reconnaissance Squadron with RC-135s

3 Airborne Command and Control Squadrons (two with EC-135s, one with E-4s)

Missiles 1,170 Minuteman (including missiles in depot modification), 57 Titan II, 1,396 SRAM, 10 Thor Boosters

Missile Units 6 Titan II Squadrons (9 UE) fully equipped, 20 Minuteman Squadrons (50 UE), 9 with Minuteman IIF series missiles and 11 with Minuteman IIIG series

Active Bases 25 CONUS, 1 in Guam, and 2 in Greenland

Budget and Financial Status
(FY 79 as of 30 September 1979)

Operation and Maintenance $675,948,829, includes supplies, communications, civilian pay, minor equipment purchased

Assets $17,558,164,331, includes real property, inventories, equipment, and weapon systems

Operating Expenses $2,468,209,405, includes O&M listed above, military pay, troop subsistence, and aviation petroleum, oil, and lubricants (POL)

Military Family Housing $92,734,903, includes O&M expenses (Military Family Housing Defense Appropriation) in support of housing units

Organization

SAC and the Aerospace Defense Command Reorganization. After several years of planning, Headquarters USAF directed that the Aerospace Defense Command (ADCOM) be reorganized and the management of its resources be divided among the Tactical Air Command, Air Force Communications Service, and Strategic Air Command. Under the reorganization, SAC acquired resource management responsibilities for ADCOM's space surveillance and missile warning systems. The North American Air Defense Command (NORAD) retained operational control over these systems. SAC began assuming its new responsibilities on 1 October when it acquired Peterson AFB, Colorado, and several units located there. The transfer actions were completed on 1 December, at which time SAC received the space surveillance and missile warning system units and several installations and small sites throughout the United States and at various overseas locations. In addition to Peterson, SAC acquired Thule and Sondrestrom ABs in Greenland and Clear AFS in Alaska. The forces that SAC inherited may be divided into five functional categories: intercontinental ballistic missile (ICBM) warning, submarine-launched ballistic missile (SLBM) warning, space surveillance sensor, communications, and support. Included among the assets transferred were the modified Thor missiles that ADCOM's 10th Aerospace Defense Squadron used to launch satellites for the Defense Meteorological Satellite Program (DMSP) at Vandenberg AFB, California. Prior to the transfer, the 10th was inactivated and its Thor missiles, personnel, and functions were absorbed by SAC's 394th ICBM Test Maintenance Squadron, also located at Vandenberg. On-orbit command and control of the DMSP satellites were already under SAC's 4000th Aerospace Applications Group, located at Offutt AFB, Nebraska.

Operations

First B-52 Contingency Deployment to an Overseas Forward Operating Base. Although B-52's flew in contingency exercises in support of Korea in March 1977 and in support of NATO in Europe in September 1978, these missions were done from permanent bases in U.S. territory. The first post–Southeast Asia B-52 contingency deployment to an overseas forward operating base occurred in May 1979. Three B-52Ds from the 96th Bomb Wing, Dyess AFB, Texas, deployed to RAF Upper Heyford, United Kingdom, from 9 to 23 May to participate in Exercises Flintlock and Dawn Patrol.

Global Shield '79. From 8 to 16 July SAC exercised for the first time every phase of its role in the Single Integrated Operational Plan (SIOP) short of nuclear warfare. This exercise, one of the most comprehensive in SAC history, featured participation by the command's active forces and SAC-gained Air Force Reserve units. Hundreds of bombers, tankers, and missiles were put on alert with the aircraft dispersing to preselected bases supported by ground teams and flying sorties over radar bomb-scoring sites.

Adverse weather conditions hindered the operation, including Hurricane Bob, which menaced exercise bases in Louisiana and Mississippi.

General Richard H. Ellis, CINCSAC, called the exercise "well planned" and "an extremely valuable training experience for the aircrews, missile crews, and support personnel who participated in it."

Spaatz Trophy. The 307th Air Refueling Squadron, Travis AFB, California, was selected as the best air refueling unit in SAC for 1979.

P. T. Cullen Trophy. The 55th Strategic Reconnaissance Wing, Offutt AFB, Nebraska, was selected for the 1979 award for its contribution to SAC's photographic and signals intelligence efforts.

Omaha Trophy. The 91st Strategic Missile Wing, Minot AFB, North Dakota, was selected the outstanding wing in SAC for 1979 and became the first missile wing to win the Omaha Trophy.

Bombing Competition

Twenty-third Competition, Three Major Trophies Won by Non-SAC Units. The 1979 Bombing Competition was conducted on the three-phase basis that had been instituted in 1976. SAC participants included all CONUS-based units except those involved in combat crew training at Castle AFB, California. Royal Air Force and the Tactical Air Command units competed in the bombing exercise, while the Air National Guard and Air Force Reserve participated with KC-135s. With tabulations completed on the final missions of 19 November, SAC units were found to be in second place for the first time in three major contests. A Tactical Air Command unit won two of these events, while an Air National Guard unit captured the third award. Trophies were presented as follows on the evening of 29 November at Barksdale AFB, Louisiana:

Fairchild Trophy, highest percentage of possible points in bomber and tanker missions, 509th Bomb Wing, FB-111.

Doolittle Trophy, numbered air force whose B-52 units achieved highest percentage of possible points in low-level bombing and SRAM activity, Eighth Air Force.

Mathis Trophy, top unit in high and low bombing, Tactical Air Command's 27th Tactical Fighter Wing.

Meyer Trophy, top FB-111 unit compiling most points in low-level bombing and electronic countermeasures activity, 27th Tactical Fighter Wing.

Dougherty Trophy, FB-111 or B-52 unit compiling most points for simulated SRAM launches, 379th Bomb Wing, B-52.

Saunders Trophy, top tanker unit in competition, 380th Bomb Wing, KC-135.

Crumm Trophy, B-52/Vulcan unit with best high altitude bombing results, 28th Bomb Wing, B-52.

Bartsch Trophy, B-52 unit compiling the most points in electronic countermeasure activity, 92nd Bomb Wing.

Bombing Trophy, bomber crew compiling most points in high- and low-level bombing, 380th Bomb Wing/FB-111.

Navigation Trophy, tanker unit compiling most points in navigation, 157th Air Refueling Group.

RAF Bombing Competition. In the 1979 RAF Bombing Competition, held from 20 through 28 June at RAF Station Marham, SAC entered three B-52H aircraft and crews representing the 28th, 319th, and 410th Bomb Wings. While these wings had performed well in the 1978 SAC Bombing Competition (their selection for the RAF meet was based upon this performance) they were unsuccessful in winning either of the two trophies (Blue Steel and Camrose) for which they were eligible to compete.

Munitions Loading Competition. Again held at Ellsworth AFB, South Dakota, the Munitions Loading Competition took place between 10 and 19 September. The Barrentine Trophy for the Best Munitions Competition Team went to the 5th Bomb Wing, Minot AFB, South Dakota. The other major award winners were:

Best Security Police Team, 97th Bomb Wing, Blytheville AFB, Arkansas
Best Munitions Load Crew, 5th Bomb Wing, Minot AFB, North Dakota
Best Crew Chief, 92d Bomb Wing, Fairchild AFB, Washington
Best Combined Load Crew, 7th Bomb Wing, Carswell AFB, Texas

Missiles

Missile Launches. Total missiles and space systems launched during the year from Vandenberg AFB: SAC—11; Other Agencies—16.

Full Scale Engineering Development for Missile-X. On 12 June 1979, President Carter approved full-scale engineering development for Missile-X (MX), intended to be the mainstay of the U.S. ICBM fleet from the late twentieth century. On 7 September, President Carter announced selection of horizontal shelter basing for the new missile.

Refurbishment of Titan II Launch Complex at McConnell AFB. On 13 March, General Lew Allen, Jr., USAF chief of staff, approved project PACER DOWN, the restoration of Titan II Launch Complex 533-7 which was damaged in 1978. This launch complex and the ICBM that it contained were severely corroded through exposure to nitrogen tetroxide and its chemical derivatives. Restoration of the launch complex would cost an estimated $13 to $14 million, that of the ICBM, $5 million.

Global Shield ICBM Launch. On 10 July 1979, SAC launched two Minuteman III ICBMs from Vandenberg AFB, California, during exercise Global Shield, a comprehensive exercise of SAC's nuclear forces. One of these Global Shield missions, Glory Trip 40GM, was the last Phase I Minuteman III flight test.

Titan II Guidance System. In early December 1979, SAC completed installation of the Titan II Universal Space Guidance System (USGS) at the 381st Strategic Missile Wing and the 390th Strategic Missile Wing, completing deployment of the USGS throughout the Titan II fleet.

Missile Competition

Twelfth Competition. The 390th Strategic Missile Wing, a Titan II unit at Davis-Monthan AFB, Arizona, compiled the highest score for all exercises in this competition, which was held from 27 April through 3 May at Vandenberg AFB, California (Titan II maintenance evaluation was at McConnell AFB, Kansas), and won the Blanchard Perpetual Trophy. The 390th also received trophies for the Best Titan Wing and the Best Missile Communications Team.

Other major awards and their winners were:

Best Minuteman Wing and Best Missile Maintenance Team, 341st Strategic Missile Wing, Malmstrom AFB, Montana

Best Missile Operations, 321st Strategic Missile Wing, Grand Forks AFB, North Dakota

Best Missle Security Police Team, 91st Strategic Missle Wing, Minot AFB, North Dakota

Best Missile Civil Engineering Team, 44th Strategic Missile Wing, Ellsworth AFB, South Dakota

1980

Resources

Personnel 127,599 (19,662 officers, 91,722 airmen, 16,175 civilians)
Tactical Aircraft 1,102 (419 B-52, 68 FB-111, 612 EC/KC-135, 3 E-4)
Aircraft Units 18 Heavy Bomb Wings (one 33 UE, one 28 UE, two 18 UE, one 17 UE, three 16 UE, ten 14 UE), one Strategic Wing (14 UE) with B-52s

2 Medium Bomb Wings (one 36 UE, one 30 UE) with FB-111As

35 Heavy Air Refueling Squadrons (four 20 UE, three 19 UE, three 18 UE, one 17 UE, two 16 UE, 12 15 UE, nine 14 UE, one 13 UE) with KC-135s, 2 Strategic Reconnaissance Wings (one with U-2s and SR-71s, one with RC-135s)

1 Strategic Reconnaissance Squadron with RC-135s

3 Airborne Command and Control Squadrons (two with EC-135s, one with E-4s)

Missiles 1,094 Minuteman (including missiles in depot modification), 58 Titan II, 288 Hound Dog, 355 Quail, 1,431 SRAM

Missile Units 6 Titan II Squadrons (9 UE) fully equipped, 20 Minuteman Squadrons (50 UE), 9 with Minuteman IIF series missiles, 11 with Minuteman IIIG series

Active Bases 25 CONUS and 1 in Guam, 2 in Greenland

Budget and Financial Status
(FY 76 as of 30 June 1976)

Operation and Maintenance $658,204,983, includes supplies, communications, civilian pay, minor equipment purchased

Assets $17,804,995,267, includes real property, inventories, equipment, and weapon systems

Operating Expenses $2,412,063,735, includes O&M listed above, military pay, troop subsistence, and aviation petroleum, oil, and lubricants (POL)

<table>
<tr><td>Military Family
Housing</td><td>$64,226,232, includes O&M expenses (Military Family Housing Defense Appropriation) in support of housing units</td></tr>
</table>

Organization

Organization of Consolidated Contingency Steering Group. On 6 August, Headquarters SAC's newly formed Consolidated Contingency Steering Group (CCSG) held its first meeting. Formed in July and August at the direction of Lieutenant General Lloyd R. Leavitt, Jr., the CCSG was responsible for planning and coordinating SAC's conventional aircraft operations. The CCSG was composed of contingency experts from all major Headquarters SAC staff agencies and operated under the Deputy Chief of Staff (DCS) for Operations Plans. In addition to the DCS/Operations Plans, the prime contributors to the group were DCS/Operations, DCS/Logistics, and DCS/Intelligence. With the exception of the DCS/ Intelligence, the contingency experts of the main contributors were collocated in Corridor 3-C of the Headquarters SAC Administration Building, an area which was soon called affectionately, "Contingency Country."

Joint Strategic Connectivity Staff Established. Twenty years after the Joint Strategic Target Planning Staff (JSTPS) was formed, a second specialized JCS agency was created at Offutt AFB, Nebraska, when the Joint Strategic Connectivity Staff (JSCS) was established on 1 July 1980. As in the JSTPS, CINCSAC was the director while a Navy officer was vice director; Rear Admiral Paul A. Tomb assumed this position in September 1980 when the agency became operational. The JSCS analyzes and recommends improvements to strategic command and control and communications systems linking the national command authorities, the commanders of nuclear forces, and the nuclear forces.

Operations

Round-the-World Flight, 12–14 March 1980 and the Eleventh Mackay Trophy. In March 1980, two B-52Hs of the 410th Bomb Wing, K. I. Sawyer AFB, Michigan, made a nonstop, round-the-globe flight in 42½ hours. It was the third such operation in SAC history, the others having occurred in February 1949 and January 1957 and involving a B-50A and three B-52Bs, respectively.

The two seven-man crews involved in this third flight, commanded by Majors William H. Thurston and John M. Durham, flew to Headquarters SAC, Offutt AFB, Nebraska, a week before the mission for a briefing on myriad logistical, diplomatic, and meteorological problems. Thanks to the thorough preparation of the crews and the work of SAC support personnel and U.S. and foreign officials around the world, the flight proceeded smoothly along a 19,353 nautical-mile course across Canada, the North Atlantic, several European countries, the Mediterranean Sea, the Indian Ocean, the Strait of Malacca, the South China Sea, and the North Pacific, before ending at its starting point, K. I. Sawyer. In contrast to the earlier round-the-world missions, this flight included reconnaissance/surveillance activities, which had become increasingly important to SAC, in conjunction with U.S. naval forces in the Indian Ocean.

Aerial refuelings over eastern Canada, the North Atlantic, the Mediterranean, the Indian Ocean, and the western Pacific made the operation possible; each aircraft received almost 600,000 pounds of fuel from SAC KC-135 tankers. After the flight, General Richard H. Ellis, SAC commander-in-chief, praised the crew for demonstrating the command's "ability to rapidly project U.S. military power to any point in the world in a matter of hours." At a ceremony at Headquarters SAC on 15 May, General Lew Allen, Jr., USAF chief of staff, presented Majors Thurston and Durham with Distinguished Flying Crosses and their crewmen with Air Medals. He also selected the crews to receive the Mackay Trophy, awarded annually for the most meritorious flight by an Air Force member or organization.

Creation of Strategic Projection Force. In early 1980, the Joint Chiefs of Staff developed the Rapid Deployment Joint Task Force (RDJTF), composed of various elements of U.S. military forces, which could respond immediately with conventional weapons to crisis situations. SAC's contribution to the RDJTF was the Strategic Projection Force (SPF) formed primarily from B-52H and KC-135 aircraft of the 57th Air Division, which had its headquarters at Minot AFB, North Dakota. In addition to the bombers and tankers of the 5th Bomb Wing, also located at Minot, and the 319th Bomb Wing, Grand Forks AFB, North Dakota, the Strategic Projection Force consisted of SR-71, U-2, and RC-135 strategic reconnaissance aircraft and EC-135 and E-3A command, control and communications aircraft. SAC's 55th Strategic Reconnaissance Wing, Offutt AFB, Nebraska, supplied the EC-135s; the 9th Strategic Reconnaissance Wing, Beale AFB, California, furnished the U-2s and SR-71s; and the Tactical Air Command provided the E-3A aircraft.

Strategic Projection Force Tested. From 22 through 25 September, SAC successfully tested the Strategic Projection Force in an exercise called Busy Prairie. Fourteen B-52H bombers of the 5th Bomb Wing deployed from Minot to Whiteman AFB, Missouri, which served as a simulated forward operating base. They were augmented at Whiteman by EC-135, RC-135, U-2, DC-135, and C-5 aircraft (Military Airlift Command transports used to airlift cargo). From Whiteman, the B-52s conducted simulated combat operations over a training range in central Nevada to demonstrate the crews' ability to penetrate enemy territory and bomb targets. The 319th Bomb Wing's B-52 bombers operating out of their home base, Grand Forks, participated in the flying portion of the exercise as did SR-71s operating out of Beale.

Global Shield '80. The no-notice command exercise, which was first held in 1979, gave the entire combat force experience in Single Integrated Operational Plan warfare under simulated conditions. Conducted between 20 and 29 June, the operation, which involved the use of 44 bases and the services of almost 100,000 command personnel, featured 437 aircraft flying 1,035 sorties for a total of 5,506 flying hours.

Spaatz Trophy. The 452d Air Refueling Squadron, March AFB, California, was selected as the best air refueling unit in SAC for 1980. This marked the first time a unit of Air Reserve Forces received the Spaatz Trophy.

P. T. Cullen Trophy. The 9th Strategic Wing, Beale AFB, California, was selected for the 1980 award for its contribution to SAC's photographic and signal intelligence efforts.

Omaha Trophy. The 410th Bomb Wing, K. I. Sawyer AFB, Michigan, was selected the outstanding wing in SAC for 1980.

Bombing Competition

Twenty-fourth Competition, First Royal Australian Air Force Participation. For its 1980 Bombing Competition, conducted similarly to the four previous meets, SAC expanded its guest list to include the Royal Australian Air Force, which entered two F-111C crews in the final two phases. The Royal Air Force participated with four Vulcan crews while the Tactical Air Command entered two F-111 crews. The Air National Guard and the Air Force Reserve competed with two and four KC-135 crews, respectively. SAC, as usual, excluded its overseas B-52 and KC- 135 units as well as the 93d Bomb Wing, the B-52 combat crew training unit at Castle AFB, California.

Major trophies presented during the 20 November awards ceremony at Barksdale AFB, Louisiana, were as follows:

Fairchild Trophy, bomber and tanker unit compiling highest percentage of points in the bomber and tanker mission, 320th Bomb Wing, B-52/KC-135.

Doolittle Trophy, numbered air force whose B-52 units achieved highest percentage of points in low-level bombing, release time control, and SRAM activity, Eighth Air Force.

Mathis Trophy, unit with most points for high and low bombing and time control, 319th Bomb Wing, B-52.

Dougherty Trophy, B-52 unit compiling most points in simulated SRAM launches, 320th Bomb Wing, B-52.

Saunders Trophy, top tanker unit, 384th Air Refueling Wing, KC-135.

Meyer Trophy, Top F/FB-111 unit compiling most points in low-level bombing, low time control, and low electronic countermeasures, 509th Bomb Wing.

Crumm Trophy, B-52/Vulcan unit with best high-altitude bombing, 7th Bomb Wing, B-52.

Bartsch Trophy, B-52 unit compiling highest points in electronic countermeasure activity, 42nd Bomb Wing.

The General Curtis E. LeMay Bombing Trophy Awarded for First Time. Donated by Norden Systems, Inc., the trophy was named for General Curtis E. LeMay, former commander-in-chief of SAC (CINCSAC), and was designated for presentation to the bomber crew compiling the most points in high- and low-level bombing. It replaced the Bombing Trophy. As with other major trophies, the LeMay Trophy would be retained for one year by the winning unit and then presented to the next winning unit. Norden Systems also donated a number of smaller bombing trophy replicas for individual recognition programs. A 380th Bomb Wing FB-111 crew was the first to receive the trophy.

Navigation Trophy, top tanker unit in navigation, 305th Air Refueling Wing, KC-135.

Royal Air Force Bombing Competition. Unsuccessful in its 1979 bid to win major trophies with B-52H aircraft, SAC sent four B-52G aircraft and crews to the 1980 RAF Bombing Competition, which was again held at RAF Station Marham in the United Kingdom from 21 to 29 July. Once again the SAC representatives (68th, 97th, 320th, and 379th) failed to bring home either the Blue Steel or Camrose Trophy.

Munitions Loading Competition. The SAC Munitions Loading competition was held at Ellsworth AFB, South Dakota, from 8 through 17 September. The Barrentine Trophy for the Best Munitions Competition Team was won by the 97th Bomb Wing, Blytheville AFB, Arkansas. The other major awards were:

Best Security Police Team, 97th Bomb Wing.

Best Munitions Load Crew, 509th Bomb Wing, Pease Air Force Base, New Hampshire.

Best Crew Chief, 416th Bomb Wing, Griffiss AFB, New York.

Best Combined Load Crew, 509th Bomb Wing, Pease Air Force Base, New Hampshire.

Missiles

Missile Launches. Total missiles and space systems launched during the year from Vandenberg AFB: SAC—9 ; other agencies—18.

Titan II Launch Complex Restoration at McConnell AFB. In early March 1980, engineers at Martin-Marietta Denver reported that they could restore the Titan II ICBM damaged in the August 1978 propellant spillage mishap to operational service by February 1982. After receiving permission from the House Armed Services Committee to exceed a $2.8 million limit, Headquarters SAC, on 5 September 1980, awarded a $4.17 million contract to the Mayfair Construction Company to restore McConnell Launch Complex 533-7.

Ogden-ALC Titan II Assessment. Completing a congressionally mandated investigation in May 1980, Ogden-Air Logistics Center declared that Titan II equipment and procedures together with programmed modifications adequately protected public safety and national interests.

Titan II Mishap—Little Rock. Between 18–19 September 1980, a Titan II mishap at Launch Complex 374-7, 308th Strategic Missile Wing, Little Rock AFB, Arkansas, resulted in an explosion, obliterating the launch complex, its assigned ICBM, and killing one airman. Formed in the wake of this tragedy, a Titan II Executive Committee chaired by General Bennie L. Davis, Commander of the Air Force Training Command, certified the safety and effectiveness of the Titan II in December 1980.

Missile Competition

Thirteenth Competition—Blanchard Perpetual Trophy Missing—Replacement Procured. On 15 March 1980, less than six weeks before SAC's annual missile competition began, the 390th Strategic Missile Wing reported that the Blanchard Perpetual Trophy was missing. The trophy, which had been in the 390th's possession since the 1979 competition, was apparently stolen from a display case in the wing headquarters building at Davis-Monthan AFB, Arizona, on either 14 or 15 March. Although an extensive search was made, the trophy could not be found. A replacement similar in design to the original was procured in time for presentation at the conclusion of the competition, which was held from 24 through 30 April.

As in the two previous meets, the Titan II maintenance evaluations were conducted at McConnell AFB, Kansas, while the remainder of the competition was held at Vandenberg AFB, California. McConnell's 381st Strategic Missile Wing, having compiled the highest combined score for all exercises, received the new Blanchard Perpetual Trophy as well as the Best Titan II Wing award. This marked the third time for the 381st to win the top award. Another Titan II unit, the 308th Strategic Missile Wing, Little Rock AFB, Arkansas, won the Best Missile Operations and Best Missile Civil Engineering Team awards.

The remainder of the major awards went to the following units:

Best Minuteman Wing and Best Missile Security Police Team, 90th Strategic Missile Wing, Francis E. Warren AFB, Wyoming

Best Missile Maintenance Team, 390th Strategic Missile Wing, Davis-Monthan AFB, Arizona

Best Missile Communications Team, 44th Strategic Missile Wing, Ellsworth AFB, South Dakota

1981

Resources

Personnel	118,799 (18,708 officers, 87,055 airmen, 13,036 civilians)
Tactical Aircraft	960 (344 B-52, 62 FB-111, 544 EC/KC-135, 4 E-4)
Aircraft Units	Beginning this year, the term PAA (Primary Aircraft Authorization) replaced UE

17 Heavy Bomb Wings (one 33 PAA, one 30 PAA, one 28 PAA, one 20 PAA, three 17 PAA, ten 14 PAA), one Strategic Wing (14 PAA) with B-52s

2 Medium Bomb Wing (one 34 PAA, one 26 PAA) with FB-111As

33 Heavy Air Refueling Squadrons (one 25 PAA, six 19 PAA, one 18 PAA, three 16 PAA, eight 15 PAA, four 14 PAA, five 13 PAA, one 12 PAA, two 10 PAA, one 9 PAA) with KC-135s, one 6 PAA with KC-10As

2 Strategic Reconnaissance Wings (one U-2s, SR-71s, and TR-1s, one RC-135s)

1 Strategic Reconnaissance Squadron with RC-135s

3 Airborne Command and Control Squadrons (two with EC-135s, one with E-4s)

Missiles	1,164 Minuteman (including missiles in depot modification), 56 Titan II, 1,374 SRAM, 14 ALCM
Missile Units	6 Titan II Squadrons (9 PAA) fully equipped, 20 Minuteman Squadrons (50 PAA), 9 with Minuteman IIF series missiles, 11 with Minuteman IIIG series
Active Bases	25 CONUS and 1 in Guam, 2 in Greenland

Budget and Financial Status
(FY 81 as of 30 September 1981)

Operations and Maintenance	$1,153,081,511, includes supplies, communications, civilian pay, minor equipment purchased
Assets	$19,991,945,678, includes real property, inventories, equipment, and weapon systems

168

Operating Expenses	$3,956,655,432, includes O&M listed above, military pay, troop subsistence, and aviation petroleum, oil, and lubricants (POL)
Military Family Housing	$106,582,348, includes O&M expenses (Military Family Housing Defense Appropriation) in support of housing units

Organization

No significant changes in the organization occurred in 1981.

Operations

President Reagan Announced Decisions Affecting SAC Bomber and Missile Forces. On 2 October, President Reagan issued several decisions that would influence the future of SAC. Reversing the decision made by President Carter in 1977, President Reagan announced that he had "directed the Secretary of Defense to revitalize our bomber forces by constructing and deploying some 100 B-1 bombers, as soon as possible. . . ." The Air Launched Cruise Missile program that President Carter had approved would continue as would new efforts to develop an advanced radar-evading stealth bomber for the 1990s.

President Reagan endorsed continuing development of the MX missile, but he announced that the new missile would not be deployed in multiple protective shelters as advocated by the Carter administration. A limited number of these new missiles would be deployed initially in existing missile silos while studies continued on a permanent basing mode. As explained in subsequent announcements by Secretary of Defense Caspar W. Weinberger, the initial MX deployment, approximately 36 missiles, would be made in refurbished silos of Minuteman or Titan II missiles. The latter were earmarked to be phased out of operation.

Exercise Bright Star 82. On 23 November, eight bombers of SAC's Strategic Projection Force took off on what was to be the longest nonstop B-52 bombing mission in the history of SAC. The two flights of B-52Hs, four from the 319th Bomb Wing, Grand Forks AFB, North Dakota, delivered their loads of conventional munitions on a simulated runway target in Egypt. En route to the target the crews accomplished three heavyweight air refuelings. Excellent navigation and precision bombing made the 31-hour, 15,000-mile flight a complete success. Rapid Deployment Joint Task Force Exercise Bright Star 82 vividly demonstrated the Strategic Projection Force's capability to strike rapidly in any part of the world.

First Air Launched Cruise Missiles Delivered. On 11 January, the first two Air Launched Cruise Missiles (ALCMs) were delivered to the 416th Bomb Wing, Griffiss AFB, New York, where they were used initially for environmental testing and maintenance training. The ALCM was a turbofan-powered, inertially guided missile that could be launched from a B-52G and deliver a nuclear

169

weapon to a target 1,500 miles away. It was manufactured by the Boeing Company, which had won the production contract after a competitive fly-off with the General Dynamics Corporation.

The missile's Terrain Contour Matching (TERCOM) feature enables it to fly at extremely low altitude to avoid detection by enemy radar. While the 416th Bomb Wing's aircraft were the first to be equipped with the ALCM, the entire SAC force of 172 B-52G aircraft would be modified to carry the new missiles, six under each wing in jettison-capable pylons and eight on a rotary launcher in the bomb bay.

First ALCM/OAS-Modified B-52G Delivered. On 15 August, Boeing, Wichita, Kansas, delivered the first modified B-52G, capable of carrying the Air Launched Cruise Missiles. With the ALCM modification, the B-52Gs were also outfitted with the Offensive Avionics System (OAS) designed to improve navigation and weapons delivery techniques.

B-52 Deployment to Australia. In March, after several years of negotiations, the government of Australia agreed to the landing of B-52s. On 5 May, a B-52H of the 410th Bomb Wing arrived at RAAF Base Darwin for a two-day public display. The first operational sortie to fly from Darwin was a sea-search mission on 22 June.

SAC Strategic Training Range Complex Opened. In 1978, SAC began to develop a flying training range that would provide all the benefits of the TAC Red Flag Range while more accurately simulating conditions of a strategic penetration of northern Russia. The Strategic Training Range Complex (STRC) opened on 1 July 1981 with three mobile radar bombing sites in Wyoming and one in Idaho. These mobile sites would be replaced by fixed sites as other fixed sites in the CONUS were closed.

Global Shield '81. For the third consecutive year, SAC practiced its Emergency War Order procedures in a command-wide, no-notice exercise, the largest in SAC history. From 26 January to 16 February, over 100,000 SAC personnel in the United States and Guam responded to a simulated escalation in cold war tensions by dispersing more than 120 bombers and tankers to 30 secure locations, improving the command's ability to survive a surprise attack. Other unarmed bombers flew airborne alert missions on low-level routes over Colorado, New Mexico, Kansas, and Texas. At the same time, SAC missile crews launched two Minuteman III intercontinental ballistic missiles from Vandenberg AFB, California, along the Western Test Range toward Kwajalein Atoll.

Shortly before the simulated attack on the United States, about 400 SAC bombers and tankers conducted positive-control launches from some 70 locations in the CONUS. These were minimum interval takeoff operations in which aircraft at each location, using common runways, launched at twelve 30-second intervals. This procedure ensured that the entire command would become airborne within minutes.

Delivery of First KC-10A. On 17 March, the first KC-10A tanker/cargo aircraft (serial number 79-0434) was delivered to SAC. Delivery actually took place at the Douglas Aircraft Company plant in Long Beach, California. Lieutenant General Edgar S. Harris, Jr., commander of the Eighth Air Force, accepted the new aircraft and flew it to Barksdale AFB, Louisiana. It was initially assigned to Detachment 2 of the 4200th Test and Evaluation Squadron for testing and evaluation purposes. On 1 November, this aircraft and five others that had been produced by Douglas were assigned to the 32d Air Refueling Squadron, a newly activated unit of the 2d Bomb Wing, also located at Barksdale. Nicknamed the Extender, the KC-10A was substantially larger and capable of carrying more fuel than the KC-135. It was outfitted with both the boom and the extended hose refueling systems, providing the ability to refuel a wide variety of aircraft. The versatile Extender, with a crew of four (pilot, copilot, flight engineer, and boom operator), was able to refuel fighter aircraft on overseas flights and carry equipment and personnel to support the fighters at deployment bases.

Delivery of First TR-1. On 15 September, SAC received its first TR-1A reconnaissance aircraft (serial number 80-1066). It was assigned to the 4029th Strategic Reconnaissance Training Squadron of the 9th Strategic Reconnaissance Wing, Beale AFB, California. The TR-1, built by Lockheed-California, essentially was an improved and enlarged version of the U-2 aircraft that had been assigned to SAC since 1957. It was designed to conduct day and night all-weather reconnaissance operations at high altitudes (over 70,000 feet) in support of U.S. and allied air and ground forces. The TR-1 has a crew of one.

Spaatz Trophy. The 305th Air Refueling Squadron, Grissom AFB, Indiana, was selected as the best air refueling unit in SAC for 1981.

P. T. Cullen Trophy. The 922d Strategic Wing, Hellenikon AB, Greece, was selected for the 1981 award for its contribution to SAC's photographic and signals intelligence efforts.

Omaha Trophy. The 19th Bomb Wing, Robins AFB, Georgia, was selected the outstanding wing in SAC for 1978.

Bombing Competition

Twenty-fifth Competition. In the 1981 SAC Bombing and Navigation Competition, the B-52 and FB-111 wings competed alone. The Royal Air Force units were converting from Vulcan to Tornado bombers and by-passed the meet as did the Tactical Air Command wings that were involved with other commitments. The Royal Australian Air Force, a 1980 competitor, also was not represented. It had adopted a policy of competing every other year. Each SAC unit that participated (the 93d Bomb Wing, Castle AFB, California, and the overseas B-52 and KC-135 units were excluded) entered two aircraft and crews. Major awards presented on 18 November, based upon the two final phase missions of 2-to-5 and 7-to-10 November, were:

Fairchild Trophy, highest percentage of possible points in bomber and tanker missions, 509th Bomb Wing, FB-111/KC-135

Doolittle Trophy, numbered air force whose B-52 units achieved highest percentage of possible points in low-level bombing and SRAM activity, Eighth Air Force

Mathis Trophy, top bombing unit, 509th Bomb Wing, FB-111

Meyer Trophy, top FB-111 unit compiling most points in low- level bombing and electronic countermeasures activity, terrain following, and low-time control, 509th Bomb Wing

Dougherty Trophy, unit compiling most points for simulated SRAM launches, 320th Bomb Wing, B-52

Saunders Trophy, top tanker unit, 379th Bomb Wing, KC-135

Crumm Trophy, unit with best high-altitude bombing results, 97th Bomb Wing, B-52

Bartsch Trophy, unit compiling the most points in electronic countermeasure activity, 320th Bomb Wing, B-52

LeMay Trophy, bomber crew compiling most points in high- and low-level bombing and time control, 509th Bomb Wing/FB-111

Navigation Trophy, tanker unit compiling most points in navigation, 92d Bomb Wing

RAF Bombing Competition. SAC selected four B-52H aircraft and crews (two representing the 319th Bomb Wing and one each representing the 5th and 410th Bomb Wings) to compete in the RAF Strike Command Bombing and Navigation Competiton that was held from 6 to 14 July. Their selection was based on high overall performances in low-level bombing in 1980. The SAC wings, operating out of RAF Station Marham, did not fare well in the competition, placing 13th, 15th, 19th, and 22d in a field of 22.

Missiles

Missile Launches. Total missiles and space systems launched during the year from Vandenberg AFB: SAC—8; other agencies—13.

Phaseout of Thor Boosters. In August and September, SAC disposed of 10 modified Thor missile boosters it had acquired from ADCOM in 1979. These missiles were shipped from Vandenberg to Norton AFB, California, with the last one departing on 4 September.

Missile Competition

Fourteenth Competition. From 1 through 7 May, the 1981 competition was held at Vandenberg AFB. The winners of the major awards were:

Blanchard Perpetual Trophy for highest combined score in all exercises and Best Minuteman Wing, 351st Strategic Missile Wing, Whiteman AFB, Missouri

Best Titan II Wing and Best Missile Operations, 308th Strategic Missile Wing, Little Rock AFB, Arkansas

Best Missile Maintenance Team, 91st Strategic Missile Wing

Best Missile Security Police Team, 90th Strategic Missile Wing, F. E. Warren AFB, Wyoming

Best Missile Communications Team, 390th Strategic Missile Wing, Davis-Monthan AFB, Arizona

Best Missile Civil Engineering Team, 381st Strategic Missile Wing, McConnell AFB, Kansas

1982

Resources

Personnel 122,697 (18,674 officers, 89,918 airmen, 14,105 civilians)

Tactical Aircraft 918 (300 B-52, 62 FB-111, 540 EC/KC-135, 12 KC-10, 4 E-4)

Aircraft Units 15 Heavy Bomb Wings (one 30 PAA, one 26 PAA, three 19 PAA, five 16 PAA, five 13 PAA), one Strategic Wing (14 PAA) with B-52s

2 Medium Bomb Wings (one 32 PAA, one 24 PAA) with FB-111As.

34 Heavy Air Refueling Squadrons, 32 (one 25 PAA, six 19 PAA, five 16 PAA, eight 15 PAA, three 14 PAA, five 13 PAA, one 12 PAA, two 10 PAA, one 9 PAA) with KC-135s, two (one 7 PAA, one 3 PAA) with KC-10s

2 Strategic Reconnaissance Wings (one with U-2s, SR-71s and TR-1s, one with RC-135s)

1 Reconnaissance Wing with TR-1s

1 Strategic Reconnaissance Squadron with RC-135s

3 Airborne Command and Control Squadrons (two with EC-135s, one with E-4s)

Missiles 1,153 Minuteman, 53 Titan II, 1,332 SRAM, 288 ALCM

Missile Units 6 Titan II Squadrons (four 9 PAA, one 8 PAA, one 7 PAA), 20 Minuteman Squadrons (50 PAA), 9 with Minuteman IIF series missiles, 11 with Minuteman IIIG series missiles

Active Bases 25 CONUS and 1 in Guam, 2 in Greenland

Budget and Financial Status
(FY 82 as of 30 September 1982)

Operations and Maintenance $1,262,109,571, includes supplies, communications, civilian pay, minor equipment purchased

Assets $19,765,794,580, includes real property, inventories, equipment, and weapon systems

Operating Expenses	$4,469,551,737, includes O&M listed above, military pay, troop subsistence, and aviation petroleum, oil, and lubricants (POL)
Military Family Housing	$128,778,230, includes O&M expenses (Military Family Housing Defense Appropriation) in support of housing units

Organization

Oveaseas Air Divisions Assigned to Numbered Air Forces. On 31 January 1982, the 3d and 7th Air Divisions were reassigned to Fifteenth and Eighth Air Forces, respectively. Prior to this, since their first activation in the early 1950s, SAC's overseas air divisions had been assigned to Headquarters SAC.

CONUS Air Division Realignment. The Eighth Air Force was realigned to place the command's Titan II expertise under a single commander for the coming phase-out of the Titan II missile. Other changes that were made balanced division strengths and distances between division headquarters and subordinate units. Similarly, the Fifteenth Air Force realignments were intended to better distribute units, personnel, and the overall workload across all the air divisions.

Operations

Global Shield '82. Between 15 and 23 July, the largest exercise of the year, the command's annual readiness exercise, was conducted. Global Shield '82, involving extensive participation by agencies outside the command, provided the most realistic test to date of SAC's ability to function in a prolonged nuclear war. To test fighter intercept techniques, the North American Air Defense Command conducted a concurrent exercise pitting U.S. and Canadian fighters against SAC bombers.

In-flight Emergency and the Twelfth Mackay Trophy. On 15 September 1982, a B-52G crew of the 19th Bomb Wing, Robins AFB, Georgia, performed an outstanding feat of airmanship and bravery that was unparalleled in the annals of Strategic Air Command. The B-52, while returning to Robins from a training mission, lost both rudder elevator hydraulic systems, severely crippling it and placing the crew's lives in danger. After considering all factors, including weather, runway gradient, and crew experience, Captain Robert L. Cavendish, the pilot, decided to try to land the aircraft. Captain Cavendish was fully aware that this type operation had never been accomplished by a SAC combat crew. With the entire crew performing at peak efficiency in carrying out all critical areas of operation, Captain Cavendish landed the aircraft and saved the crew. Captain Cavendish and his crew received the Mackay Trophy, presented annually by the Chief of Staff, USAF, for the most meritorious flight. Other members of the crew were: Second Lieutenant Frank A. Boyle, copilot; Captain Ronald D. Nass, radar navigator; First Lieutenant James D. Gray, navigator;

First Lieutenant Michael J. Connor, electronic warfare officer; Technical Sergeant Ronald B. Wright, gunner; and First Lieutenant Gerald E. Valentine.

First All-Female Crew ("Fair Force One"). SAC's first all-female crew made an historic flight on 10 June. The crew from the 924th Air Refueling Squadron at Castle AFB, California, performed a five-hour training mission that included a mid-air refueling of a B-52. Nicknamed "Fair Force One" by operations specialists, the crew was commanded by Captain Kelly S. C. Hamilton, SAC's only female aircraft commander at the time. The other crew members were: First Lieutenant Linda Martin, copilot; Captain Cathy Bacon, instructor navigator; First Lieutenant Diane Oswald, navigator; and Sergeant Jackie Hale, boom operator.

Two other all-female teams supported the "Fair Force One" mission. The airmen who scheduled the mission were Technical Sergeant Lorrie Roberts and Staff Sergeant Laurie Moffatt, both assigned to the 93d Bomb Wing's training operations branch. "Fair Force One" was not a permanent crew, but the all-female ground crew who supported the flight had worked together for some time. Its three members, who made up the first all-female ground crew at Castle AFB, California, included crew chief Staff Sergeant Judy Ricks assisted by Airman First Class Gwendolyn Hoyle and Airman First Class Terese Sessums. Although she was pleased to have taken part in the special 10 June 1982 mission, Captain Hamilton pointed out that permanent all-female aircrews would not become policy since doing so "would defeat the concept of further integrating women with men in the Air Force. . . ."

B-1 Program. President Reagan's revival of the B-1 gained momentum in 1982. The initial B-1B production contract with Rockwell International Corporation was signed on 20 January. It covered the first aircraft and parts for the next seventeen. Flight testing of B-1As two and four resumed. In September, B-1A number four flew from Edwards AFB, California, to the Farnborough Air Show in England (2–3 September). On the return trip it stopped for display at Andrews AFB, Maryland (14–17 September), and Offutt AFB, Nebraska (19–21 September).

KC-135 Re-engining Program. On 22 June, the rollout of the first KC-135R (S/N 61-0293) at the Boeing Military Aircraft Corporation Plant in Wichita, Kansas, and its first flight on 4 August highlighted the re-engining of the KC-135 air tanker, one of the largest aircraft modernization programs in Air Force history. SAC placed 16 KC-135s under contract to Boeing for re-engining in 1982. The new, advanced technology CFM-56 engines significantly increased the aerial refueling capacity of the aircraft and reduced its maintenance costs with improvements in fuel efficiency and other subsystems.

Spaatz Trophy. The 46th Air Refueling Squadron, K. I. Sawyer AFB, Michigan, was selected as the best air refueling squadron in SAC for Fiscal Year 1982.

P. T. Cullen Award. The 306th Strategic Wing, RAF Mildenhall, England, received the 1978 award for its contribution to the national intelligence collection efforts of the Strategic Air Command.

Omaha Trophy. The 308th Strategic Missile Wing, Little Rock AFB, Arkansas, was selected the best wing in the Strategic Air Command for the year.

Bombing Competition

Twenty-sixth Competition. The 1982 SAC Bombing and Navigation Competition allowed participating units to evaluate their planning and execution of a series of missions, similar to those required during Emergency War Order implementation. Each SAC unit selected the top two bomber and tanker crews in the first phase of the competition. The 7th, 93d, and 380th Bomb Wings Combat Crew Training School and instructor personnel were excluded from the competition. Four F-111 crews represented the Royal Australian Air Force, which participated every other year. In addition, the competition included units from the Air Force Reserve, Air National Guard, and the Air Defense Tactical Air Command fighter interceptor squadrons. For the first time, KC-10 tanker crews competed for trophies.

McDonnell-Douglas Trophy Presented for First Time. In honor of the first appearance of the new tanker in the competition, the Douglas Aircraft Company presented the new James S. McDonnell and Donald W. Douglas, Sr., KC-10 Trophy, for the best active or reserve KC-10 squadron.

General John D. Ryan Trophy Awarded for First Time. Another new trophy, the General John D. Ryan Trophy, was provided by the Boeing Military Aircraft Company to recognize the B-52 unit with the best bombing score. This new trophy resolved concerns over the inequitable competition in bombing accuracy between B-52 units and units with the more modern FB-111. The major awards, based on the final phase missions of 1 to 8 November, were presented on 24 November during ceremonies at Barksdale AFB, Louisiana.

The 509th Bomb Wing, a FB-111 and KC-135 unit, Pease AFB, New Hampshire, set a competition record by winning five trophies:

The Fairchild Trophy, Best Combined Bombing and Navigation Team Score for Both Bombers and Tankers.

The Mathis Trophy, Best Bomber Unit.

The Saunders Trophy, Best Tanker Unit.

The John C. Meyer Memorial Trophy, Best FB-111 Unit in Low- Level Bombing and Electronic Countermeasure.

The Navigation Trophy, Outstanding Tanker Unit in Celestial Navigation.

Other major awards and their recipients were:

Doolittle Trophy, awarded to the numbered air force whose B-52 units achieved the highest percentage of possible points in low-level bombing, was won by the Fifteenth Air Force.

William J. Crumm Linebacker Memorial Trophy, for the B-52 unit with the most points in high altitude bombing, was won by the 5th Bomb Wing, Minot AFB, North Dakota.

General Curtis E. LeMay Bombing Trophy, for the bomber crew with the most points in high- and low-level bombing and time control, was awarded to the 380th Bomb Wing (FB-111), Plattsburgh AFB, New York.

General Russell E. Dougherty Short Range Attack Missile (SRAM) Trophy, for the unit with the most points in simulated SRAM launches, was won by the 42d Bomb Wing, Loring AFB, Maine.

Major James M. Bartsch Electronic Warfare Trophy, for the B-52 unit compiling the most points in electronic countermeasures activity, went to the 319th Bomb Wing, Grand Forks AFB, North Dakota.

General John D. Ryan B-52 Trophy, awarded to the B-52 unit achieving the most points on bombing competition missions for high- and low-level altitude bombing, was won by the 416th Bomb Wing, Griffiss AFB, New York.

McDonnell-Douglas Trophy, presented to the KC-10 squadron that compiled the most points in five navigation exercises, was won by the 2d Bomb Wing, Barksdale AFB, Louisiana.

Weapons Loading Competition. With the term "munitions" changed to "combat weapons," SAC's annual loading competition, known as Giant Sword, was held at Ellsworth Air Base, South Dakota, from 13 through 21 September. The winner of the Barrentine Trophy for the Best Munitions Competition Team was the 28th Bomb Wing from Ellsworth. The other major award winners were:

Best Security Police Team, 44th Strategic Missile Wing, Ellsworth.

Best Munitions Load Crew, 410th Bomb Wing, K. I. Sawyer AFB, Michigan.

Best Crew Chief, 28th Bomb Wing, Ellsworth.

Best Combined Load Crew, 93d Bomb Wing, Castle AFB, California.

Missiles

Missile Launches. Total missiles and space systems launched during the year from Vandenberg AFB: SAC—9; other agencies—8

Titan II Deactivation (Rivet Cap). Although immediate deactivation of the Titan II was ordered by the Reagan administration in October 1981, for the first seven months of 1982 congressional debate cast doubt on the deactivation schedule. To compensate for delaying the MX interim deployment, the Senate Armed Services Committee voted in March to retain the Titan II through FY 1983.

The uncertain status of the Titan II program generated concern in SAC over adequate logistics. Air Force planning for Rivet Cap proceeded on the assumption that deactivation would take place as quickly as possible. In August, Rivet Cap received the long-awaited go-ahead order when a House-Senate authorization conference deleted Titan II funds. The 390th Strategic Missile Wing, Davis-Monthan AFB, Arizona, was the first Titan II unit to inactivate. Site 570-9, already off alert since 2 July for testing, was the first site to be deactivated. Site 571-6 was the first to be removed from alert for deactivation on 30 September.

Storage of Titan II components presented many problems, particularly with propellants. Oxidizer disposal was resolved through temporary storage, sale to manufacturers, and burning of unsalable lots. Downloaded fuel was shipped directly to Vandenberg's Space Launch Complex for use in Titan III launches. The deactivation of Titan II signaled the end of the era of liquid-propellant ICBMs.

MX Basing Controversy. Debate over the deployment and basing of the MX advanced ICBM continued in Congress through 1982. On 22 November, President Reagan informed the American public that MX in Closely Spaced Basing would be deployed at F. E. Warren AFB, Wyoming. During his speech urging the "dense pack" basing mode, the president officially named MX "Peacekeeper." In late December, Congress passed an FY 1983 continuing resolution authority deleting Peacekeeper procurement funding, restricting obligation or expenditure of funding for full-scale engineering development on any Peacekeeper basing mode, and prohibiting flight testing until both houses of Congress decided on a basing mode. Congress also asked the Department of Defense to conduct a comparative assessment of basing modes. President Reagan then appointed a special commission headed by Lieutenant General Brent Scowcroft (USAF, Ret) to examine U.S. strategic modernization with special emphasis on intercontinental ballistic missiles.

Missile Competition

Fifteenth Competition. The annual competition to recognize excellence in numerous missile specialties was held from 23 through 29 April at Vandenberg AFB, California. The competition proved to be a close race as the 44th Strategic Missile Wing from Ellsworth AFB, South Dakota, captured first place and the Blanchard Perpetual Trophy by one point. In addition to the Blanchard Trophy, the 44th Strategic Missile Wing won awards for Best Minuteman Wing and Best Missile Operations. Awards for Best Titan Wing and Best Security Police went to the 381st Strategic Missile Wing, McConnell AFB, Kansas. The award for Best Missile Maintenance was won by the 308th Strategic Missile Wing, Little Rock AFB, Arkansas. The 390th Strategic Missile Wing, Davis-Monthan AFB, Arizona, won the Best Missile Communications Award, while the 351st Strategic Missile Wing, Whiteman AFB, Missouri, won an award for Best Missile Civil Engineering.

1983

Resources

Personnel 120,043 (17,767 officers, 89,267 airmen, 13,009 civilians)

Tactical Aircraft 888 (262 B-52, 61 FB-111, 541 EC/KC-135, 20 KC-10, 4 E-4)

Aircraft Units 14 Heavy Bomb Wings (two 20 PAA; three 19 PAA; six 16 PAA; one 14 PAA; two 10 PAA), one Strategic Wing (14 PAA) with B-52s

2 Medium Bomb Wings (one 32 PAA; one 24 PAA); with FB-111As

34 Heavy Air Refueling Squadrons, 32 (one 25 PAA, one 24 PAA, five 19 PAA, four 16 PAA, six 15 PAA, four 14 PAA, eight 13 PAA, two 10 PAA, one 9 PAA) with KC-135s, two (9 PAA) with KC-10s

2 Strategic Reconnaissance Wings (one with U-2s, SR-71s, and TR-1s, one with RC-135s)

1 Reconnaissance Wing with TR-1s

1 Strategic Reconnaissance Squadron with RC-135s

3 Airborne Command and Control Squadrons (two with EC-135s, one with E-4s)

Missiles 1,149 Minuteman, 43 Titan II, 1,327 SRAM, 736 ALCM

Missile Units Five Titan II Squadrons (four 9 PAA, one 8 PAA), 20 Minuteman Squadrons (50 PAA), nine with Minuteman IIF series missiles, 11 with Minuteman IIIG series missiles

Active Bases 24 CONUS and 1 in Guam

Budget and Financial Status
(FY 83 as of 30 September 1983)

Operations and Maintenance $1,104,172,129, includes supplies, communications, civilian pay, minor equipment purchased

Assets $22,025,147,157, includes real property, inventories, equipment, and weapon systems

Operating Expenses	$4,232,596,562, includes O&M listed above, military pay, troop subsistence, and aviation petroleum, oil, and lubricants (POL)
Military Family Housing	$84,968,517, includes O&M expenses (Military Family Housing Defense Appropriation) in support of housing units

Organization

Joint Strategic Connectivity Staff Transferred. On 1 October the Joint Strategic Connectivity Staff (JSCS), an agency of the Joint Chiefs of Staff (JCS) located at Offutt AFB, Nebraska, since 1980, was disestablished. Its command control communications function and most of its manpower were transferred into the Command Control Communications System Directorate of the JCS.

SAC and the Space Command. Shortly after the Space Command was established on 1 September 1982, Headquarters USAF decided that the new command would be assigned the Missile Warning and Space Surveillance Systems that SAC acquired from the Air Defense Command in 1979. Consequently, approximately 3,600 personnel, 31 units, and four Air Force installations were transferred from SAC to the Space Command on 1 April and 1 May.

Operations

A Phantom Save and the Thirteenth Mackay Trophy. On 5 September 1983, Captain Robert J. Goodman and his KC-135 crew, which were assigned to the 42d Bomb Wing, Loring AFB, Maine, saved an F-4E Phantom fighter over the North Atlantic. While deploying to the European Tanker Task Force, Captain Goodman and his crew were participating in the in-flight refueling of a group of F-4Es on a Crested Cap I mission. One of the fighters lost power in one engine and was diverted to the nearest airfield, Gander International Airport, Newfoundland, Canada, approximately 500 miles away. Captain Goodman was directed to escort the crippled fighter across the ocean to Gander. Shortly thereafter, the F-4E crew was forced to shut down one engine entirely and reduce power in the other, which caused the aircraft to drop altitude by nearly 20,000 feet and lose airspeed. With its centerline tank jettisoned, the F-4E almost ran out of fuel. Through four in-flight refueling hookups, all of which were interrupted by disconnects, the KC-135 was finally able to refuel, tow, and escort the Phantom fighter toward Gander.

At times the flight became extremely perilous with the F-4E dropping to an altitude of 2,000 feet above the frigid ocean. Finally, the fighter was able to take on enough fuel and to gain sufficient engine thrust to maintain a safe flight altitude into Gander where it landed without mishap. For this most meritorious flight of the year in the Air Force, Captain Goodman and his crew received the Mackay Trophy. Other members of the KC-135 crew were: Captain

Michael R. Clover, copilot; First Lieutenant Karol R. Wojcikoski, navigator; and Staff Sergeant Douglas D. Simmons, boom operator.

Last B-52Ds Retired. On 1 October, the last B-52D, the aircraft that bore the brunt of the Arc Light bombing in Southeast Asia from 1966 through 1973, was removed from operations. Probably due to their role in the Vietnam War, retired B-52Ds were in great demand for display purposes. A total of 24 B-52Ds were preserved for display during 1982 and 1983. On 4 October the 7th Bomb Wing's 55-0674 was the last B-52D to go to the storage facility at Davis-Monthan AFB, Arizona. Seven B-52Ds remained at Carswell AFB, Texas, and Andersen AFB, Guam, until their display facilities were ready. The very last B-52D (S/N 56-0687) left Carswell on 20 February 1984 for Orlando International Airport, Florida.

First B-52 Deployment to Spain. Although small groups of B-52s had been deployed to temporary forward operating bases in England for several years, the deployment of three B-52Gs from the 42d Bomb Wing, Loring AFB, Maine, to Moron Air Base, Spain, for three weeks in October-November was the first such use of a Spanish base. The B-52s, participating in NATO exercise Eternal Triangle (27–28 October) and Crisex (31 October–8 November) a joint U.S.-Spanish exercise, took part in high- and low-altitude bombing, sea-search and ECM and fighter-intercept exercises. On 2 November, Spain's King Don Carlos observed a B-52 bombing exercise.

First B-1B Base Selected. On 31 January 1983, Secretary of the Air Force Verne Orr announced that Dyess AFB, Texas, would be the home of the first B-1 squadron and the combat crew training school.

Urgent Fury. When more radical elements of the leftist government of Grenada staged a coup and killed the prime minister, the United States and other countries in the Caribbean decided to take action to prevent injury to the more than 1,100 U.S. citizens on the island and to preserve peace in the Caribbean. SAC KC-135 and KC-10 tankers operating from several CONUS bases provided air refueling support to numerous types of USAF aircraft participating in the Grenada invasion from 22 October through 4 November.

Largest B-52 Aerial Mining Exercise. On 7 March, in the largest B-52 mining exercise of its kind to date, ten SAC B-52D/G aircraft from the 43d Strategic Wing, and the 2d and 19th Bomb Wings, dropped mines off the coast of South Korea. The mining exercise, a part of Team Spirit 83, included U.S. Navy and Marine minelayers and fighters, SAC and Navy tankers, and South Korean fighters.

Harpoon Anti-Shipping Missile Operational for B-52s. In addition to sea-search and aerial mining, SAC's collateral maritime mission included the interdiction of enemy sea power. After looking at other weapons, SAC began to modify some B-52Gs in 1982 to carry the AGM-84 Harpoon. The first flight tests took place between 15 and 28 March 1983 on the Pacific Missile Test Range. A limited operational capability for the 42d Bomb Wing B-52Gs with Harpoon was achieved on 6 October.

Spaatz Trophy. Awarded to the 42d Bomb Wing (42d and 407th Air Refueling Squadrons), Loring AFB, Maine, for outstanding air refueling operations in FY 1983.

Omaha Trophy. Awarded to the 90th Strategic Missile Wing, Francis E. Warren AFB, Wyoming, in recognition of being the outstanding wing in SAC.

P. T. Cullen Award. The 6th Strategic Wing, Eielson AFB, Alaska, received this award in recognition of its contribution to SAC's photo and signal intelligence mission.

Bombing Competition

Twenty-seventh Competition. In the 1983 SAC Bombing and Navigation Competition, the SAC crews were joined by two F-111D entries from the Tactical Air Command as well as Air National Guard and Air Force Reserve KC-135 crews. The Royal Air Force missed the meet for the third consecutive year because its Tornado aircraft conversion was still underway. Major awards presented during the 10 November ceremony at Barksdale AFB, Louisiana, were:

Fairchild Trophy, best combined bomber and tanker scores, 509th Bomb Wing, FB-111/KC-135.

Doolittle Trophy, numbered air force whose units had the best combined scores in low-level bombing and SRAM accuracy, Fifteenth Air Force.

McDonnell-Douglas Trophy, numbered air force KC-10 team (each numbered air force team consisted of one active squadron and one reserve associate squadron crew), Fifteenth Air Force.

Mathis Trophy, unit with most points for high- and low-level bombing and time control, 28th Bomb Wing, B-52.

Ryan Trophy, B-52 unit with most points in bombing, 28th Bomb Wing.

Meyer Trophy, F/FB-111 unit with best low-level bombing and electronic countermeasures, 509th Bomb Wing.

Dougherty Trophy, unit with most points in simulated SRAM launches, 379th Bomb Wing, B-52.

Crumm Trophy, B-52 unit compiling most points in high-altitude bombing, 28th Bomb Wing.

Saunders Trophy, KC-135 unit with most points in all tanker operations, 190th Air Refueling Group (Air National Guard).

Bartsch Trophy, B-52 unit with most points in all electronic countermeasures activity, 410th Bomb Wing.

LeMay Trophy, B-52 or F/FB-111 crew compiling most points in high- and low-level bombing and time control, 28th Bomb Wing, B-52.

Navigation Trophy, outstanding KC-135 unit in navigation, 452d Air Refueling Wing (Air Force Reserve).

Weapons Loading Competition. The SAC Combat Weapons Loading Competition was again held at Ellsworth AFB, South Dakota, from 20 through 27 September. The Barrentine Trophy for the Best Munitions Competition Team went to the 416th Bomb Wing, Griffiss AFB, New York. The other major award winners were:

Best Security Police Team, 320th Bomb Wing, Mather AFB, California.
Best Munitions Load Crew, 43d Strategic Wing, Andersen AFB, Guam.
Best Crew Chief, 42d Bomb Wing, Loring AFB, Maine.
Best Combined Load Crew, 410th Bomb Wing, K. I. Sawyer AFB, Michigan.

Missiles

Missile Launches. Total missiles and space systems launched during the year from Vandenberg AFB: SAC—9; other agencies—19.

Titan II Deactivation (Rivet Cap). Work continued at Davis-Monthan AFB, Arizona, on deactivating the Titan II missiles. The program, nicknamed Rivet Cap, progressed to the final stage—site dismantlement. The first headworks of a launch site, 570-7, was successfully demolished by a contractor on 30 November. The first Titan II unit inactivation, that of the 571st Strategic Missile Squadron, occurred on 2 December. By the end of 1983, 8 sites had been deactivated, for a total of 12.

ICBM Modernization. As a result of the continuing public and congressional debate on the need for a new ICBM and basing modes, President Reagan appointed a commission on strategic forces to review these questions. Known as the Scowcroft Commission after its chairman, retired Air Force Lieutenant General Brent Scowcroft, it recommended, on 6 April: (1) development of a small single warhead ICBM; (2) deployment of 100 Peacekeepers in existing Minuteman silos; (3) further study of silo and shelter hardness and basing modes; and (4) continuation of other ongoing strategic programs (ABM, Trident, Bombers, ALCM, Command Control). The president accepted the findings on 19 April, followed by Congress on 24 and 25 May.

First Peacekeeper Flight Test. The first Peacekeeper (MX) test missile was launched from Vandenberg AFB, California, on 18 June. The multiple warheads impacted in the Kwajalein Target Area. Two more Peacekeeper tests were flown in 1983.

Missile Competition

Sixteenth Competition. In the 1983 competition, held at Vandenberg AFB, California, from 29 April through 5 May, the three Titan II wings set the pace by capturing the first three spots in competing for the Blanchard Perpetual Trophy. This trophy, given to the wing with the highest combined score in the meet, went to the 381st Strategic Missile Wing, McConnell AFB, Kansas. In addition to winning this trophy, the 381st received recognition as the Best Titan II Wing, Best Missile and Engineering Team, Best Missile Crew, and Best Missile Operations. Other major awards and their recipients were:

Best Minuteman Wing, 321st Strategic Missile Wing, Grand Forks AFB, North Dakota

Best Missile Maintenance Team, 308th Strategic Missile Wing, Little Rock AFB, Arkansas

Best Missile Security Police Team, 44th Strategic Missile Wing, Ellsworth AFB, South Dakota

Best Missile Communications Team, 390th Strategic Missile Wing, Davis-Monthan AFB, Arizona

1984

Resources

Personnel   118,484 (17,165 officers, 88,458 airmen, 12,861 civilians)

Tactical Aircraft   897 (262 B-52, 60 FB-111, 543 EC/KC-135, 28 KC-10, 4 E-4)

Aircraft Units   14 Heavy Bomb Wings (one 23 PAA; two 20 PAA; two 19 PAA; one 18 PAA; four 16 PAA; one 14 PAA; three 10 PAA), one Strategic Wing (14 PAA) with B-52s

2 Medium Bomb Wings (one 32 PAA, one 24 PAA) with FB-111As

35 Heavy Air Refueling Squadrons, 33 (one 25 PAA, four 19 PAA, six 16 PAA, six 15 PAA, six 14 PAA, six 13 PAA, two 10 PAA, two 9 PAA) with KC-135s, two (one 14 PAA, one 13 PAA) with KC-10s

2 Strategic Reconnaissance Wings (one with U-2s, SR-71s and TR-1s, one with RC-135s)

1 Reconnaissance Wing with TR-1s

1 Strategic Reconnaissance Squadron with RC-135s

3 Airborne Command and Control Squadrons (two with EC-135s, one with E-4s)

Missiles   1,140 Minuteman, 31 Titan II, 1,309 SRAM, 1,209 ALCM

Missile Units   4 Titan II Squadrons (one 9 PAA, two 8 PAA, one 4 PAA), 20 Minuteman Squadrons (50 PAA), 9 with Minuteman IIF series missiles, 11 with Minuteman IIG series missiles

Active Bases   24 CONUS and 1 in Guam

Budget and Financial Status
(FY 84 as of 30 September 1984)

Operations and Maintenance $943,376,274, includes supplies, communications, civilian pay, minor equipment purchased

Assets $23,675,204,301, includes real property, inventories, equipment, and weapon systems

Operating Expenses	$3,147,563,869, includes O&M listed above, military pay, troop subsistence, and aviation petroleum, oil, and lubricants (POL)
Military Family Housing	$85,325,960, includes O&M expenses (Military Family Housing Defense Appropriation) in support of housing units

Organization

Consolidation of Information Systems in One Agency. On 1 July, a new consolidation of communications and data processing responsibilities went into effect at SAC. The process began during 1982 when Headquarters USAF addressed the issue of the growing overlapping of communications and data processing management agencies. On 1 June 1983 the Assistant Chief of Staff for Information Systems was created in the Air Staff. This new agency was responsible for communications, computer systems, and office automation equipment. A similar consolidation was already under study by SAC. At that level the issue was complicated by SAC's relationship with Air Force Communications Command (AFCC).

In July, the consolidation was completed with SAC's new Deputy Chief of Staff, Information Systems, who would also be the AFCC Strategic Information Systems Division Commander. At all levels of the command, SAC Data Processing and Office Automation Agencies were merged with AFCC Communications-Electronics Units.

Operations

Gallant Eagle '84. From 4 through 12 September, SAC participated in Gallant Eagle '84, the largest military exercise in the United States since 1962. This U.S. Central Command exercise involved 44 SAC bombers, tankers, reconnaissance, and command and control aircraft. SAC, TAC, MAC, and Army elements operated from a number of installations in the western U.S. including SAC's Vandenberg, March, and Beale Air Force Bases in California and Minot AFB, North Dakota. Also B-52Hs from Ellsworth AFB, South Dakota, deployed to Biggs Army Airfield, Texas. The B-52s flew 182 sorties while the KC-135s and KC-10s flew 309 sorties.

KC-10 Support of Antarctic Supply Drop. On 21 June a 22d Air Refueling Wing KC-10A, operating for the first time from Christchurch International Airport, New Zealand, provided three air refuelings to a Military Airlift Command C-141B Stratolifter. The operation enabled the transport to conduct the midwinter air supply drop for the U.S. Antarctic bases at the South Pole and McMurdo Sound. A second flight to McMurdo Sound was accomplished on 23 June.

B-1B Rollout and First Flight. On 4 September the first B-1B (S/N 82-0001) was shown to the public in a rollout ceremony at Rockwell International's

Palmdale, California, assembly plant. The bomber aircraft made its first flight on 18 October. Both events were ahead of schedule.

SAC Receives First Re-engined KC-135R. On 20 June, the first KC-135R (S/N 61-0293) was transferred to SAC's 384th Air Refueling Wing, McConnell AFB, Kansas, by Boeing at the Wichita, Kansas, plant. The transfer followed the completion of a two-year operational test and evaluation program. The aircraft was formally accepted by General Davis from the Aeronautical Systems Division Commander Lieutenant General Thomas H. McMullen in a ceremony on 2 July. The KC-135R, with new fuel-efficient CFM-56 engines, had one and one-half times the fuel off-load capability of the KC-135A. The new engines also allowed reduced maintenance costs, operation from shorter runways, and met federal noise and emission standards. SAC's entire KC-135 tanker force would be re-engined over the next few years.

Spaatz Trophy. The 906th Air Refueling Squadron, Minot AFB, North Dakota, was selected for outstanding air refueling operations in FY 1984.

P. T. Cullen Award. The 55th Strategic Reconnaissance Wing, Offutt AFB, Nebraska, was selected for its contribution to the National Intelligence Collection efforts for SAC.

Omaha Trophy. The 380th Bomb Wing, Plattsburgh AFB, New York, was awarded the trophy in recognition of being the outstanding wing in SAC.

Bombing Competition

Twenty-eighth Competition—RAF Returns. In addition to SAC bombers and tankers, Air Reserve Forces tankers and TAC, USAFE, and Australian (RAAF) F-111s, the RAF brought its new Tornado fighter/bombers to the 1984 SAC Bombing and Navigation Competition. The RAF appearance ended a three-year absence while converting from Vulcans to Tornados. The USAFE F-111s were first-time competitors for the European command. Air National Guard and RCAF interceptors also participated.

For the first time, inert practice bombs were dropped on the Nellis Range during Phase One of the competition. All other scoring was electronic. At the beginning of the competition the Barksdale AFB Auditorium was renamed Hoban Hall in honor of Lieutenant General Richard M. Hoban, a former Second and Eighth Air Force commander, who was instrumental in refurbishing the building in 1974 as a permanent bombing competition headquarters.

Major awards presented at the 31 October ceremony were:

Fairchild Trophy, best combined bomber and tanker scores in bombing and navigation, 380th Bomb Wing, Plattsburgh AFB, New York

Saunders Trophy, best tanker unit, 380th Bomb Wing (310th and 380th Air Refueling Squadrons)

Mathis Trophy, best bombing unit, 416th Bomb Wing, Griffiss AFB, New York

Ryan Trophy, best B-52 units in high- and low-level bombing, 416th Bomb Wing

Dougherty Trophy, best SRAM results, 416th Bomb Wing

Crumm Trophy, best B-52 unit in high-altitude bombing, 379th Bomb Wing, Wurtsmith AFB, Michigan

Bartsch Trophy, best B-52 unit in electronic countermeasures activity, 320th Bomb Wing, Mather AFB, California

LeMay Trophy, best bomber crew in high- and low-level bombing, RAF2, 617 Squadron, RAF Marham

Meyer Trophy, F/FB-111 or Tornado unit achieving the highest damage expectancy rating, RAF2, 617 Squadron, RAF Marham

Navigation Trophy, best KC-135 unit in celestial navigation, 9th Strategic Reconnaissance Wing, Beale AFB, California

Doolittle Trophy, numbered air force with best overall combined scores in low-level bombing and SRAM accuracy, Eighth Air Force

McDonnell-Douglas Trophy, numbered air force with best KC-10 unit, Eighth Air Force

During the Bombing Competition Symposium, the Memphis, Tennessee, Chamber of Commerce donated an award in honor of General Bennie L. Davis for the most improved unit in the competition versus last year's results. The award went to the 97th Bomb Wing, Blytheville AFB, Arkansas.

Weapons Loading Competition. This year's Combat Weapons Loading Competition was held at Ellsworth AFB, South Dakota, from 5 through 12 September. The 28th Bomb Wing from Ellsworth won the Barrentine Trophy for the Best Munitions Competition Team. The other major award winners were:

Best Security Police Team, 44th Strategic Missile Wing, Ellsworth AFB, South Dakota

Best Munitions Load Crew, 93d Bomb Wing, Castle AFB, California

Best Crew Chief, 28th Bomb Wing, Ellsworth AFB, South Dakota

Best Combined Load Crew, 410th Bomb Wing, K. I. Sawyer AFB, Michigan

Missiles

Missile Launches. Total missiles and space systems launched during the year from Vandenberg AFB: SAC—8; other agencies—15.

Titan II Deactivation. The last Titan II site (570-5) of the 390th Strategic Missile Wing, Davis-Monthan AFB, Arizona, was removed from alert on 21 May. The missile left the site on 28 June. The remaining squadron, the 571st, and the wing were inactivated on 31 July. Work was already underway at the second Titan II wing, the 381st at McConnell AFB, Kansas. The first site (533—8) was removed from alert on 2 July. Three more were deactivated by the end of the year.

Missile Competition

Seventeenth Competition. SAC's Missile Combat Competition took place between 3 and 10 May. The competition was once again held at Vandenberg

AFB, California. Only eight wings participated this time as the 390th was getting ready to inactivate. The winner of the Blanchard Perpetual Trophy as the Best Missile Wing was the 90th Strategic Missile Wing, F. E. Warren AFB, Wyoming. The 90th also won the Best Minuteman Wing, Best Missile Operations, Best Missile Maintenance Team, and Best Missile Communications Team Awards. The other major award winners were:

Best Titan II Wing, 308th Strategic Missile Wing, Little Rock AFB, Arkansas

Best Missile Security Police Team, 351st Strategic Missile Wing, Whiteman AFB, Missouri

Best Missile Civil Engineering Team, 91st Strategic Missile Wing, Minot AFB, North Dakota

1985

Resources

Personnel	118,976 (17,475 officers, 88,341 airmen, 13,160 civilians)
Tactical Aircraft	901 (2 B-1, 261 B-52, 60 FB-111, 535 EC/KC- 135, 39 KC-10, 4 E-4)
Aircraft Units	1 Heavy Bomb Wing (2 PAA) with B-1s
	13 Heavy Bomb Wings (one 33 PAA, two 20 PAA, two 19 PAA, one 18 PAA, three 16 PAA, two 14 PAA, one 12 PAA), one Strategic Wing (14 PAA) with B-52s
	2 Medium Bomb Wings (one 32 PAA, one 24 PAA) with FB-111As
	36 Heavy Air Refueling Squadrons, 33 (one 25 PAA, three 19 PAA, five 16 PAA, six 15 PAA, six 14 PAA, nine 13 PAA, two 12 PAA, two 11 PAA) with KC-135s, three (one 19 PAA, one 16 PAA, and one 3 PAA) with KC-10s
	2 Strategic Reconnaissance Wings (one with U-2s, SR-71s and TR-1s, and one with RC-135s)
	1 Reconnaissance Wing with TR-1s
	1 Strategic Reconnaissance Squadron with RC-135s
	3 Airborne Command and Control Squadrons (two with EC-135s, one with E-4s)
Missiles	1,140 Minuteman, 21 Titan II, 1,309 SRAM, 1,271 ALCM
Missile Units	3 Titan II Squadrons (one 8 PAA, one 7 PAA and one 6 PAA), 20 Minuteman Squadrons (50 PAA), 9 with Minuteman IIF series missiles and 11 with Minuteman IIIG series missiles
Active Bases	24 CONUS and 1 in Guam

Budget and Financial Status
(FY 85 as of 30 September 1985)

Operations and Maintenance	$955,825,677, includes supplies, communications, civilian pay, minor equipment purchased

Assets	$25,283,589,329, includes real property, inventories, equipment, and weapon systems
Operating Expenses	$3,715,956,369, includes O&M listed above, military pay, troop subsistence, and aviation petroleum, oil, and lubricants (POL)
Military Family Housing	$99,191,292, includes O&M expenses (Military Family Housing Defense Appropriation) in support of housing units

Organization

No significant changes.

Operations

Another In-Flight Emergency and the Fourteenth Mackay Trophy. On 21 January 1985, Lieutenant Colonel David E. Faught, a member of the 97th Bombardment Wing, saved the lives of eight KC-135 crew members and prevented the loss of his tanker through a conspicuous act of courage during flight. In his capacity as evaluator pilot, Lieutenant Colonel Faught was instructing a pilot proficiency exercise and after having supervised four uneventful touch-and-go landings, was making the final approach for a full stop landing. Suddenly, the tanker's nose gear would not extend and the aircraft, which had been in the air for approximately six hours, could not land at Blytheville AFB, Arkansas, its home base.

While the crew was making numerous unsuccessful attempts to lower the nose gear, other problems developed. Fuel became low and the weather deteriorated. A tanker aircraft was in the local traffic area and a refueling was finally conducted in the turbulent skies over Arkansas. Lieutenant Colonel Faught and his crew continued trying to lower the nose gear, and about every 20 minutes another refueling was required. No more than 8,000 pounds of fuel could be onloaded at one refueling time because of critical center of gravity limitations and the necessity to keep the aircraft in landing configuration.

A KC-10 tanker arrived to provide relief. Later, the KC-10 began to run low on fuel, and a strip alert tanker at Blytheville was called on to refuel the KC-10, which in turn, refueled the KC-135. Finally, after being airborne for over 13 hours, and with darkness approaching, Lieutenant Colonel Faught decided to make a nose up landing at Blytheville. The landing was successful. The tanker suffered only minor damage. For his superior performance on this flight, Lieutenant Colonel Faught was named recipient of the 1985 Mackay Trophy.

First B-1 Delivered. On 7 July, the first operational B-1B (S/N 83-0065) was accepted by SAC and the 96th Bomb Wing on its arrival at Dyess AFB, Texas. The controversial bomber was flown from Edwards AFB, California, to Offutt AFB, Nebraska, on 27 June with Secretary of the Air Force Verne

Orr on board. General Davis was to fly the B-1B to Dyess on 29 June, the 30th anniversary of the SAC acceptance of the first B-52. The first operational B-1B, 83-0065, unfortunately suffered engine damage from ingesting nuts and bolts from a faulty air conditioner. To keep the acceptance on schedule, General Davis went to Edwards on 29 June to pick up the only other existing B-1B, S/N 82-0001, the fleet prototype. He then flew it to Dyess for the acceptance ceremonies.

E-4 Modification Program Completed. On 30 January, the last of three E-4As modified to an E-4B configuration was returned to the 55th Strategic Reconnaissance Wing, Offutt AFB, Nebraska. Added to the one E-4 built as an E-4B, SAC now had four improved E-4 National Emergency Airborne Command Post (NEACP) aircraft with nuclear effects shielding, advanced command and control electronics, a 1200 KVA generator (the largest power generator ever flown), and 13 external communications systems using 50 antennas to cover a broad frequency spectrum from super-high to very-low.

ALCM Test Flight in Canada. On 19 February, a 319th Bomb Wing B-52 launched the first ALCM flight test missile over the Beaufort Sea north of Canada. The ALCM flew south into Canada on a four and one-half hour flight down a 1,500 by 50-mile corridor from the MacKenzie River Delta along the east slope of the Rockies to Dawson Creek, British Columbia, and then east to the Primrose Lake Air Weapons Range near Canadian Forces Base, Cold Lake, Alberta. The missile made a successful parachute-assisted landing in the target area.

Spaatz Trophy. The 906th Air Refueling Squadron, Minot AFB, North Dakota, was awarded the trophy for outstanding air refueling operations in FY 1985. This was the first time that a unit had won two consecutive Spaatz Trophies.

P. T. Cullen Award. The 9th Strategic Reconnaissance Wing, Beale AFB, California, won the award for exemplary contributions to intelligence gathering efforts for SAC.

Omaha Trophy. The 5th Bombardment Wing, Minot AFB, North Dakota, was selected the outstanding wing in SAC for 1985.

Headquarters SAC "PEACE IS OUR PROFESSION" Sign Removed. On 12 April, the "Peace is our Profession" sign that had been in front of the SAC entrance gate to Offutt AFB, Nebraska since 1958 was removed. All gate and directional signs at Offutt were replaced by the standard Air Force signs. The 1958 sign was given to the SAC Aerospace Museum at Offutt.

Bombing Competition

Twenty-ninth Competition. For only the second time since 1974, a B-52 unit won the SAC Bombing and Navigation Competition. For a number of years, the FB-111s, with more modern avionics equipment, had a distinct advantage. With the B-52s receiving new avionics along with the ALCM, they had a better competitive position. In addition to the SAC bomber and tanker units and Air

Reserve Forces tanker units, TAC F-111s and RAF Tornados joined the competition. Major awards presented at the 14 November ceremony were:

Fairchild Trophy, best combined bomber and tanker scores in bombing and navigation, 97th Bomb Wing, Blytheville AFB, Arkansas

Saunders Trophy, best tanker unit, 452d Air Refueling Wing, March AFB, California

Mathis Trophy, best bombing unit, 97th Bomb Wing, Blytheville AFB, Arkansas

Ryan Trophy, best B-52 unit in high- and low-level bombing, 7th Bomb Wing, Carswell AFB, Texas

Dougherty Trophy, best SRAM results, 319th Bomb Wing, Grand Forks AFB, North Dakota

Crumm Trophy, best B-52 unit in high-altitude bombing, 416th Bomb Wing, Griffiss AFB, New York

Bartsch Trophy, best B-52 unit in electronic countermeasures activity, 7th Bomb Wing

LeMay Trophy, best bomber crew in high- and low-level bombing, RAF1, 27 Squadron, RAF Marham

Meyer Trophy, FB-111 or Tornado unit achieving the highest damage expectancy rating, RAF2, 27 Squadron, RAF Marham

Navigation Trophy, best KC-135 unit in celestial navigation, 452d Air Refueling Wing

Doolittle Trophy, numbered air force with best overall combined scores in low-level bombing and SRAM accuracy, Fifteenth Air Force

McDonnell-Douglas Trophy, numbered air force with best KC-10, Eighth Air Force

Davis Trophy, for the most improved unit since the last competition, 319th Bomb Wing

Weapons Loading Competition. The SAC Combat Weapons Loading Competition again was held at Ellsworth AFB, South Dakota, from 19 through 26 September. The winner of the Barrentine Trophy for the Best Munitions Competition Team was the 509th Bomb Wing, Pease AFB, New Hampshire. The 509th also won the Best Munitions Load Crew and Best Combined Load Crew Awards. The other major award winners were:

Best Security Police Team, 96th Bomb Wing, Dyess AFB, Texas.

Best Crew Chief, 5th Bomb Wing, Minot AFB, North Dakota.

Missiles

Missile Launches. Total missiles and space systems launched during the year from Vandenberg AFB: SAC—6; other agencies—11.

TAC GLCM Launched from Vandenberg. On 22 October 1985 Tactical Air Command launched its first missile from Vandenberg. This ground-launched cruise missile was the first of its kind flown from Vandenberg.

New Minuteman Modification Program Begun. For the first time since the completion of the Force Modernization Program in 1975, SAC's Minuteman fleet was to undergo a major upgrade and modification program. On 1 April, the Rivet Mile (Minuteman Integrated Life Extension) program began at the 341st Strategic Missile Wing, Malmstrom AFB, Montana, when four launch facilities were transferred to Air Force Logistics Command for modification.

Titan II Deactivation. During 1985 7 more Titan II sites of the 381st Strategic Missile Wing, McConnell AFB, Kansas, were deactivated, for a total of 12. The 533d Strategic Missile Squadron was inactivated on 1 November. Titan II deactivation began at the third wing, the 308th Strategic Missile Wing, Little Rock AFB, Arkansas, in April at Site 374-8, which was already off alert for maintenance. Three more sites at Little Rock were deactivated by the end of the year.

Female Crews for Minuteman and Peacekeeper Authorized. In 1984, Headquarters USAF asked SAC to restudy the placement of women on Minuteman and Peacekeeper crews. This issue was originally addressed in the late 1970s when women were added to the Titan II crew force. At that time it was not desirable to have two-person mixed (male and female) crews in Minuteman. However, in August 1984, Headquarters USAF requested that SAC investigate the use of gender-specific Minuteman crews. An extensive SAC study resulted in a 4 February 1985 CINCSAC announcement instituting all-female crews in Minuteman. A phased-approach (one wing at a time) was initiated. The first class of six female Titan II Launch Control Officers began Minuteman initial qualification training at Vandenberg AFB, California, in October. They were scheduled for assignment to the 351st Strategic Missile Wing, Whiteman AFB, Missouri, in January 1986.

Missile Competition

Eighteenth Competition. The SAC Missile Combat Competition was held from 26 April through 2 May at Vandenberg AFB, California. The 308th Strategic Missile Wing, Little Rock AFB, Arkansas, in its 18th try, won its first Blanchard Perpetual Trophy. The 308th also won the Best Titan Wing, Best Missile Operations Team, Best Missile Maintenance Team, and Best Missile Civil Engineering Team Awards. The other major award winners at the, were:

Best Minuteman Wing and Best Missile Security Police Team, 341st Strategic Missile Wing, Malmstrom AFB, Montana

Best Missile Information Systems Team, 351st Strategic Missile Wing, Whiteman AFB, Missouri

1986

Resources

Personnel   118,671 (106,630 military, 12,041 civilians)

Organization

No significant changes in the organization occurred in 1986.

Operations

25th Anniversary of Looking Glass. On 3 February 1986, the SAC Airborne Command Post, carried on board EC-135 aircraft known affectionately as Looking Glass, completed 25 years of continuous duty. General Welch flew the official anniversary mission which landed at Offutt AFB at 2:30 p.m. As had been the practice for the past 25 years, a replacement Looking Glass aircraft had been launched and in the air for several minutes before General Welch's aircraft landed.

40th Anniversary of SAC. On 21 March, the Strategic Air Command observed its 40th anniversary. The event was highlighted at Headquarters SAC, with General Welch presiding over a cake-cutting ceremony in the SAC cafeteria. This brief ceremony marked the beginning of a yearlong observance of the anniversary under the theme "Forty and Forward," which was part of SAC's 40th anniversary logo.

SAC Digital Network (SACDIN) Completes Test. On 31 January, the SAC Digital Network (SACDIN) successfully completed its second Initial Operational Test and Evaluation (IOT&E). SACDIN would replace the 1960s-vintage SAC Automated Command Control System (SACCS) Data Transmission Subsystem (DTS) to provide two-way direct and secure record data communications from CINCSAC to all SAC ground-based commanders charged with executing the Single Integrated Operational Plan (SIOP). The Digital Network, which had been planned in the 1970s, had failed its first Initial Operational Test and Evaluation in August 1984. The system was scheduled to reach Initial Operational Capability (IOC) in September 1986 at Offutt AFB, Nebraska, and Whiteman AFB, Missouri. Final Operational Capability was projected for January 1988.

IDHS-80 Achieved Full Operational Capability. On 26 January, the SAC Intelligence Data Handling System for the mid-1980s (IDHS-80) achieved full operational capability, successfully concluding a five-year hardware and software procurement and development effort. To achieve this goal, computer support for several major intelligence functions was transitioned from two obsolete computers to IDHS-80. The supported areas included electronic intelligence exploitation and production, delegated production of basic military intelligence, target intelligence development, and threat assessment. During the transition process every effort was made to maintain the appearance of user screen displays, while improving processing time. In fact, the average terminal response decreased from 34 seconds, under the previous system, to 8 seconds for IDHS-80.

Joint SAC/US Navy Harpoon Missile Exercise. On 20 April, a B-52G bomber from the 42d Bomb Wing, Loring AFB, Maine, joined five U.S. Navy platforms, including an A-6E Intruder, in firing the AGM-84 Harpoon missile, and achieving a perfect six out of six target hits. The B-52 began the exercise, part of the Navy's FLEETEX 2-86, by putting its Harpoon into the target at extended range.

This was the first launch of the missile by a B-52 in a Navy fleet exercise. The four Navy ship participants were two submarines, the battleship IOWA (BB 61), and the cruiser JOSEPHUS DANIELS (CG 27). Aircraft from carrier FORRESTAL (CV 59) also participated.

B-1B Bomber Initial Operational Capability. On 1 October the new B-1B bomber reached its Initial Operational Capability at the 96th Bomb Wing, Dyess AFB, Texas. Three of the 15 bombers could not assume alert status, however, because of a delay in the delivery of parts for their Electronic Countermeasures (ECM) equipment.

All of the B-1Bs experienced minor fuel leaks that were subsequently reduced to minor seepage. Dyess received its first B-1B in June 1985.

Bombing Competition

Thirtieth Competition, 92d Bomb Wing Dominated. The competition was dominated by the Fairchild AFB, Washington wing, which also claimed the Muir S. Fairchild Trophy for Highest Competition Effectiveness, named for the wing's host base's namesake. Trophies were presented as follows:

Fairchild Trophy, highest percentage of possible points in bomber and tanker missions, 92d Bomb Wing, B-52

Doolittle Trophy, numbered air force whose B-52 units achieved highest percentage of possible points in low-level bombing and SRAM activity, Eighth Air Force

Mathis Trophy, top unit in high and low bombing, 92d Bomb Wing, B-52

Meyer Trophy, top FB-111 unit compiling most points in low-level bombing and electronic countermeasures activity, 380th Bomb Wing

Dougherty Trophy, FB-111 or B-52 unit compiling most points for simulated SRAM launches, 92d Bomb Wing, B-52

Saunders Trophy, top tanker unit in competition, 92d Bomb Wing, B-52

Crumm Trophy, B-52 unit with best high-altitude bombing results, 92d Bomb Wing, B-52

Bartsch Trophy, B-52 Unit compiling the most points in electronic counter-measure activity, 319th Bomb Wing

LeMay Bombing Trophy, bomber crew compiling most points in high- and low-level bombing, 92d Bomb Wing

Holloway Navigation Trophy, tanker unit compiling most points in navigation, 7th Bomb Wing

Davis Most Improved Trophy, 340th Air Refueling Wing

Ellis Best KC-10 Unit, 2d Bomb Wing

Missiles

Peacekeeper Lawsuit Dismissed. On 20 February, the U.S. District Court in Lincoln, Nebraska, dismissed lawsuits against the placement of Peacekeeper missiles in Minuteman sites at Frances E. Warren AFB, Wyoming. The State of Colorado and several other individual plaintiffs appealed the dismissal to the Eighth Circuit Court of Appeals in St. Louis. Oral arguments were to be heard three to four months later, with a decision anticipated in spring 1987.

Peacekeeper Completed Over 70 percent of Scheduled Test Firings. On 18 September, the LGM-118A Peacekeeper ICBM successfully completed the 14th test of a planned total of 20. The flight from a modified Minuteman III silo at Vandenberg AFB was about 4,200 miles and took 30 minutes. All six of the re-entry vehicles it carried (it is capable of carrying up to 10) hit the target area on the Kwajalein Missile Test Range. The test came less than a month after the previous one on 23 August.

On 5 December, another Peacekeeper was successfully launched from Vandenberg to Kwajalein carrying a full complement of 10 unarmed re-entry vehicles. Two of the RVs did not deploy, but all other test objectives were achieved.

Last ALCM Delivered Ahead of Schedule. On October 7, the last AGM-86B Air-Launched Cruise Missile was delivered to the Air Force. The final delivery was made ahead of schedule and $90 million under budget. Boeing Aerospace, the primary contractor, was awarded the contract to build the ALCM in 1980 and in December 1982, the 416th Bomb Wing, Griffiss AFB, New York, became the first unit to reach operational capability.

1987

Resources

Personnel   118,799 (18,708 officers, 87,055 airmen, 13,036 civilians)

Organization

First Advanced Technology "Stealth" Bomber Operational Base. In early January, Representative Ike Skelton (D-Mo) announced and the Air Force confirmed that the first operational B-2 ATB base would be Whiteman AFB, Missouri. Military construction budgeted at $89.3 million had been provided for FY 1988 to prepare the base for the Stealth bombers.

Operations

General Chain—Nuclear and Conventional Modernization. In early 1987, SAC Commander-in-Chief John T. Chain presented testimony before the Senate Defense Appropriations Subcommittee that stressed the need for strategic modernization of both nuclear and conventional capabilities. The CINCSAC said, "It is imperative that we help bolster the nation's conventional capabilities to make nuclear war less likely. Theater commanders require a large, long-range fully capable conventional bomber force to do their mission. Our strategic bombers are an essential element of their warfighting capability. When timeliness, range, and payload are considered, there are conventional missions that cannot be accomplished and areas of the world that cannot be reached without SAC bombers." Chain added, ". . . we need to dedicate non-ALCM B-52Gs to a conventional role."

B-1B Bomber and Long Flight Records. On 14 April, a six-month-old B-1B record was broken by a Dyess AFB B-1B that flew continuously for 21 hours and 44 minutes. The new record was set with the aircraft flying at an average speed of 440 knots over 9,411 miles. The previous record was set over a distance of 5,940 miles for 13 hours and 20 minutes.

B-1B Bomber Set Four More World Records. On 4 July, a B-1B unofficially broke four world records for speed, distance, and payload. It also unofficially established 14 new records. The B-1B was on an acceptance flight after taking off from the Rockwell plant in Palmdale, California, with a 66,140-lb payload.

The plane flew two distance legs, first, 620 miles with an average speed of 678.48 mph and then 1,240 miles with a speed of 669.52 mph.

Members of the crew were Lt. Colonel Robert A. Chamberlain, aircraft commander; Captain Michael E. Waters, copilot; Major Richard K. Fisher, offensive systems officer; and Captain Nathan E. Gray, defensive systems officer.

First Successful B-1B SRAM Launch. On 3 June, the first launch from a B-1B of an AGM-69A Short Range Attack Missile was successfully conducted at the Tonopah Test Range, Nevada. The bomber, based at Dyess AFB, Texas, flew a low-level 1,200-mile track to the test range, evaluating the aircraft's performance enroute.

B-1B Sets Nine Payload and Speed Records. On 17 September, a B-1B unofficially broke nine payload and speed records while on its acceptance flight over five western states. After take-off from the Rockwell plant at Palmdale, California, the B-1B flew the 2,700-nautical-mile course in four hours and forty-six minutes for an average speed of 655 mph.

The crew consisted of Major H. Brent Hedgpeth and Lt. Colonel Robert A. Chamberlain, pilots; Captain Alexander F. J. Ivanchiskin, offensive systems officer; and Captain David J. Novick, defensive systems officer. Colonel Chamberlain was the aircraft commander during the record-breaking B-1B flight of 4 July. The two flights together amassed a total of 36 class records for the B-1B.

B-1B Sustains Bird Strike and Crashes. On September 28, a B-1B on a training sortie out of Dyess AFB, Texas, crashed into a mesa at the La Junta Strategic Training Range in southeastern Colorado. Originally, the plane was thought to have sustained multiple bird strikes, ingesting the birds into the engines, losing power in two of the engines, and crashing. The final USAF report, released on 20 January, concluded that a 15- to 20-lb bird (probably a white pelican) collided with the airframe, causing a fire and failure of three of the four hydraulic systems. The collision with the bird occurred at 600 feet with a speed of 560 knots. Three of the six crewmen survived.

Modernized Stratotanker Milestone. On 2 October, the 100th KC-135R Stratotanker was delivered to the 340th Air Refueling Wing at Altus AFB, Oklahoma, by Boeing Military Airplane Company. The tanker modernization program involved the re-engining of the KC-135s with turbofan powerplants, an auxiliary power unit, and strengthened landing gear.

MacKay Trophy for B-1B Record Flights. The 36 class records set by the July and September B-1B flights earned the 1987 MacKay Trophy for the Rockwell International's USAF Contract Management office and to the B-1B System Program Office (SPO) at the Aeronautical Systems Division (AFSC), Wright-Patterson AFB, Ohio. The MacKay Trophy is awarded for the most meritorious flight(s) of the year.

416th Bombardment Wing Daedalian Maintenance Award Winner. The 416th's maintenance complex was named the Daedalian Maintenance Award

Winner, recognizing the outstanding USAF maintenance organization for FY 1987. The wing won the award for two of the previous three years.

Missiles

Secretary of Defense Announced Advanced Cruise Missile Deployment. In January, Secretary Caspar Weinberger announced that the first operational Advanced Cruise Missiles would be deployed to K. I. Sawyer AFB, Michigan, in 1989 or 1990. The missile is considered to be a "stealthy" follow-on to the AGM-86 Air-Launched Cruise Missile (ALCM).

Small ICBM Motor Test. On 24 April, the first test-firing of the SICBM's second-stage motor was successfully conducted at the Arnold Engineering Development Center, Tennessee. The test of the solid-propellant motor lasted 40 seconds and was staged in a test cell that simulates high-altitude conditions. The first-stage motor was fired successfully on 3 April.

New Short-Range Missile Contract. On 30 April, a contract to develop a new Short Range Attack Missile (SRAM) was awarded to Boeing Aerospace Company. The contract, worth over $214 million, requires an advanced design phase, with options for full-scale development and production of the first 400 missiles.

Titan II ICBM Era Over. On 5 May, the last Titan II was taken off strategic alert at Little Rock AFB, Arkansas. The LAM-25C had been operational in SAC since 1963. The crews continued to work at the site, dismantling the missile and completing the deactivation.

SICBM Guidance System Test. On September 1, a successful test of two navigation systems, Litton's ring-laser gyroscope Inertial Measurement Unit (IMU), and General Electric's Star Sensor IMU, was conducted at Vandenberg AFB. The test compared data from the two systems during the flight to Kwajalein to select one as the guidance system for the Small ICBM (SICBM).

MX Casting Facility Explosion Kills Five. In late December, an explosion destroyed a Morton Thiokol solid-propellant casting facility and killed five workers. The accident occurred as workers were disassembling the casting equipment used to fill an MX first stage with fuel.

Missile Team of Lieutenants Wins Power Award. A young team of 1st Lieutenant David W. Dale and 2d Lieutenant John B. Shuman won the Power Trophy for the outstanding missile crew for 1987.

1988

Resources

Personnel	116,805 (105,023 military, 11,782 civilian)
Tactical Aircraft	(98 B-1, 262 B-52, 62 FB-111, EC/KC-135, 4 E-4)

Organization

301st Air Refueling Wing Reactivated. In January the 301st Air Refueling Wing was reactivated at Malmstrom AFB, Montana. With the reactivation, Malmstrom regained a flying mission to complement the 341st Strategic Missile Wing. The 301st, SAC's first all-jet refueling wing, had been deactivated for 10 years. On 3 October, the first three of the planned 16 KC-135R tankers arrived. It was the first fixed-wing flying mission for the base in 25 years.

Blytheville AFB Renamed for General Ira C. Eaker. On 26 May, Blytheville AFB, Arkansas, home of the 97th Bomb Wing, was renamed for one of the most famous air pioneers, General Ira C. Eaker. Appropriately, General Eaker was the first commander of the Eighth Air Force in World War II. The ceremony featured a flyby of each type of Eighth Air Force's assigned aircraft—the B-1B, B-52, FB-111, KC-10, and KC-135.

Units Celebrate Silver, or More, Anniversaries. A few SAC units commemorated their 25th anniversaries in 1988. On 1 July, the 90th Strategic Missile Wing at F. E. Warren AFB, Wyoming, celebrated its 25th anniversary. The wing has evolved from the LGM-30B Minuteman I, to the LGM-30G Minuteman III, to the installation of the first LGM-118A Peacekeeper (MX) on 12 June 1986. The base is the only site where the Peacekeeper will be kept in silos.

On 23 October, the 44th Strategic Missile Wing celebrated its birthday; 25 years earlier, the final Minuteman I missile was placed on strategic alert.

Finally, on 27 October, the 25th Air Division celebrated its 40th anniversary at McChord AFB, Washington. The 25th AD was the first unit organized specifically for the continental air defense.

Operations Information on the B-2 Stealth Bomber. On 20 April, the U.S. Air Force released information on the controversial but highly classified Stealth bomber. The first released picture of the bomber was an artist's concept that revealed little detail. As anticipated, the general shape of the aircraft resembled a flying wing, reminding older observers of Northrop's XB-35 and

YB/YRB-49, built in the mid-1940s. A primary concern with the older prototypes, and the new Stealth, is stability and control. Like the XB-35, the B-2 does not have vertical stabilizers. The B-2 is powered by General Electric engines, probably similar to the GE powerplants used in the B-1B. The design of the bomber is intended to make the plane virtually invisible to enemy radar. The first flight of the B-2 was expected in the fall.

Later in the year, on 4 August, more information on the B-2 was released, including the crew size (two), the engines (four GE F118s), and some other characteristics. The Air Force stated that the first six of the B-2s would undergo flight-testing at Edwards AFB, California. The second B-2 was well into assembly.

Honda B-2 Model Donated to SAC. In late 1988, Honda donated to SAC its full-scale model of the B-2 bomber, used in its "for the record, ours was first" advertising campaign. The conceptual model will be displayed at Ellsworth AFB, South Dakota. Honda paid to have the plane disassembled and shipped to the Black Hills base, total costs estimated as $30,000.

First Production B-1B Grounded. In mid-1988, the Strategic Air Command took delivery of its first production B-1B. The Rockwell bomber flew from Edwards AFB, California, to Ellsworth AFB, South Dakota, after completing 617 hours of tests. At Ellsworth, it will be used as a ground trainer for weapons loading.

The Last B-1B Rolls Out. On 20 January, the final, 100th B-1B was rolled out at the Rockwell plant in Palmdale, California. The rollout was two months ahead of schedule. After final checkout and painting, the plane will be delivered to McConnell AFB, Kansas. Meanwhile, on 4 January, the first B-1B to be stationed at McConnell arrived from Palmdale. The base was the fourth and last base to receive the B-1B.

B-1B Accidents in November. As the beginning of the year noted the delivery of the final B-1B to the SAC inventory, the end of the year brought the loss of two of the controversial bombers. In an 11-day period in November, two B-1Bs were lost. On 8 November, a bomber out of the 96th Bomb Wing, Dyess AFB, Texas, crashed during take-off for a training sortie. All four crewmen ejected safely. A command-wide safety inspection was ordered by SAC for the remaining 98 aircraft.

Then, on 18 November, a 28th Bomb Wing B-1B crashed on approach to Ellsworth AFB, South Dakota. Again, the crew ejected safely without significant injury.

The preliminary investigation of the 8 November crash indicated the cause as being a fire from a fuel leak in the left overwing fairing. Flow-rate measurements indicated the leak.

The second accident was attributed to pilot error. According to the official report, the aircraft commander, Major Thomas C. Skillman failed to "establish sufficient visual cues to determine the runway environment." The copilot was also cited for failing to advise the pilot that the correct procedures had not been followed.

Hagar's a Gasser. The 501st Organizational Maintenance Squadron commander, Major Chris J. McWilliams, used the influence of his father to create some original nose art for a Pease AFB, New Hampshire KC-135 Stratotanker. The creator and artist of the cartoon strip, "Hagar the Horrible" was a personal friend of Major McWilliams's father, and the major wrote the cartoonist for permission to use the likeness of the character for one of the planes. The artist, Dik Browne, did one better and sent two original drawings to paint onto the nose of the KC-135, "Valhalla Express."

KC-135A Record Setters. On 19 November, a number of class records, including three previously held by a Soviet Yak-42 commercial airliner, were broken or set by a SAC KC-135A Stratotanker. The aircraft was fitted with the new General Electric/CFM International F108-CF-100 engines that produce marked improvements in fuel efficiency, allowing the plane to carry more fuel farther. Four different SAC refueling crews set a total of 13 previously unclaimed time-to-climb records; one of the crews, from the 19th Air Refueling Wing at Robins AFB, Georgia, broke the Soviet-held records as well as setting two others. The other three record-setting crews were from the 340th Air Refueling Wing, Altus AFB, Oklahoma, the 319th Bomb Wing, Grand Forks AFB, North Dakota, and the 384th Bomb Wing, McConnell AFB, Kansas.

Last KC-10A Leaves Plant. On 29 November, the 60th and last KC-10A Extender left the McDonnell Douglas plant in Long Beach, California, bound for the company's testing facility at Yuma, Arizona. Ironically, the last produced was the first modified with wing-mounted aerial refueling pods. All earlier KC-10s will be retrofitted with the pods. The pods will allow the tanker to refuel three aircraft simultaneously.

General Curtis E. LeMay Strategic Aircrew Award. The award for 1988 was presented to the S-01 crew of the 42d Bomb Wing, Loring AFB, Maine, for superior airmanship and performance. The crew earned the award through their sustained performance of excellence for over a year. Members of the B-52 crew were: Lt. Colonel (selectee) Chuck Patrum, aircraft commander; 1st Lieutenant Craig Thomas, pilot; Captain Steve Kasemeier, radar navigator; 1st Lieutenant Mike Byrne, navigator; Captain Mitch Namendorf, electronic warfare operator; and Technical Sergeant Dan Danish, gunner.

Bombing Competition

Thirty-second Competition. The Proud Shield '88 competition had a couple of firsts even before the points began to be counted. EC-135 crews were permitted to compete for the first time in the KC-135 phase, since they still had the capability for in-flight refueling. Additionally, F-111 crews were entered in the competition for the first time, to compete for the Fairchild Trophy. Probably most significant was that for the first time B-1B crews would be participating in the competition.

A new award was added this year, the Billy Mitchell Trophy, for a bomber unit for accuracy in conventional bombing, survival in an electronic countermeasures environment, and avoiding fighters. The B-1B crews were not eligible because their mission is nuclear deterrence.

Major awards presented at the 14 November ceremony were:

Fairchild Trophy, best combined bomber and tanker scores in bombing and navigation, 5h Bomb Wing, Minot AFB, North Dakota

Saunders Trophy, best tanker unit, 42d Bomb Wing, Loring AFB, Maine

Mathis Trophy, best bombing unit, 96th Bomb Wing, Dyess AFB, Texas

Ryan Trophy, best unit in high- and low-level bombing, 28th Bomb Wing, Ellsworth AFB, South Dakota

Dougherty Trophy, best SRAM results, 96th Bomb Wing, Dyess AFB, Texas

Bartsch Trophy, best B-52 unit in electronic countermeasures activity, 43d Bomb Wing, Andersen AFB, Guam

LeMay Trophy, best bomber crew in high- and low-level bombing, Crew R-76, 27th Tactical Fighter Wing, Cannon AFB, New Mexico

Meyer Trophy, best F/FB-111 unit, 509th Bomb Wing, Pease AFB, New Hampshire

Holloway Trophy, best KC-135 unit in celestial navigation, 42d Bomb Wing, Loring AFB, Maine

Davis Trophy, for the most improved unit since the last competition, 96th Bomb Wing, Dyess AFB, Texas

Ellis Trophy, for the best KC-10 crew, 22d Air Refueling Wing, March AFB, California

Eaker Trophy, for the best B-1B unit, 96th Bomb Wing, Dyess AFB, Texas

Mitchell Trophy, for most points in conventional bombing, electronic combat, and fighter intercept, 27th Tactical Fighter Wing, Cannon AFB, New Mexico

Weapons Loading Competition. The SAC Combat Weapons Loading Competition again was held at Ellsworth AFB, South Dakota, from 19 through 26 September. The winner of the Barrentine Trophy for the Best Munitions Competition Team was the 509th Bomb Wing, Pease AFB, New Hampshire. The 509th also won the Best Munitions Load Crew and Best Combined Load Crew Awards. The other major award winners were:

Best Security Police Team, 96th Bomb Wing, Dyess AFB, Texas

Best Crew Chief, 5th Bomb Wing, Minot AFB, North Dakota

Missiles

Mixed Male/Female ICBM Crews. On 1 January, a change to SAC missile crew assignment policy was implemented, allowing both sexes to serve on the same crew. Mixed launch crews were allowed in Minuteman and Peacekeeper silos. In 1985, two females were first permitted to serve on a crew.

Fate of the Small ICBM. On April 1, the Air Force announced that just under $1 billion was cut from seven development contracts for the SICBM, or Midgetman, essentially halving the original allocation. Although the Defense Department had recommended that the program be terminated, it requested sufficient funds in the budget to keep the program alive until the next presidential administration could decide the missile's fate.

MX Accident. In June an MX missile experienced a system failure when it became unmoored and slipped 6-to-8 inches down into its canister. The accident caused the power and coolant umbilical cords to become severed, indicating a "missile away" report in the launch control center. The ten warhead package of the missile was subsequently removed, along with the warheads of four other missiles from the same production batch. It is believed that a faulty epoxy bond in the support skirt of the Stage 1 motor was the cause of the accident.

More Successful Missile Launches. In July two more successful launches of the Minuteman III LGM-30G were achieved, one by an air crew and the other by a ground crew. The missiles were fired from Vandenberg AFB, California, and traveled the 4,200-mile course to the Western Missile Test Range at Kwajalein. The two firings were the 133d and 134th in the Follow-on Operational Test (FOOT) series.

On 27 October, the first Minuteman III assembled by personnel permanently assigned at Vandenberg AFB, California, was successfully launched. Previously, a crew from the launching unit would be sent temporarily to Vandenberg to conduct the launch. Staff Sergeant John Brantly, a nuclear weapons specialist, suggested the establishment of a permanently assigned assembly team. The 394th ICBM Test Maintenance Squadron, certified to reassemble re-entry systems for the Minuteman II and Peacekeeper missiles as well, represents a savings of over $45,000 a year to the U.S. Air Force in temporary duty funds.

Top Strategic Combat Missile Crew. The General Thomas S. Power Strategic Missile Crew Award for 1988 was received by a crew of the 90th Strategic Missile Wing, F. E. Warren AFB, Wyoming. The Peacekeeper crew consisted of Captain Stephen G. Cullen and 1st Lieutenant Rodney L. Holder.

Missile Competition

Twenty-first Competition. SAC's Missile Combat Competition took place between 10 and 17 April. Again, the competition was held at Vandenberg AFB, California. The winner of the Blanchard Perpetual Trophy as the Best Missile Wing was the 91st Strategic Missile Wing, Minot AFB, North Dakota, edging out the 44th Strategic Missile Wing, Ellsworth AFB, South Dakota.

The other major award winners were:

Best Minuteman Wing, 91st Strategic Missile Wing

Best Missile Operations, 44th Strategic Missile Wing

Best Missile Maintenance Team, 91st Strategic Missile Wing

Best Missile Communications Team, 90th Strategic Missile Wing, F. E. Warren AFB, Wyoming

Best Missile Security Police Team, 91st Strategic Missile Wing

Best Missile Civil Engineering Team, 321st Strategic Missile Wing, Grand Forks AFB, North Dakota

1989

Organization

Two Malmstrom Wings Combined in 40th Air Division. On 7 July the 301st Air Refueling Wing and the 341st Strategic Missile Wing were placed under the 40th Air Division at Malmstrom AFB, Montana. The 301st is a KC-135 wing and the 341st is a Minuteman ICBM unit.

Operations

Largest Pacific Deployment Since 1975. In late April the Fifteenth Air Force completed the 30-day Giant Warrior exercise, with over 900 sorties flown. More than 2,000 people and 163 aircraft participated. Aircraft that participated included the largest deployment of B-1B bombers to date, from Ellsworth AFB and Dyess AFB, and B-52s from Mather AFB, Andersen AFB, and Minot AFB. Over 1,600 practice and live bombs were dropped. SAC tankers and reconnaissance aircraft also participated.

SR-71 Blackbird Lost at Sea. On 20 April a SR-71 was lost in the south China Sea following engine failure soon after take-off. It was reported to be the first Blackbird to have been lost in 17 years.

Oldest Active B-52G Retired. On 10 July SAC's oldest active B-52G bomber, serial number 58-0232, was retired. That Stratofortress entered service in 1959 and, appropriately, was nicknamed "Eldership" by the 320th Bomb Wing. The Mather AFB, California wing was the aircraft's last assignment before it was flown to SAC Headquarters to enter the SAC museum. The crew for the last flight was commanded by Colonel Dave Johnson.

During part of the Vietnam War the B-52 was assigned to Andersen AFB, Guam. The aircraft also made headlines in 1987 when it hit a bald eagle during a low-level training flight.

First Flight of B-2 Stealth. On 17 July the first flight of the Northrop B-2A Advanced Technology Bomber Stealth was successfully conducted at the Air Force Plant 42 in Palmdale, California. The crew consisted of aircraft Commander Bruce J. Hinds, Northrop chief test pilot; and Colonel Richard S. Couch, USAF, director, B-2 Combined Test Force. The 112-minute flight was successful, with the aircraft landing at the Air Force Flight Test Center at Edwards AFB. The flight test followed a delay from the originally scheduled flight on 15 July, due to a faulty fuel gauge. Low-speed taxi tests were completed on 10 July and high-speed tests were completed on 13 July.

B-52G Destroyed at Kelly AFB. On 24 July a B-52G was destroyed at Kelly AFB, Texas, after an improperly manufactured vent plug was not removed, permitting the fuel system to become overpressurized. A spill resulted, leading to an explosion that destroyed the bomber.

New Graduate School. In August, the General Curtis E. LeMay Strategic Warfare Center (SWC) was activated at Ellsworth AFB, South Dakota. The center is scheduled for full operations in 1992 and will consist of three branches: SAC Tactics School, Strategic Weapons School, and Strategic Training Center. The SWC has the designation of the 99th Strategic Weapons Wing, becoming the third active wing at Ellsworth, unprecedented for a SAC base.

Two Stratotankers Destroyed in Accidents. On 20 September, a KC-135E assigned to the Alaska Air National Guard exploded while parking after a training flight. Two boom operators were killed and all others on board, including two passengers, were injured. On 4 October, a KC-135A of the 42d Bomb Wing, Loring AFB, Maine, had completed a six-hour training mission and was returning to the home base when it exploded in mid-air over Canada. No indication of problems was given by the crew to the base radar approach control just minutes before the accident. Four of the crew were killed. Following the second accident, KC-135s were grounded until an inspection could be conducted of the fuselage electrical wiring and fuel cells.

Successful Recovery of B-1B with Failed Nose Gear. Another potential incident on 4 October was avoided when a B-1B from the 96th Bomb Wing, Dyess AFB, Texas, had to make an emergency landing. The plane's nose gear would not extend, and after circling for five hours, a successful landing was achieved at Edwards AFB, California. Several attempts to lower the gear were attempted with hard touch-and-go landings and high-g maneuvers. The pilot was Captain Jeffery Bean, who brought the bomber safely home. The failure was blamed on a malfunction in the number two hydraulic system.

Lockheed's Bill Park Leaves the "Skunk Works." On 29 September, Bill Park, director of flying operations at Lockheed's "Skunk Works," retired. Although not a member of SAC, or the military, Bill Park had a long list of firsts in the pilot's seat for some of the greatest accomplishments of SAC aircraft. He was the first pilot to fly the SR-71A Blackbird to its designated speed of over Mach 3; he was the first to land a U-2 onto the deck of an aircraft carrier; and the first to make a dead-stick landing in a U-2. His flying career ended in 1978 in an F-117 Stealth fighter crash.

Last U-2/TR-1 Delivered. On October 3 the last of 37 Lockheed U-2R/TR-1A/B delivered to SAC was turned over to the Air Force at Palmdale, California. The original contract for this procurement was awarded to Lockheed in 1979 and was a follow-on to the initial U-2 production that ended in 1969.

Stealth Bomber Refueled for First Time. On 8 November the first aerial refueling of a B-2 Stealth bomber was achieved during the sixth test flight of the plane. The entire flight took just over six hours. The crew consisted of

Northrop chief test pilot Bruce Hinds and Lieutenant Colonel John Small, USAF. A KC-10 tanker from March AFB, California, conducted several hook-ups and disconnects before taking on over 40,000 lbs of fuel.

The B-1B's First Low-Level Night Sortie. On 8 November the first low-level night sortie for the B-1B bomber, using fully automatic terrain-following equipment, was flown by a crew from the 96th Bomb Wing, Dyess AFB, Texas. The first flight was made over relatively flat terrain. A second flight on 14 November was made over undulated terrain, varying greatly in altitude. All previous low-level flights were made during the day and with good weather.

Ending SR-71 Operations. In early November the House and Senate military authorization conference effectively ended the life of the Blackbird reconnaissance aircraft. The passage of the compromise budget authorization bill brought to an end the plane's operation. Due to the high costs of operating the Mach 3 aircraft, including dedicated KC-135Q tankers, the Air Force had been working to drop the program for two years. The planes will gradually be retired from the 9th Strategic Reconnaissance Wing, Beale AFB, California, and its detachments at RAF Mildenhall, England, and Kadena AB, Okinawa.

Females Eligible for U-2 and TR-1 Pilot Positions. In late November, for the first time women were declared eligible for U-2 and TR-1 pilot opportunities. The decision was influenced by a study conducted on the possible adverse effects from high-altitude radiation, decompression, recompression, and hypothermia. Women assigned as pilots of the U-2 or TR-1 will be required to take a pregnancy test every two weeks because of potential hazards to a fetus.

Stealth Bomber Tests Continue. Also in late November, a Northrop B-2A Stealth bomber completed its seventh and eighth flights during a four-day period. On 18 November, during the seventh flight, the General Electric's engines were shut down and air started for the first time. The total flight lasted 7 hours and 17 minutes. On 22 November, the eighth flight lasted 5 hours and 48 minutes and continued the series of planned flight control and systems checkouts. The Air Force pilot for both flights was Lt. Colonel John Small; the Northrop pilots were Bruce Hinds (7th flight) and Leroy Schroeder (8th flight).

SAC Refueling Crews Play Role in Operation Just Cause. In late December, beginning on the 20th, SAC tankers from fifteen units flew more than 170 missions and logged more than 1,600 flying hours in support of the invasion of Panama, to capture dictator Manuel Noriega. More than 12 million lbs of fuel were offloaded to 270 receiver aircraft by SAC's KC-135 Stratotankers and KC-10A Extenders with a 100 percent mission success rate.

General Curtis E. LeMay Strategic Aircrew Award. The award for 1989 was presented to the S-01 crew of the 441st Bomb Squadron, 320th Bomb Wing, Mather AFB, California, for superior airmanship and performance. The crew earned the award through sustained excellence in performance, including leading several higher headquarters missions. Members of the B-52 crew were: Major Cameron K. Green, aircraft commander; 1st Lieutenants James O. Preaskorn and Allan K. Click, pilots; Major David E. Snodgrass, radar navigator; 1st Lieutenant Richard T. Gindhart, navigator; Captain James M. Tinnesz, electronic warfare operator; and Technical Sergeant Noah L. "Skip" Elliot, Jr., gunner.

General Jerome F. O'Malley Reconnaissance Crew Award. For 1989, the award was given to Major John J. Smith, a U-2/TR-1 flight commander with the 99th Strategic Reconnaissance Squadron. He was recognized for his outstanding airmanship when "with minimum navigational aids [he] was able to locate the takeoff base and accomplish flameout-landing procedures in rapidly deteriorating weather conditions, thus saving a valuable strategic reconnaissance asset," according to his nomination statement.

Omaha Trophy. The 2d Bomb Wing, Barksdale AFB, Louisiana, was selected the outstanding wing in SAC for 1989.

Weapons Loading Competition. This year's Combat Weapons Loading Competition, Giant Sword, was held at Fairchild AFB, Washington, in mid-August. It marked the first competition in which all four B-1B wings and their support crews participated in all parts of the competition. The 2d Bomb Wing from Barksdale AFB, California, won the Barrentine Trophy for the Best Munitions Competition Team, edging out a Pease AFB, New Hampshire, team. The award winners were:

Best Munitions Maintenance Unit, Best Combined Weapons Load, and Best Air-Launched Cruise Missile Load Crew, 2d Bomb Wing

Best Security Police Tactics Exercise Team, 96th Bomb Wing, Dyess AFB, Texas

Best Munitions Load Crew, 509th Bomb Wing, Pease AFB, New Hampshire

Bombing Competition

Thirty-third Competition. The Proud Shield '89 was just the second year that B-1 crews participated in the annual SAC bombing competition, but that's all it took for a B-1B unit to win the Fairchild Trophy for the bomber/tanker team with the highest competition effectiveness. The 28th Bomb Wing, Ellsworth AFB, South Dakota, slipped past the 380th Bomb Wing from Plattsburg AFB, New York.

Other major awards presented at the ceremony were:

Saunders Trophy, best tanker unit, 384th Bomb Wing, McConnell AFB, Kansas

Mathis Trophy, best bombing unit, 380th Bomb Wing, Plattsburg AFB, New York

Ryan Trophy, best unit in high- and low-level bombing, 93d Bomb Wing, Castle AFB, California

Dougherty Trophy, best SRAM results, 319th Bomb Wing, Grand Forks AFB, North Dakota

Bartsch Trophy, best B-52 unit in electronic countermeasures activity, 416th Bomb Wing, Griffiss AFB, New York

The B-2 bomber touching down at Edwards AFB following its successful first flight on 17 July 1989. During the flight, the aircraft climbed to 10,000 feet and functional checks of the basic subsystems were performed. The plane then returned to base for landing.

LeMay Trophy, best bomber crew in low-level bombing, 509th Bomb Wing, Pease AFB, New Hampshire

Meyer Trophy, best F/FB-111 unit, 380th Bomb Wing, Plattsburg AFB, New York

First aerial refueling of the B-2 Stealth bomber on 8 November 1989. The B-2 received 40,000 lbs. of JP-8 fuel from the KC-10. This was the sixth successful test mission of the flying-wing bomber, lasting six hours and three minutes.

Holloway Trophy, best KC-135 unit in celestial navigation, 301st Air Refueling Wing, Malmstrom AFB, Montana

Davis Trophy, for the most improved unit since the last competition, 319th Bomb Wing, Grand Forks AFB, North Dakota

Ellis Trophy, for the best KC-10 crew, 22d Air Refueling Wing, March AFB, California

Eaker Trophy, for the best B-1B unit, 28th Bomb Wing, Ellsworth AFB, South Dakota

Crumm Trophy, for the bomber unit with most points in all activities except electronic countermeasures and simulated SRAM firing, 28th Bomb Wing, Ellsworth AFB, South Dakota

Doolittle Trophy, for the numbered Air Force with units receiving the highest percentage of total points, 15th Air Force

Mitchell Trophy, for most points in conventional bombing, electronic combat, and fighter intercept, 93d Bomb Wing, Castle AFB, California

A new trophy, the Maynard "Snuffy" Smith B-52 Gunnery Trophy, was awarded for the first time to the B-52 unit with the most points in gunnery and fighter defense activity, to the 379th Bomb Wing, Wurtsmith AFB, Michigan.

Missiles

Advanced Cruise Missile Over Canada. On 2 March, a B-52 crew from the Air Force Flight Test Center, Edwards AFB, California, conducted the first captive-carry flight of the AGM-129A Advanced Cruise Missile. The flight was the first test of the ACM outside the United States.

First Midgetman SICBM Launch Fails. On 11 May, the first launch of the Small ICBM was attempted at Vandenberg AFB, California, from an above-ground silo. Although the flight looked normal through first-stage separation, the missile began to tumble and had to be destroyed by the range safety officer after a flight of about 70 seconds.

Subsequent investigation determined the blame for the failure was the second-stage nozzle. The Air Force claimed that 80 percent of the test objectives were met before the flight was terminated.

Another Minuteman III Successful Test. On 6 July an unarmed Minuteman III ICBM was successfully launched from Vandenberg AFB, California, by a 321st Strategic Missile Wing crew from Grand Forks AFB, North Dakota. The test marked the 138th Follow-on Operational Test (FOOT) of the Boeing LGM-30F missile. It few 4,200 miles to Kwajalein Missile Test Range in approximately 30 minutes.

Bases Named for Peacekeeper Rail-Garrison Deployment. On 29 November the Air Force announced the seven bases where the rail-garrison Peacekeeper ICBMs will be deployed. The missiles will be assigned to Barksdale AFB, Louisiana; Grand Forks AFB, North Dakota; Fairchild AFB, Washington; Dyess AFB, Texas; Little Rock AFB, Arkansas; Wurtsmith AFB, Michigan;

and F. E. Warren AFB, Wyoming. The missiles are currently housed in modified Minuteman III silos.

Twenty-five trains carrying two missiles each will be on alert in hardened shelters at each base. The first train is expected to be turned over to SAC in 1992, and the remaining scheduled to be turned over by 1994.

Top Strategic Combat Missile Crew. The General Thomas S. Power Strategic Missile Crew Award for 1989 was presented to a crew of the 351st Strategic Missile Wing, Whiteman AFB, Missouri. The Minuteman crew consisted of Captain Dennis R. Benson and Lieutenant Julia A. Gibbons. Lieutenant Gibbons made history in 1986 when she was selected to be the deputy missile combat crew commander for the first SAC male-female Minuteman crew.

1990

Resources

Personnel	Approximately 119,000 (Total)
Tactical Aircraft	960 (274 B-52, 61 FB-111, 97 B-1B, 616 ED/KC-135, 60 KC-10A, 4 E-4)
Aircraft Units	1 Bomb Wings (B-52, KC-10, KC-135)
	2 Bomb Wings (B-52)
	9 Bomb Wings (B-52, KC-135)
	2 Bomb Wings (FB-111, KC-135)
	4 Bomb Wings (B-1, KC-135)
	4 Air refueling Wings (KC-135)
	1 Air refueling Wings (KC-10)
	1 Air refueling Wings (KC-135, KC-10)
	2 Strategic Reconnaissance Wings (RC-135)
	1 Strategic Reconnaissance Wings (U-2/TR-1, KC-135)
Missiles	450 Minuteman II, 500 Minuteman III (200 with 335 kt warhead/300 with 300 kt), 50 MX Peacekeeper, 1,500 SRAM, 1,715 ALCM
Missile Units	5 Minuteman Wgs, 1 Peacekeeper/Minuteman Wg

Operations

SR-71 Blackbird Completes Last Operation. On 18 January Captain Steve Grzebiniak conducted the final operational flight of an SR-71 Blackbird from southern Japan. Kadena AB, Okinawa, the first U.S. overseas deployment base for the spy plane, also will be the first to close its SR-71 operation.

The SR-71 Blackbird Retires in Record Style. On 6 March, the SR-71 retired with style with a record-shattering flight from the West Coast to the East Coast. The Blackbird departed Edwards AFB, California, refueled over the ocean, then overflew the base, leaving a sonic boom in its wake. After a flight of 1 hour, 8 minutes, 17 seconds, equaling 1,227 miles per hour, the plane entered Washington airspace at Dulles International Airport.

The SR-71, tail number 17972, with Lieutenant Colonel Raymond Yeilding as pilot and Lieutenant Colonel Joseph T. Vida as reconnaissance officer, set four flight-time records; in addition to the 2,404.5-mile, national coast-to-coast record, the plane set three world city-pair records, for flights from Kansas City, Kansas, to Washington and from St. Louis to Cincinnati, and from Los Angeles to Washington. The SR-71 was officially retired 26 February, but Lockheed requested that one of them publicly break some records on its last flight.

The SR-71 that flew the highest number of combat sorties, 64-17976, will be displayed at the USAF Museum, Wright-Patterson AFB, Ohio. Other Blackbirds will be allocated to other museums; the Smithsonian National Air and Space Museum will house the record-breaking final-flight SR-71.

KC-135 Explosion. On 11 January the third KC-135 explosion in less than six months occurred at Pease AFB, New Hampshire. An E-model Stratotanker, belonging to the state's Air National Guard, exploded on the ramp. One firefighter was the only person injured. No one was in the tanker at the time and no other aircraft were affected.

The Peace Dividend and SAC Programs. The decline of Soviet influence and military capability in Eastern Europe has nurtured speculation on how the fiscal fallout, the so-called peace dividend, will affect the U.S. military. U.S. Defense leaders warned against a too rapid cutback in current and future weapons programs and a dramatic decrease in personnel strengths, while many members of Congress and other agencies have put in bids for the redistribution of the perceived savings.

President Bush, in the aftermath of his proposal for the fiscal year 1991 defense budget, stated that he did not intend to cut any of the most expensive weapons systems. The Congress was expected to demand faster and deeper Pentagon cutbacks.

Two areas that affect SAC and were expected to receive especially close scrutiny are the B-2 Stealth bomber and the Peacekeeper missile. The Stealth was slated for over $5.5 billion to produce five planes in FY 1991; the Stealth is expected to be one of the most inviting targets for cuts in the Pentagon budget. The MX Peacekeeper's requested budget was nearly $2.9 billion to purchase 12 more multiple-warhead missiles and to continue development and procurement of a system for basing the MX on rail cars.

President Bush Gives Pep Talk to SAC Alert Crews. On 8 February the president used the Red Phone to remind SAC crews standing alert that U.S. strategic forces have not had their mission changed despite the historical changes in Eastern Europe. President Bush spoke to the crews from the SAC Command Post, telling them,

> On behalf of all Americans, I thank you for your sacrifices. For you air crews, keep 'em flying. And for you missile crews, the pointy end is up and keep 'em in the green.

The commander-in-chief's four-minute talk was transmitted to SAC bases worldwide. He also was photographed giving the "thumbs-up" from the cockpit of a B-1B bomber.

Soviet Delegation Briefed on SAC. On 13 February, a delegation from the Supreme Soviet's Committee on Defense and State Security toured Headquarters

SAC. The 10 visitors received a briefing on SAC's view of Soviet improvements in mobile missile systems, submarines, strategic bombers, and air defenses. CINCSAC, General John T. Chain, Jr., stated that his responsibility "is to worry about capability, not intentions," in a talk that the press described as "a stern lecture."

The visit was part of a tour of U.S. military installations for the Soviet visitors.

CINCSAC Fights for Strategic Systems. On 6–7 March General Chain testified before the House and Senate Armed Services committees to reinforce the earlier warning that Chairman of the Joint Chiefs of Staff General Colin L. Powell made during the initial round of testimony on the FY 1991 defense budget. Chain recently asserted that support for the Strategic Arms Reduction Treaty (START) would be reconsidered by the top military leadership if Congress killed the B-2 program and refused to fund either of the programs to put the Peacekeeper missiles on rail cars or to put a new single-warhead Midgetman missile on tractor-trailer trucks to evade a Soviet nuclear attack.

General Chain was told by the Congress during the hearing that, "the B-2 is in trouble; it really is," by Representative William Dickinson (R-Alabama), the ranking Republican on the panel. House Committee Chairman Les Aspin (D-Wisconsin) told General Chain that "a full B-2 buy now looks extremely unlikely—the ultimate number may be closer to the 15 we've authorized to date than the 132 originally envisioned."

The CINCSAC argued to the committee that, in the event of war, he needs a bomber to penetrate Soviet air defenses and locate Soviet mobile missiles and command centers. "The B-52 can do it today. The B-1 can do it tomorrow, but we need the B-2 to do it in the out years," he said.

B-52 Makes Emergency Landing. On 16 March a B-52 made a safe emergency landing at Griffiss AFB, New York, after one of its hydraulic systems malfunctioned. The Stratofortress was on a routine night training mission from Kansas to Loring AFB, Maine, when it lost one of six on-board hydraulic systems. The in-flight emergency was described as "routine" with no danger posed to aircraft or crew at any time. The plane carried a 500-pound concrete dummy bomb upon landing; another dummy bomb had been dropped during the training mission.

Final KC-10 Joins SAC Fleet. On 4 April the 60th and final KC-10 Extender completed extensive flight testing that began in December 1988. The tests included examining the wing-mounted air refueling pod system. The underwing hose-and-drogue pods will allow the KC-10 to simultaneously refuel two to three aircraft. The Extender advanced tanker/cargo aircraft built by McDonnell Douglas will be based at Seymour Johnson AFB, North Carolina.

Missiles

Contract Awarded for Minuteman Transporters. On 10 January the Air Force awarded Martin Marietta Corporation a $33 million contract to design and build 55 missile payload transporter trailers for the Minuteman ICBM. The transporters will be used to transfer missile components from operating bases to silos and to place the warheads onto the missiles.

Another Successful Minuteman Launch. On 6 February, the 142d test launch of an unarmed Minuteman ICBM was conducted successfully from an underground silo at Vandenberg AFB.

Strategic Bomber Aircraft

B-29

The Boeing B-29 Superfortress was the most advanced bomber aircraft to see operational service in World War II. It was used in conventional and low-level, night incendiary attacks against Japan. (The former were not particularly successful, leading General Curtis LeMay to resort to the latter tactic which was highly so.) The aircraft was also employed most profitably in the aerial mining of Japanese home waters. The B-29 was the world's first nuclear delivery vehicle with aircraft from the 393rd Bombardment Squadron (Very Heavy) of the 509th Composite Group dropping atomic bombs on Hiroshima and Nagasaki in August 1945. Another B-29 from the 509th (redesignated as a very heavy bomb group) dropped an atomic bomb in the Bikini atomic tests of July 1946.

B-29s were the only bomber aircraft assigned to SAC when that command was established in 1946. They again were used in the conventional bombing role during the Korean War (1950-1953). The last were retired as bomber aircraft in 1954, after which many continued to serve SAC in specialized roles. Eighty-eight B-29s were transferred to the RAF in the early 1950s with the designation Washington B.I. These were the only U.S. strategic bombers to serve with a foreign air force in the post-World War II period.

The aircraft was designed to meet a U.S. Army 1940 requirement for a bomber to carry 2,000 pounds of bombs against targets 2,500 miles away, with a maximum bomb load of 16,000 pounds, with a heavy defensive armament. Boeing, with considerable multi-engine bomber experience (primarily the four-engine XB-15 and B-17) responded with Model 345 that promised to meet all Army requirements except speed (only 382 mph vice stipulated 400 mph). Competitors were the Lockheed B-30, Douglas B-31, and Consolidated B-32. Only the last went beyond the design stage and 115 B-32s were built, with 15 actually being used in Pacific combat.

More than 1,500 production B-29s were ordered between September 1941 and September 1942, when the first of several prototypes was flown. This large-scale pre-flight production was unprecedented in aviation history. B-29s were produced by Bell (668 aircraft) and Martin (536) in addition to Boeing (2,766).

The B-29 was a streamlined aircraft, with two separate pressurized sections in the fuselage, connected by a tunnel above the two bomb bays, and a pres-

141.2'

28.5'

99.0'

27.8'

14.1"

NOSE COMP. | PILOT'S COMP. | NAV. & RADIO COMP. | FWD. BOMB BAY | WING BAY | REAR BOMB BAY | REAR UPPER TURRET | RADAR OPERATOR | CAMERA | LOWER TURRET | TAIL AMMO | TAIL TURRET

surized tail gunner's position. The heavy defensive armament consisted of five remotely controlled gun turrets; two dorsal turrets with twin .50-caliber MGs, with the forward turret having four guns in later aircraft; two ventral turrets with twin .50-caliber MGs; and a tail turret, normally with twin .50-caliber MGs plus a single 20-mm cannon. For low-level fire bomb raids against Japanese cities and oil refineries, many B-29s were stripped of all armament except tail guns, an improved configuration made possible with night-bombing tactics and minimal Japanese fighter opposition. Most of the F-13 reconnaissance aircraft had only tail guns or were completely unarmed.

In the post-war period B-29s served in a variety of special-mission roles, with four being flown by the U.S. Navy (P2B-1 series).

Status: Retired; 3,970 produced through May 1946 (several thousand additional B-29s were cancelled at the end of World War II).

Variants:

XB-29	Prototype aircraft; first flight 21 September 1942; 3 built.
YB-29	Service test aircraft; first flight 26 June 1943; 14 built.
B-29	Production aircraft; 101,082 lbs. combat, 133,500 lbs. normal maximum; 11 crew; 3,659 built (plus 311 completed as B-29Bs).
B-29A	Production aircraft; modified wing and improved engines (fuel decreased by 213 gallons, but overall range increased); 101,480 lbs. combat, 133,500 lbs. normal maximum; 11 crew; 1,119 built.
RB-29/RB-29A	Conversion to photographic reconnaissance; designated F-13/F-13A until 1948; no guns in most aircraft; fitted with cameras and additional fuel tanks in bomb bays; 118 converted from B-29/B-29A.
B-29B	Final production aircraft; all guns deleted except tail turret; fitted with APG-15 gun control radar system; 311 built.
B-29C	Planned production variant; improved engines; cancelled in 1945.
B-29D	Improved design; designation changed to B-50 in 1946.
XB-29E	Aircraft fitted for fire control tests; 1 converted from B-29 in 1946.

B-29 Super Fortress (Boeing photo)

B-29A Super Fortress

B-29F	Aircraft winterized for arctic operations; 6 converted from B-29.
XB-29G	Engine test aircraft with retractable turbojet in bomb bay; 1 converted from B-29B.
XB-29H	Aircraft fitted for armament tests; 1 converted from B-29A in 1947.
YB/RB-29J	Improved reconnaissance aircraft; 6 converted from B-29.
YKB-29J	First flying-boom tankers; 2 converted from RB-29J in 1948.
CB-29K	Aircraft stripped for cargo; 1 converted from B-29 in 1949.
B-29L	Initial designation of KB-29M.
KB-29M	Aircraft converted to hose-drogue tankers; armament deleted and additional fuel tanks and hose fitted; 92 converted from B-29 from 1948 onward.
B-29MR	Standard bomber aircraft fitted for long-range operations capable of refueling in-flight from KB-29Ms; 74 modified.
B-29N	Apparently not used.
KB-29P	Flying-boom tankers; armament deleted, additional fuel tanks and special radar installed; 116 converted from B-29 from 1949-1951.
B-29Q	Apparently not used.
B-29R	Apparently not used.
B-29S	Apparently not used.
YKB-29T	Triple-point hose tanker aircraft; 1 converted from KB-29M.
QB-29	Radio-controlled target drone configuration; several converted from 1954 onward.
SB-29	Search-and-rescue variant; fitted with large droppable lifeboat; all weapons deleted; 16 converted.
WB-29	Weather reconnaissance aircraft; several converted.
P2B	Navy designation for B-29s acquired for long-range search missions; 1 modified for air launching of D-558-II research aircraft; 2 designated P2B-1S and 2 P2B-2S; all acquired 1947.
XB-39	First YB-29 as refitted with in-line piston engines.
XB-44	B-29A with improved engines; initially redesignated B-29D; Reordered as B-50.
Washington B.I	British designation for 88 B-29/B-29A aircraft transferred for service from 1950 to 1955.

Characteristics: (B-29A)

Crew 11 (pilot, copilot, bombardier, navigator, flight engineer, radio operator, radar operator, 4 gunners)

Weight 72,206 lbs. empty; 101,480 lbs. combat; 133,500 lbs. maximum normal takeoff, 140,000 lbs. maximum overload takeoff

Dimensions Span 141.2 ft., length 99 ft., height 27.8 ft., wing area 1,736 ft.^{2}

Engines 4 Wright R-3350-57 or 57A radial piston (2,200 hp each)

Fuel 9,150 gallons internal

Speed 365 mph at 25,000 ft.; 220 mph cruise

Range 1,932-mile radius with 10,000-lb. bomb load; 1,561-mile radius with 20,000-lb. load; 5,420-mile ferry range

Ceiling 31,850 ft.

Payload 1 gravity nuclear weapon (when modified) or 4 × 2,000-lb. bombs or 8 × 2,000-lb. bombs or 12 × 1,600-lb. bombs or 12 × 1,000-lb. bombs or 40 × 500-lb. bombs (20,000 lbs. maximum)

Guns 10 or 12 × .50-caliber MG with 500 rounds per barrel; 1 × 20-mm cannon in some later aircraft with 60 rounds (replaced by MG in some aircraft)

Electronics APQ-7 or APQ-23A bombing-navigation radar

B-50

The Boeing B-50 Superfortress was basically a B-29 with improved engines, the prototype being a B-29A originally designated XB-44 with R-4360-33 Major Wasp engines by Pratt & Whitney. This change and other improvements were incorporated in the B-29D variant which was put into production by Boeing in 1945. However, the aircraft's designation was changed to B-50 prior to the start of deliveries.

A low production rate of B-50s continued after World War II as the aircraft replaced the B-29 as the primary SAC bomber. Production was increased with the worsening U.S.-Soviet relations in the late 1940s, with B-50s remaining in SAC in the bomber role until October 1955.

The B-50 could be easily distinguished from its antecedent by the larger engine nacelles, taller tail fin, and 1,500-gallon wing tanks. The B-50 also had improved wing materials, undercarriage, and hydraulic controls. There were several special mission configurations.

Status: Retired; 370 produced through March 1953.

Variants:

B-50A	Production aircraft; 168,408 lbs. gross; 11-12 crew; first flight 25 June 1947; 79 built.
TB-50A	B-36 conversion trainer; 11 converted from B-50A.
B-50B	Production aircraft; 170,000 lbs. gross; 11-12 crew; first flight 14 January 1949; 45 built.
EB-50B	Test aircraft; 1 B-50B converted.
RB-50B	Reconnaissance aircraft; fitted with 9 cameras and weather monitoring equipment; 700-gallon wing tanks; 44 B-50B converted.
YB-50C	Prototype aircraft based on B-50A with improved engines; designation changed to B-54A; 14 B-54As and 29 RB-54As were ordered, but none completed.
B-50D	Production aircraft; 173,000 lbs. gross; 11 crew; fitted with 700-gallon wing tanks; first flight 23 May 1949; 222 built.
DB-50D	Aircraft modified for launching GAM-63 Rascal air-to-surface missile; 1 B-50D converted.
TB-50D	B-36 conversion trainer; 11 B-50D converted.

BOMB	PILOT	ENG & AUX CREW MEMBER	NAV RADAR OPER	FORWARD BOMB BAY	RADOME	REAR BOMB BAY	GUNNER	TURRET	RADIO RCM OPER	EQUIP	TURRET	AMMO	TAIL TURRET

WB-50D	Weather reconnaissance aircraft; several B-50D converted.
RB-50E	Reconnaissance aircraft; 14 RB-50B converted.
RB-50F	Improved reconnaissance configuration; 14 RB-50B converted.
RB-50G	Improved reconnaissance configuration; 15 RB-50B converted.
TB-50H	Training aircraft for B-47 bombardier/navigators; no guns or in-flight refueling capability; 164,500 lbs. gross; 15 crew; first flight 29 April 1952; 24 built.

TB-50D Super Fortress; note "chins" on large engine nacelles

B-50 Super Fortress

WB-50H	Weather reconnaissance aircraft; several TB-50H converted.
KB-50J	Flying-boom tanker; fitted with 2 J-47 turbojet pods in place of wing tanks; 101 B-50D and 11 TB-50D converted.
KB-50K	Flying-boom tanker; similar to KB-50J configuration; 24 TB-50H and WB-50H converted.

Characteristics: (B-50A)

Crew	11-12 (pilot, copilot, bombardier, navigator, flight engineer, radio operator, 1-2 radar operators, 4 gunners)
Weight	81,050 lbs. empty; 121,700 lbs. combat; 168,480 lbs. maximum
Dimensions	Span 141.2 ft., length 99 ft., height 32.75 ft., wing area 1,736 ft.^{2}
Engines	4 Pratt & Whitney R-4360 Wasp Major radial piston (3,500 hp each)
Fuel	
Speed	385 mph at 25,000 ft.; 235 mph cruise
Range	2,325-mile radius with 10,000-lb. bomb load; 5,270-mile ferry range
Ceiling	37,000 ft.
Payload	1 gravity nuclear weapon or 20,000 lbs. bombs (load options as B-29)
Guns	13 × .50-caliber MG with 500 rounds per barrel
Electronics	APQ-24 bombing-navigation radar

B-36

The Convair B-36—unofficially known as the "Peacemaker"—was the world's largest bomber in terms of length and wingspan. Conceived in 1941, when it still appeared the German armies might land in Britain, the B-36 was planned as a trans-Atlantic bomber to strike Europe from bases in the United States. The design goal was to carry a 10,000-pound bomb load against targets 5,000 miles away. Development of the B-36 was delayed by the Convair B-24 and then B-32 bomber production, but the giant bomber was ordered into production in mid-1943 for eventual use against the Japanese home islands. Still, the prototype XB-36 did not fly until three years later.

After World War II the aircraft was pursued as a strategic nuclear bomber amidst considerably controversy. General George C. Kenney, the first commander SAC, stated: "The B-36 is a night bomber. I would not use it in the daytime," and further declared the plane might be suitable for the Navy's anti-submarine mission. Kenney's successor, General LeMay, supported the B-36, claiming "We can get a B-36 over a target and not have the enemy know it is there until the bombs hit." Another aspect of the controversy was Navy opposition to a U.S. defense strategy based only on nuclear attack, which the Navy leadership felt was personified by the B-36 and reductions in Navy funds. The Navy's opposition was labeled the "Admiral's revolt" and resulted in special Congressional hearings into the B-36 program.

The huge B-36 had a relatively conventional design except for the six-piston pusher engines. From the B-36D variant onward these were supplemented by four turbojets in twin pods under the wings. These boosted top speed from 381 mph to 435 mph. The aircraft had pressurized crew compartments forward and amidships, connected by an 80-foot-long tunnel; a sled on tracks carried crewmen between the compartments. The RB variants had a third pressurized compartment. The tail gun was a remote, radar-controlled system. Four separate weapon bays were provided with a maximum bomb load being two 42,000-pound "Grand Slam" high-explosive bombs in the B-36D. Normal maximum bomb load was 72,000 pounds.

Defensive armament from the B-36 onward consisted of eight remotely controlled gun turrets, each with two 20-mm cannon. The six fuselage turrets could retract and be faired over while in flight to reduce aerodynamic drag, leaving only the nose and tail turrets exposed. An unusual defensive scheme was the proposal to have the B-36 carry its own fighter escort. Using part of the bomb bay capacity, the aircraft was to carry and launch a fighter, which could also be recovered in flight. The XF-85 Goblin was designed for this role, but only the GRF-86F Thunderstreak, a reconnaissance aircraft, was operationally carried by the GRB-36D variant.

Some B-36D/H/J aircraft were stripped of all armament except the tail cannon and, with a crew of nine or more, could fly high-altitude missions. These were called "featherweight" bombers.

Status: Retired; 446 produced through August 1954.

Variants:

XB-36   Prototype aircraft; 265,000 lbs. gross; first flight 8 August 1946; 1 built.

PILOT'S COMPARTMENT | TURRET BAY | BOMB BAYS 1 - 2 - 3 - 4 | TURRET BAY | AFT COMPARTMENT | TAIL SECTION

YB-36   Prototype aircraft; change to YB-36A with modified landing gear; 1 built.

B-36A   Production aircraft; raised "green house" cockpit; no armament; used primarily for training; first flight 28 August 1947; 22 built.

B-36B   Production aircraft; fully armed; 328,000 lbs. gross, 15 crew (including 4 relief); first flight 8 July 1948; 73 built. (First fully operational aircraft.)

YB-36C   Proposed variant with 6 tractor engines; design cancelled and 34 aircraft on order completed as B-36B.

B-36D   Production aircraft; fitted with 4 turbojet engines; improved navigation-bombing radar and gun fire control; 357,500 lbs. gross; 15 crew; first flight 26 March 1949; 64 converted from B-36B and 22 built.

RB-36D   Reconnaissance variant with 2 bomb bays modified for 14 cameras (bomb capability retained in 2 bays); guns retained; 357,500 lbs. gross; 22 crew; first flight 18 Decem-

B-36D with four J47 turbojet engines in twin pods

B-36B

ber 1949; 7 converted from B-36B and 17 built; 12 subsequently modified to GRB-36D to carry "parasite" fighter.

RB-36E	Reconnaissance variant similar to RB-36D; 22 converted from B-36A.
B-36F	Production aircraft; similar to B-36D; first flight 18 November 1950; 28 built.
RB-36F	Reconnaissance aircraft; similar to RB-36E with longer range; 24 built.
YB-36G	Turbojet-propelled variant; designation changed to YB-60.
B-36H	Production aircraft; similar to B-36F; first flight 5 April 1952; 81 built.
RB-36H	Reconnaissance variant; improved RB-36F; 73 built.
NB-36H	Aircraft modified to serve as nuclear engine test platform; fitted with reactor (did not power aircraft); 47 flights made from 1955 to 1957; 1 converted from B-36H.
B-36J	Production aircraft; 410,000 lbs. gross; 15 crew; first flight 3 September 1953; 33 built.

Characteristics: (B-36J)

Crew	15 (pilot, copilot, 2 navigators, bombardier, flight engineer, radio operator, radar operator, 2 ECM operators, 5 gunners)
Dimensions	Span 230 ft., length 162.1 ft., height 46.6 ft., wing area 4,772 ft.^{2}
Engines	6 Pratt & Whitney R-4360 Major Wasp in-line piston (3,800 hp each) and 4 General Electric J47-GE-19 turbojet (5,200

The XF-85 fighter was launched and recovered from an airborne bomber with an articulated trapeze. The fighter had a wing span of 21.1 feet and a length of 14.9 feet to permit carrying in a B-36 bomb bay. The "parasite" aircraft concept was used by the U.S. Navy before World War II when the airships Akron and Macon operated trapeze aircraft.

	lbs. static thrust each for 30 minutes; 4,730 lbst continuous)
Fuel	33,400 gallons internal; in addition, two bomb bays could each be fitted with 2,996-gallon tanks for long-range missions
Speed	411 mph at 36,400 ft.; 391 mph cruise
Range	3,990-mile radius with 10,000-lb. bombs; 2,399-mile radius with 72,000-lb. load; 9,443-mile ferry range
Ceiling	39,900 ft. combat; 45,200 ft. maximum
Payload	4 gravity nuclear weapons or 2 × 42,000-lb. bombs or 12 × 4,000-lb. bombs or 28 × 2,000-lb. bombs or 72 × 1,000-lb. bombs or 132 × 500-lb. bombs (normal maximum 72,000 lbs.)

A B-29 was modified to serve as an experimental mother aircraft for the XF-85 Goblin "parasite" fighter. The diminutive—4,850 pounds gross weight—fighter was to have been carried by B-36s to provide fighter escort as the bombers neared enemy territory. Only one XF-85 was built by McDonnell Aircraft. (McDonnell photo)

Guns	16 × 20-mm cannon with 600 rounds per barrel except 400 rounds per barrel in nose turret
Electronics	K-3A bombing-navigation radar, APG-41A tail gunfire control radar

B-47

The Boeing B-47 Stratojet was the first swept-wing, jet-propelled bomber produced in large numbers by any nation. It was in many respects a revolutionary aircraft. Bill Gunston, a leading aviation writer, has observed that the B-47 was "a design so advanced technically as to appear genuinely futuristic." In addition to its high speed and sleek configuration, the B-47 was highly automated, permitting a reduction in crew from the 11 men in a B-50—of roughly the same gross weight—to only three men, and the deletion of all gun armament except for a remotely controlled tail turret. Speed and defensive electronics permitted the elimination of the large number of guns found in earlier bombers.

The U.S. Army Air Forces issued its first requirement for a jet bomber late in 1943. Boeing initiated several designs, with post-war examination of German aircraft data indicating the advantages of the swept-wing configurations. Subsequently, Boeing developed a design with thin, laminar-flow wings swept back 35 degrees, with six turbojet engines mounted in twin and single pods beneath the wings. These were supplemented with provisions for solid-fuel rockets in the rear fuselage for accelerated takeoffs. (These rockets were incorrectly designated as JATO for *Jet* Assisted TakeOff.) The main landing gear was fitted in tandem, extending from the fuselage, with smaller wheels on outriggers extending from the wings. Between the main landing gear wells was the single bomb bay, which could accommodate a single gravity nuclear weapon or 10,000 pounds of conventional bombs (up to 22,000 pounds maximum in overload condition).

Gun armament in some B-47As and most B-47Bs consisted of two .50-caliber MGs in the remotely controlled tail turret (controlled by the co-pilot/weaponeer). Early in the B-47E program two 20-mm cannon were fitted in the tail.

Boeing production of the B-47 was supplemented by Douglas and Lockheed assembly lines to produce more of these aircraft than any other Western bomber of the post-World War II period. However, the exact number produced cannot be fully documented. Official reports list from about 2,000 B-47s to the 2,258 tabulated below, the differences being in the estimates of B-47B and B-47E aircraft.

The number of B-47s in service peaked in early 1957 with 28 medium bomb wings (each with 45 UE) flying 1,260 B-47s, with some 300 reconnaissance

116.0'

44.3'

107.1'

28.0'

NOSE COMPT.	PILOT & COPILOT COMPT.	WHEEL WELL	BOMB BAY	FUEL	WHEEL WELL	FUEL	ELECTRONICS	SURFACE CONTROLS	TAIL TURRET

variants in service, plus another 300 B-47s of various types in training, maintenance, and other categories. In the early 1960s Secretary of Defense Robert McNamara accelerated the retirement of B-47s as part of his emphasis on ICBMs in place of manned bombers. The last bombers were withdrawn from SAC in February 1966, with some RB-47s remaining in the reconnaissance role with SAC until December of the following year. However, during the next decade the U.S. Navy took three B-47Es from storage and, with contractor flight crews, operated them as EB-47Es in support of missile and electronic warfare development programs.

Status: Retired; 2,048 aircraft produced through February 1957.

Variants:

XB-47	Prototype; 125,000 lbs. gross; 3 crew; first flight 17 December 1947; 2 built.
B-47A	Service test aircraft; similar to XB-47; 160,000 lbs. gross; first flight 25 June 1950; 10 built.
B-47B	Production aircraft; provision for 2 × 1,500-gallon wing tanks and in-flight refueling; 180,000 lbs. gross; 3 crew; first flight 26 April 1951; 399 built.
YDB-47B	Aircraft modified to launch GAM-63 Rascal air-to-surface missile; 1 B-47B converted in 1953.
DB-47B	Aircraft modified for radio control of QB-47 and other target drones; 2 B-47B converted.
YRB/RB-47B	Aircraft fitted with 8-camera reconnaissance pod in bomb bay; used mostly as trainers for RB-47E; 24 B-47B converted in 1953-1954.
TB-47B	Aircraft modified as trainers for B-47E; 51 B-47B converted in 1953-1954.
WB-47B	Aircraft modified for use with Tiros weather satellite; 1 B-47B converted.
YB-47C	Modified engine configuration; aircraft reclassified XB-56 and subsequently YB-56; project cancelled.
XB-47D	Experimental turbojet/turboprop-propelled aircraft; first flight 26 August 1955; 2 B-47B converted.
B-47E	Production aircraft; 198,180 lbs. gross takeoff (could be refueled in flight to 206,700 lbs.); 3 crew; first flight 30

The 1,000th B-47 produced for the Strategic Air Command is shown with its special markings as well as the SAC shield and band on its nose. This aircraft flew for the first time exactly seven years after the first XB-47 took to the skies. (Boeing photo)

XB-47D; standard B-47B fitted with two T49 turboprop engines.

	January 1953; 1,350 built (including 274 by Douglas and 385 by Lockheed).
NB-47E	Research aircraft; 2 B-47E converted.
QB-47E	Aircraft modified as "non-destruct" radio-controlled target drones; 14 B-47E converted.
RB-47E	Reconnaissance aircraft; 11 cameras fitted in bomb bay; 3 crew; first flight 3 July 1953; 240 built.
ERB/RB-47H	Aircraft modified for training; several B-47E converted.
YB-47F	Aircraft modified for probe-and-drogue refueling from KB-47G tanker; 1 B-47B converted.
KB-47G	Aircraft modified as tanker for probe-and-drogue refueling experiments; 1 B-47B converted.
ERB-RB/47H	Special reconnaissance aircraft fitted for electronic surveillance; compartment in bomb bay housed equipment and operators; 220,000 lbs. gross takeoff (could be refueled in flight to 221,000 lbs.); 5-6 crew; first flight June 1955; 32 built.
YB-47J	Aircraft fitted to evaluate advanced bombing-navigation radar; 1 B-47E converted.
RB-47K	Aircraft fitted for weather and photographic reconnaissance; similar to RB-47E; 15 built.
EB-47L	Aircraft modified for communications relay; 35 B-47E converted in 1963.
CL-52	Aircraft transferred to Canada to test turbojet engine (fitted on starboard side of fuselage); 1 B-47B transferred in 1956.

Characteristics: (B-47E-II)

Crew	3 (pilot, copilot, bombardier/navigator)
Weight	80,756 lbs. empty; 124,875 lbs. combat takeoff; 221,000 lbs. maximum (refueled in flight)

Dimensions	Span 116 ft., length 107.1 ft., height 28 ft., wing area 1,428 ft.²
Engines	6 General Electric J-47-GE-25 turbojet (7,200 lbs. static thrust each for 5 minutes; 5,670 lbst continuous)
Fuel	14,610 gallons internal plus 3,390 gallons in drop tanks
Speed	606 mph at 16,300 ft. maximum; 557 mph at 38,500 ft. cruise
Range	2,014-mile radius with 10,000-lb. bombs; 4,647-mile ferry range
Ceiling	47,000 ft.
Payload	1 gravity nuclear weapon or 3 to 6 × 2,000-lb. bombs or 6 to 18 × 1,000-lb. bombs or 13 to 28 × 500-lb. bombs (the larger bomb loads could be carried in B-47E No. 617 and later aircraft with modification kit)
Guns	2 × 20-mm cannon with 350 rounds per barrel
Electronics	K-4A bombing-navigation radar, A-5 or MD-4 tail gunfire control radar, APS-54 warning radar

B-52

The Boeing B-52 Stratofortress has been the principal bomber of the Strategic Air Command since the 1950s; in 1990, it is operated by 12 of SAC's 18 bomb wings. The B-52 was designed to provide a high-altitude strategic bomber with intercontinental ranges. However, the range goals were not met during design, and the B-52 gross weight was "frozen" at about 480,000 lbs, with in-flight refueling to permit long-range missions.

The original Boeing XB-52 contract, awarded in July 1948, was for a turbo-prop aircraft with a 20-degree wing sweep. By the end of the year the XB-52 was redesigned with eight turbojet engines in twin pods, two per wing, slung well forward under wings swept back at 35 degrees, similar to the configuration of the B-47. The wings flex considerably during flight.

The B-52 is capable of both conventional free-fall bomb delivery and air-to-ground missile launch missions. B-52s were used in the conventional bombing role in the Vietnam War. Although originally designed as a nuclear bomber, the existing B-52 force may be deployed in various conventional missions, including show of force, precision strikes, and defense suppression. The plane's capabilities also include sea surveillance and surface ship air interdiction with anti-ship missiles.

The fuselage is long, slab-sided, and capacious. The flight deck is well forward, behind a stepped windshield and blunt nose. The two main gear legs are arranged side-by-side, ahead and behind the weapons bay. The evolution of the B-52 has seen extensive offensive avionics and electronic warfare updates as well as improvements to basic systems. In 1969, the G and H models were fitted with a Stability Augmentation System (SAS) to improve low-altitude ride and extend airframe life.

The weapons payload is carried in an internal weapon bay and on wing pylons located between the inboard pair of engines and the fuselage. About 60 percent of the B-52Gs carry 12 Air-Launched Cruise Missiles (ALCM) on pylons. The remaining non-ALCM B-52Gs are being fitted with the Integrated Conventional Stores Management System (ICSMS), a software upgrade that permits weapons computers to target and launch both nuclear and conventional weapons.

The B-52H is being fitted with the Common Strategic Rotary Launcher (CSRL) in the weapons bay that will carry free-fall nuclear weapons, Short-Range Attack Missiles (SRAM), and ALCM. All B-52Hs are scheduled to be fitted with the CSRL by the end of FY 1993. When the AGM-129 Advanced Cruise Missile (ACM) enters service, it will be deployed first on the B-52Hs; the missiles will be carried on external pylons until the aircraft are fitted with CSRLs.

The Defense Department posture statement on U.S. strategic forces stated that 98 B-52Gs and "about" 70 B-52Hs were equipped to carry ALCM. The

B-52H Stratofortress in Vietnam-era camouflage

B-52G has a remote-control tail turret with four 50-cal. machine guns and the B-52H has a tail turret with a single 20-mm Gatling-type cannon.

Status: Initial operational capability in June 1955; first flight (YB-52) was 15 April 1952. 744 B-52s were produced and over 270 B-52G/Hs remain in service in early 1990.

Variants:

XB-52	Prototype with tandem bubble canopy; 5 in crew; first flight on 2 October 1952 (after YB-52); 1 built.
YB-52	Development prototype, also with tandem bubble canopy; first flight 15 April 1952; 1 built.
B-52A	Development aircraft with J57-P-19W engines, side-by-side crew cabin, slightly longer fuselage, first with tail guns, outboard wing tanks; first flight 5 August 1954; 3 built.

YB-52 Stratofortress; note early tandem cockpit (Boeing photo)

NB-52A	B-52A modified for NASA to air launch X-15 hypersonic research aircraft; 2 modified.
B-52B	Initial production version with J57-P-19W/29WA or J57-F-19W/29WA engines, crew of 8; first flight 25 January 1955; 50 built. 27 of these were fitted with removable weapons bay pod equipped with cameras, electronic sensors, and provisions for 2 operators; redesignated RB-52B; a few, designated NB-52B, were converted to carry and launch X-15 research aircraft.
B-52C/D	Production versions similar to B-52B but with added fuel capacity, crew of 6; B-52C first flight on 9 March 1956, B-52D first flight on 4 June 1956; retired in late 1983; 205 built.
B-52E	Production version similar to B-52C/D, but with improved navigation system, first flight 3 October 1957; 100 built.
B-52F	Production version with J57-P-43WA/43WB or J57-F-3WA/43WB engines and modified wing and engine pod design; first flight 6 May 1958; 89 built.

A B-52G configured for the maritime patrol role with eight Harpoon anti-ship missiles fitted on inboard wing pylons. The B-52 also made an excellent minelayer with the CAPTOR anti-submarine homing mine. Photo courtesy of McDonnell Douglas Corp.

B-52G	Similar to B-52F with a 1-ft fuselage stretch, roll control by spoilers only, increased fuel capacity, tail crew position deleted, shorter tail fin, and air-to-ground and anti-ship (8 to 12 AGM-84 Harpoon) missile capability; first flight on 26 September 1958; 193 built, the first entering service in early 1959.

B-52H   Similar to B-52G with TF-33-P-3 engines, 1 20-mm cannon in tail turret instead of four-gun .50-cal. (12.7-mm) machine gun mount; first flight on 6 March 1961; 102 built.

Characteristics: (B-52H)

Crew   6 (2 pilots, navigator, radar operator, electronic warfare operator, gunner)

Weight   195,000 lbs empty; 488,000 lbs maximum takeoff; 60,000 lbs maximum bombload

Dimensions   Span 185 ft, length 159 ft, height 40.7 ft, wing area 4,000 ft.^{2}

Engines   8 Pratt & Whitney TF33-P-3 turbofan (approx 17,000 lbs static thrust each

Fuel   Iinternal fuel capacity 46,000 gal

Speed   650 mph (Mach 0.95); cruise speed at altitude 509 mph) (Mach 0.77)

Range   More than 10,000 miles

Ceiling   55,000 ft

Payload   Max conventional weapons load may consist of 24 X 750-lb weapons on pylons and 84 X 500-lb weapons in bay

Nuclear weapons payload consists of up to 20 X AGM-69A SRAM or X 12 AGM-86B ALCM or 4 gravity nuclear weapons in the weapons bay and 12 X SRAM or ALCM on wing pylons (approx 70 B-52G are fitted with AGM-84; Harpoon anti-ship missiles)

Guns   20-mm Gatling-type cannon (H); four 50-cal. machine guns (G)

Electronics   ASQ-38 analog bombing and navigational radar, APN-218 doppler navigation system, ASN-131 precision inertial navigation system, and APN-224 pulse radar altimeter.

The B-52G and B-52H are also fitted with a chin-mounted Electro-optical Viewing System (EVS), which consists of an AVQ-22 Low-Light-Level TV (LLLTV) and an AAQ-6 Forward Looking Infrared (FLIR) system.

Defensive avionics currently include the ALQ-155 EW power management system, ALQ-122 Smart Noise Operation Equipment (SNOE) false target generator, ALR-46 digital radar warning receiver, ALQ-117 tail-mounted deception jammer for use against radar-guided missiles (later upgraded as Pave Mint, ALQ-172), and ALQ-153 tail warning system.

B-58

The Convair B-58 Hustler is the only supersonic strategic bomber to enter squadron service in the West. It was characterized by its small size, advanced design with weapons and sensors carried in an external pod, and comparatively brief service career. The design evolved from an Air Force competition in 1949 which sought to develop a supersonic strategic bomber and reconnaissance aircraft. A relatively small number of B-58s served in SAC for the decade of the 1960s. Although the sleek-lined aircraft set several speed records, it was not well liked because of its comparatively short range and the small numbers procured required a disproportionate share SAC support resources. And, reportedly, General LeMay, after flying the B-58, declared it was too small . . . "it didn't fit my 'arse'."

The aircraft had a long, sleek fuselage and delta wing. The fuselage, with a needle nose, had an area-rule or "Coke bottle" configuration. The delta wing alleviated the need for horizontal tail surfaces. The four turbojet engines, originally proposed in twin pods, were mounted well forward on the wing, in single nacelles. In an effort to minimize aircraft size and improve performance, an internal weapons bay was deleted in favor of an external pod that could carry fuel, sensors, electronic countermeasures, and nuclear weapons. In the strategic attack role the B-58's MB-1C pod would carry fuel for the fuel for reaching the target and the nuclear weapon. The entire 62-foot pod would then be released over the target. Alternative pod concepts included cameras, EW and other special equipment in the upper half that would be retained, and the weapon and fuel tank in the lower half.

The three-man crew was seated in tandem cockpits, with a dual-control variant also being procured in small numbers. A single 20-mm rotary-barrel cannon ("Gatling" gun) was fitted in the tail.

B-58s were in service with SAC from August 1960 until November 1969.

Designation: The B-58 was the last B-series aircraft to enter SAC operational service at the time this book went to press.

Status: Retired; 116 built through October 1962.

Variants:

XB-58   Prototype; first flight 11 November 1956; 2 built.
YB-58A   Service test; 28 built.
B-58A   Production aircraft; first flight September 1959; 86 built.

Prototype B-58 Hustler

NB-58A	Test vehicle for J93 engine of XB-70 (installed in centerline nacelle); 1 converted from B-58A.
TB-58A	Training aircraft; dual controls fitted in two front cockpits; operational equipment deleted; first flight 10 May 1960; 8 converted from YB-58A.

Characteristics: (B-58A)

Crew	3 (pilot, navigator-bombardier, defensive systems operator)
Weight	55,560 lbs. empty; 163,000 lbs. maximum takeoff; 167,321 lbs. maximum (refueled in flight); weights without MB-1C mission pod, which weighed 8,555 lbs.
Dimensions	Span 56.8 ft., length 96.8 ft., height 31.4 ft., wing area 1,542.5 ft.²
Engines	4 General Electric J79-GE-5B turbojet (15,500 lbs. static thrust with afterburner 120 minutes; 10,300 lbst continuous)
Fuel	10,924 gallons internal plus 4,156 gallons in MB-1C mission pod
Speed	1,419 mph at 65,000 ft. (Mach 2) maximum; 690 mph at sea level (Mach 0.92) maximum; over 600 mph cruise (Mach 0.92)
Range	1,612-mile radius on high-altitude mission; 2,470-mile radius on maximum-range mission; 4,721-mile ferry range
Ceiling	Approximately 70,000 ft.; approximately 63,000 ft. in high-altitude combat mission
Payload	MB-1C mission pod with nuclear weapon (W39Y1-1)
Guns	1 × 20-mm M-61 rotary-barrel cannon with 1,120 rounds ammunition
Electronics	ALQ-16 radar track breaker, MD-7 gunfire control radar, ASQ-42 weapons control system

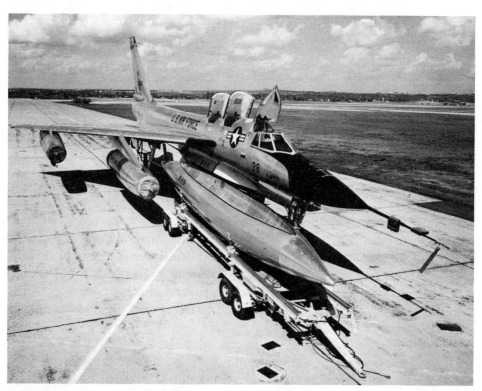

B-58 Hustler being fitted with lower portion of fuel-weapons pod; the upper portion of the pod has already been attached to the aircraft. Note tandem seating arrangement for three-man crew. (Convair/General Dynamics photo)

B-70

The North American B-70 Valkyrie was developed as a supersonic strategic bomber to succeed the B-52 as an intercontinental strike aircraft with similar range and payload, but a supersonic speed. Formal development of the aircraft began in July 1955 with North American Aviation (now Rockwell International) receiving a competitive design contract later that year. The firm was named winner of the competition in December 1957 with contracts being awarded for prototype fabrication.

Full development of the B-70 was cancelled late in 1959 by the Department of Defense with only a single prototype being approved for completion. Subsequently, Air Force efforts to restart the program led to its being reapproved as a bomber aircraft in October 1960. Then, as a counter to pressure to again halt the program, in 1961 the Air Force redesignated the aircraft as a "reconnaissance-strike" vehicle (RS-70). However, in April 1961, Secretary of Defense Robert McNamara directed the program to be reduced to three prototype aircraft without military systems. The third prototype, which was later planned to have military systems, was cancelled in 1964. (The second prototype was destroyed in a crash following a mid-air collision with an F-104 on 8 June 1966; the first prototype made 83 flights through 4 February 1969.)

The B-70 design was a precursor of the supersonic transports with a large delta wing, a small canard wing forward, needle nose, and six turbojet engines nested under the wing structure. A bomb bay was to have been provided for gravity nuclear weapons between the engine intakes (behind the nose gear well). The aircraft was originally designed to burn special high-energy ("zip") fuels.

Designation: B-70 was the next sequential number in the Air Force's bomber series (following the RB-69, Air Force designation for a planned reconnaissance version of the Navy's P2V/P-2 Neptune patrol aircraft). The change to RS-70 was undertaken primarily for political reasons, to demonstrate a more-versatile mission capability. The next U.S. bomber designation was B-1.

Status: Retired; 2 prototypes built.

CREW & EQUIPMENT | FUEL & BOMB BAY | ENGINE

Variants:

XB-70A #1 Prototype aircraft; no weapons capability; 2 crew; first flight 21 September 1964.

XB-70A #2 Prototype aircraft similar to #1; first flight 17 July 1965.

XB-70B Prototype aircraft with military systems; 4 crew; cancelled 1964.

Characteristics: (XB-70A)

Crew	2 (pilot, copilot)
Weight	231,215 lbs. empty; 341,096 lbs. combat; 521,056 lbs. maximum takeoff
Dimensions	Span 105 ft., length 185.8 ft., height 30.7 ft.
Engines	6 General Electric YJ93-GE-3 turbojet (28,000 lbs. static thrust each maximum continuous; 17,000 lbst normal continuous)
Fuel	43,646 gallons internal
Speed	2,300 mph at 65,000 ft. (Mach 3.0); 1,150 mph at 30,000 ft. (Mach. 1.5)
Range	4,291-mile range with combat payload
Ceiling	Approximately 72,500 ft.
Payload	Gravity nuclear weapons (25,000 lbs. maximum)
Guns	None
Electronics	ASQ-28 bombing-navigation radar

FB-111

The General Dynamics FB-111 is SAC's medium-range bomber, capable of flying supersonic speeds at 200 feet above the ground and twice the speed of sound above 35,000 feet. It is the strategic/theater bomber version of the F-111 multi-purpose aircraft. It differs from the tactical strike variants by having different engines, a 3 1/2-ft extension on each wingtip, strengthened landing gear and fuselage, greater fuel capacity, and improved avionics.

The FB-111 wing's low minimum sweep angle of 16 degrees and a high maximum sweep angle of 72.5 degrees allow a relatively low take-off, landing, and stall speeds as well as supersonic, low-altitude penetration flight.

The twin turbofan engines are buried in the after fuselage. The combination of the relatively economical turbofans with a variable afterburner gives the engines an unprecedented range of power settings. The broad fuselage provides a side-by-side cockpit for the pilot and navigator-bombardier. The narrow-track, main landing gear legs extend from the fuselage under the wing trailing edges and fold inward and forward into fuselage bays. The nose gear retracts forward under the cockpit. The large, low-pressure tires permit no-flare landings. The cockpit is protected by individual canopies over each seat; these are hinged on a common centerline rail and, when open at the same time, have a gull-wing appearance. The cockpit is combined in an escape pod that is ejected by a single rocket; the crew remains with the pod while it parachutes to earth where it can serve as a survival shelter.

The internal weapons bay is located between the nose and main gear. The U.S. Air Force nickname for the F/FB-111 is the Aardvark, referring to the long nose.

Designation: The FB-111 is the only current USAF bomber to be designated in the fighter series. F-111 was the highest number assigned in the USAF fighter series, with the next fighter being the F-1 (the U.S. Navy's FJ Fury, redesignated in 1962 in a joint USAF-Navy scheme).

Status: Operational in two SAC bomb wings. The bomber's initial operational capability was in October 1969; its first flight was 30 July 1967. No longer in production; 76 were built from 1968 to 1971, with about 60 in service in 1990. The first flight with the digital flight control system was on 4 May 1989.

Variants:

FB-111A   Production version only.

FB-111B   Proposed conversion of FB-111A to improve strike capability; aircraft would have been lengthened; proposal cancelled in 1979.

FB-111C   Proposed conversion and lengthening of F-111D tactical aircraft to improve strike capability; proposal cancelled in 1979.

FB-111G   Proposed enhanced-payload conversion of FB-111A; not acquired.

FB-111H   Proposed mid-1970s upgrade, incorporating the F101-GE-F100 engines of B-1 bomber in stretched fuselage; not acquired.

| **EF-111A Raven** | Converted F-111 supporting tactical strike forces and with a modified Navy ALQ-99 jammer; 42 built and assigned to tactical units. |

Characteristics:

Crew	2 (aircraft commander/pilot, navigator-bombardier)
Weight	47,481 lbs empty; 70,380 lbs combat; 119,243 lbs maximum takeoff
Dimensions	Span 70 ft extended, 33.9 ft fully swept; length 75.5 ft; height 17 ft; wing area 550 ft^2
Engines	2 Pratt & Whitney TF30-P-7 turbofan (20,350 lb static thrust each with afterburner)
Fuel	5,623 gal
Speed	Mach 2.2 (1,453 mph) at 40,000-60,000 ft; Mach 1.1 at sea level and combat weight
Range	5,751 miles at high altitude with 4 X SRAM; 4,786 miles unrefueled range with 6 X 600-gallon drop tanks; 3,077 mile radius with 4 X SRAM basic mission with low-level penetration
Ceiling	60,000 ft maximum; 35,900 ft high-level mission Payload internal weapons bay with 2 B43/B61/B83 nuclear weapons and 6 wing pylons for up to 31,500 lb weapons load including 4 SRAM or 24 750-lb M117 weapons
Guns	None
Electronics	APQ-134 Terrain-Following Radar (TFR) (after a reliability update, this radar is redesignated APQ-171). APQ-114 attack radar (being upgraded to the AN/APQ-169), AYK-6 digital computer, AYN-3 horizontal situation display, ASG-25 optical display sight, AJN-16 inertial bomb navigation system, APN-167 radar altimeter, and APN-185 Doppler radar.
	The Electronic Support Measures/Electronic Countermeasures (ESM/ECM) suite includes an AAR-34 infrared warning receiver, ALR-41 homing receiver, APS-109B Radar Homing And Warning System (RHAWS), ALQ-94 or ALQ-137 internal noise/deception jammer, and an ALE-28 countermeasures dispenser.

B-1

The Rockwell International B-1 was the product of a succession of studies that began in 1962 and led to the 1965 requirement for an Advanced Manned Strategic Aircraft (AMSA) as a successor to the B-52. The B-1 has been highly controversial throughout its interrupted life. The Air Force originally proposed a force of 244 B-1s to replace the entire B-52 force. Production was approved on 2 December 1976, but the Carter administration entered office a month later, and on 30 June 1977 the entire program was cancelled in favor of the development of the Air-Launched Cruise Missile (ALCM) and modernization of the B-52 force. When the Reagan administration took office in January 1981, President Reagan gave immediate support to the B-1 program and gained congressional funding for 100 planes.

The B-1B is a long-range strategic bomber designed for low-altitude penetration missions. The B-1 was designed to carry almost twice the weapons as the B-52, although the newer aircraft is smaller. It features variable-geometry (swing) wings mounted at mid-fuselage.

Four General Electric turbofans are paired in nacelles under the wings. They are fed through fixed-geometry intakes. In-flight refueling employs a receptacle fitted ahead of the cockpit.

The B-1B's Radar Cross Section (RCS) is approx 1/7th that of the FB-111A, 1/10th of the B-1A, and 1/100th of the B-52. This small RCS is achieved through shaping and the inclusion of Radar-Absorbent Materials (RAM) at many points on the airframe.

Although much of the B-1 structure is aluminum alloy, titanium is used where high heat is generated or where high stress is expected. The two four-wheel landing gear retract into the fuselage between the engine nacelles. The nose gear retracts forward.

The aircraft has two pilots and two weapons systems officers. The pilots use control sticks rather than wheels and have the engine throttles on consoles to the left of each seat, which is said to enhance the aircraft's fighter-like feel.

Designation: B-1 became this aircraft's designation in the 1962 revision of U.S. military aircraft designations. At that time, the higher aircraft series such as bombers (reaching B-70) were started over. (The first airplane with the B-1 designation was the Keystone XB-1 Super Cyclops, a twin-engine biplane delivered to the U.S. Army in 1928.)

Status: In the original B-1A production, four prototypes were delivered before the 240 scheduled aircraft were cancelled. The B-1B's IOC was on 1 October 1986. The first flight of the B-1A was on 23 December 1974 and the B-1B on 23 March 1983. One hundred B-1Bs were acquired by SAC but a crash in

B-1 taking off on first flight, 23 December 1974.

The three B-1 prototypes.

September 1987 and two crashes in November 1988 reduced the number in service to 97. The last aircraft was delivered on 30 April 1988.

Variants:

B-1A   Initial version oriented toward high-altitude, high-speed dash; 4 built. Planned production of 240 aircraft cancelled in 1977.

B-1B   Production version with ALCM capability, increased payload, significantly smaller radar cross-section, and ejection seats instead of the crew ejection capsule; 100 built.

B-1 with swing-wing F-111 fighter aircraft

Characteristics: (B-1B)

Crew	4 (pilot, copilot, offensive systems operators, defensive systems operator)
Weight	192,000 lbs empty; 477,000 lbs maximum takeoff; 75,000 lbs maximum internal weapons load; 59,000 lbs maximum external weapons load
Dimensions	Span 136.7 ft extended, 78.2 ft fully swept, length 147 ft, height 34 ft, wing area approx. 1,950 ft^2
Engines	4 General Electric F101-GE-F102 turbofan (approx 30,000 lbs static thrust each maximum)

A B-1B Bomber with wings extended.

Fuel	Approx. 40,000 gal
Speed	Mach 1.25
Range	6,449 miles (approx.); 1,727 miles low-altitude range with 8 SRAM and 8 B-61 bombs
Ceiling	60,000 ft
Payload	2 internal weapons bays for up to 42,000 lb of ordnance, such as 84 X Mk 82 500-lb bombs or 24 X Mk 84 2,000-lb bombs or 12 X B-28 free-fall nuclear weapons or 24 X B-61/B-83 free-fall nuclear weapons or 24 X SRAM or 8 X ALCM; and 8 hardpoints under fuselage for 14 X ALCM or SRAM or 8 X B-28 or 14 B-43/B-61/B-83 nuclear or Mk 84 conventional bombs or 44 Mk 82
Electronics	APQ-164 forward-looking radar, APQ-164 dual-channel, multi-mode Offensive Radar System, APN-224 radar altimeter systems, ALR-56M warning radar

B-2

The Northrop B-2 Advanced Technology Bomber (ATB) is a Stealth low-observable strategic bomber. The B-2 is designed to present the lowest possible visual, radar, acoustic, and infrared signatures. Its mission is to attack enemy mobile ICBMs and hardened command and control installations.

The B-2's general design resembles earlier Northrop flying wings (flown in the 1940s as the YB-35 and YB-49), a configuration that offers the smallest head-on and side-view RCS. A further reduction in RCS is achieved by using surface skins made of a composite, ferrite-based honeycomb (probably carbon-fiber) Radar Absorbent Structure (RAS), probably over titanium main structural members.

The two engine intakes are over the center section of the ATB on each side of the shallow rounded cockpit. Each intake feeds two of the four General Electric non-afterburning turbofan engines that are in the wing. Engine exhaust is emitted through narrow exhausts and over chevron-shaped channels in the wing's trailing edge. The cockpit has space for a third crew member, although the normal crew is two. If used, the third crew position would likely be a navigator/weapons systems officer.

The B-2 has approximately 200 computers with more lines of code than the space shuttle.

Status: In development. First flight had been planned for late 1987, but a $1-billion design modification to permit low-level flight delayed the program. After high- and low-speed taxi tests, the first flight took place on 17 July 1989 at Edwards AFB, Calififornia.

The Air Force estimated the total cost of the planned B-2 force to be $36.6 billion in fiscal year 1981 dollars. In December 1988, the estimate was raised to $42.5 billion in 1981 dollars and in July 1989, the cost estimate was raised to $70.2 billion. The early production rate was slow to allow correction of problems discovered during flight testing.

The Stealth bomber will continue to experience controversy and scrutiny in the 1990s as defense expenditures face the congressional ax. The fiscal year 1991 budget retained most of the high-expenditure weapons systems as submitted for approval. Although 132 bombers are planned, the Congress has suggested that far fewer will be built (see 1990 in Chronology).

The exact IOC is classified as of early 1990, but is planned for mid-1991 at Whiteman AFB, Missouri.

B-2 over California desert during test flight. There are two small "drag rudders" that provide the aircraft's only vertical control surfaces.

Variants: None

Characteristics:

Crew   2 (pilot, copilot)
Weight   approx 158,000 lbs empty; 240,000-376,000 lbs maximum takeoff
Dimensions   Span 172 ft; length 69 ft; height 17 ft; wing area more than 5,000 ft^2
Engines   4 General Electric F118-GE-100 turbofans (approx 19,000 lbs static thrust each)
Fuel   minimum 160,000 lb load
Speed   Mach 0.85
Range   4,250-7,500 miles unrefueled
Ceiling   approx 50,000 ft
Payload   16 gravity nuclear weapons B-83 or 20 B-61 gravity nuclear weapons or 16 SRAM or 8 X SRAM and 8 B-83 or 8 X SRAM and 8 B-61 or 80 X 500-lb bombs (all internal)
Electronics Hughes phased-array multi-purpose radar

Vulcan

The Vulcan is Britain's largest operational combat aircraft. Produced by Avro (Hawker Siddeley after 1962) for the strategic bomber role, it is now employed as a general-purpose strike aircraft and is also flown in the strategic reconnaissance role. The Vulcan is the last "strategic" bomber to be flown by the RAF. The Vulcan was a familiar sight at SAC bases as the aircraft participated in weapon tests and SAC bombing competitions.

The RAF Strike Command currently has six squadrons flying 48 of the Vulcan B.2 variants and one reconnaissance squadron with eight SR.2 variants. The Vulcan has been replaced in the strategic deterrence role by the Royal Navy's four nuclear-propelled submarines armed with Polaris missiles.

The Vulcan was originally conceived as a triangular wing with no fuselage or additional "wings" except for fins and rudders. Subsequently, the forward compartments were extended into a fuselage while subsequent modifications, to provide electronic equipment, extended the tail structure. The aircraft's four turbojet engines are buried in the wing roots. No guns are fitted and weapons are carried internally or semi-recessed in the weapons bay. Avro was awarded a contract to produce the Vulcan in November 1947 with two prototypes being ordered in March 1949. Wing configurations were tested with small-scale aircraft.

Status: Operational from 1957 onward; 122 aircraft produced through 1964.

Variants:

Vulcan #1	Prototype; first flight 30 August 1952.
Vulcan #2	Prototype; improved engines and wing; subsequently modified to test B.2 wing configuration; first flight 3 September 1953.
Vulcan B.1	Production aircraft; first flight 4 February 1955; 45 built.
Vulcan B.1A	Improved EW/ECM equipment with bulged tail cone (as B.2); several converted from B.1.
Vulcan B.2	Production aircraft; improved engines; designed to carry Blue Steel or Skybolt air-to-surface, stand-off missiles; all modified to conventional bombing capability (see below); first flight 19 August 1958; 75 built.
Vulcan SR.2	Strategic reconnaissance aircraft; several converted from B.2.

Vulcan B.2 (Hawker Siddeley)

Characteristics: (B.2)

Crew	5 (pilot, copilot, air electronics officer, navigator, radar operator)
Weight	200,000 lbs. maximum takeoff
Dimensions	Span 111 ft., length 99.9 ft., height 27.1 ft., wing area 3,964 ft.²
Engines	4 Bristol Siddeley Olympus Mk. 301 turbojets (20,000 lbs. static thrust each)
Fuel	70,000 lbs.
Speed	645 mph at 40,000 ft. (Mach 0.98)
Range	2,251-mile radius for low-level target attack; 3,046-mile radius for high-level target attack
Ceiling	55,000 ft.
Payload	21 × 1,000-lb. bombs
Guns	None
Electronics	

Strategic Reconnaissance Aircraft

U-2

The Lockheed U-2 is a long-range, high-altitude strategic reconnaissance aircraft that is a primary component of the U.S. "national technical means" of intelligence collection. It was developed secretly in the mid-1950s for the Central Intelligence Agency by the "Skunk Works," a small special projects division of Lockheed. The U-2 has outlived its intended successor, the SR-71 "Blackbird."

The U-2 features a glider-like configuration with mid-mounted, double-tapered, high-aspect-ratio wings designed to function like sailplane wings; the aircraft can soar without power to extend its range.

Early U-2s could be fitted with 80-gal "slipper" fuel tanks. The U-2R has a significantly larger wing with integral fuel tanks and slender, permanently fitted "superpods" carrying sensors and fuel spliced into the wing structure at mid-span.

The fuselage has a sloping nose up to a small cockpit. The rest of the fuselage has a circular section. The U-2R enjoys a 100 percent increase in fuselage volume over its predecessors.

The U-2 is one of the most difficult aircraft to land because of the narrow speed range between recommended approach speed and its stall speed. Its main landing gear is tandem bicycle-type with the larger, forward unit and a much smaller assembly near the tail; the landing gear in the U-2R is more closely spaced. Because of the great span of the wings, the U-2 landing gear also includes a balancing wheel under each wing that are jettisoned on take-off. The U-2 was designed from the outset to take off from aircraft carriers and conduct launch tests from carriers at sea.

The sensors on the U-2 series vary with the variant and the operational context. The basic aircraft used large, long-focus cameras and Electronic Intelligence (ELINT) equipment. The U-2R has wingtip Radar Homing And Warning System (RHAWS) pods and ELINT antennas.

On 14 October 1962, a U-2 piloted by Major Richard S. Heyser flew over Cuba and obtained the first photographic evidence of the Soviet offensive missiles on the island.

Designation: U-2 is in the utility series of U.S. military aircraft designations, sandwiched between the U-1, the DeHavilland Otter light cargo aircraft; and the U-3, a Cessna light cargo aircraft. Several later Army utility aircraft have

U-2 fitted for high-altitude sampling of radioactive isotopes emitted into the stratosphere by atomic weapon tests.

U-2 in landing configuration with drag chute open.

reconnaissance configurations (e.g., RU-8, RU-9, RU-21). TR indicates Tactical Reconnaissance.

Status: Operational. Initial operational capability in June 1957; first flight on 1 August 1955. Taiwan received 6 U-2 aircraft in the early 1960s, but all were subsequently lost (at least three in operations over Mainland China). Approximately 60 of the U-2 series were built in the late 1950s and early 1960s; more than 40 were lost on missions or in operational accidents. A later batch of 12 larger U-2Rs were manufactured in the late 1960s. All U-2s built before the U-2R had been retired by April 1989, the last being flown as NASA research aircraft. SAC U-2s are assigned to the 9th Strategic Reconnaissance Wing at Beale AFB, California.

Variants:

U-2	Prototype; first flight 1955; 2 built.
U-2A	Initial production version with 11,200-lb static thrust J57-P-37A engine, internal fuel capacity of 785 gal, maximum range of 2,200 miles; about 30 were built; most of these were later converted to U-2B.
WU-2A	Weather reconnaissance version of U-2A, with instrumentation in a bulged fairing on the underfuselage, below the air intakes.
U-2B	Improved version of U-2A, with J75-P-13 engine, strengthened airframe, "wet" wing. Conversions and production brought the total of U-2B aircraft to 48, and 2 of these were transferred to Taiwan.
U-2C	Electronic intelligence (ELINT) version of U-2B, with addition of long dorsal spine fairing to hold ELINT equipment. 2 flown by NASA.
U-2CT	Two-seat trainer version, with raised rear cockpit for instructor and dual controls; 2 converted.
U-2D	Two-seat, special mission version, otherwise similar to U-2C; at least 5 converted.
WU-2D	Weather/Research reconnaissance version of U-2D.
U-2EPX	Proposed Navy ocean surveillance aircraft (Electronics-Patrol-Experimental); to have had APS-116 radar; at least 2 aircraft flew in Navy markings before this program was cancelled.
U-2R	Similar to U-2C, but with longer nose and fuselage, no dorsal spine fairing, superpods, and closer-set landing wheels. Improved capability for theater reconnaissance; span 103 ft, length 63 ft, height 16 ft.
U-2R COMINT	At least 2 U-2Rs modified for Communications Intelligence (COMINT) and fitted with large airfoil-shaped radome on short dorsal pylon; radome used to relay COMINT data by satellite.

| **TR-1** | Tactical reconnaissance version; listed separately. |

Characteristics:

Crew	1
Weight	empty
	U-2C 11,700 lbs
	U-2R 14,990 lbs
	take-off
	U-2C, 16,000 lbs clean
	U-2C, with 2 89-gal wing tanks 17,270 lbs
	U-2R, 41,000 lbs
Dimensions	Span
	U-2C 80 ft
	U-2R 103 ft
	length
	U-2C 49.6 ft
	U-2R 62.7 ft
	height
	U-2C 13 ft
	U-2R 16.1 ft
	wing area
	U-2C 565 ft^2
	U-2R 1,000 ft^2
Engines	1 Pratt & Whitney J75-P-13 turbojet (17,000 lbs static thrust)
Fuel	1,140 gal internal plus 210 gal in "slipper" tanks
Speed	U-2C 528 mph maximum; 460 mph cruise
	U-2R 510 mph maximum
Range	U-2C 3,000 miles
	U-2R 3,500 miles
Ceiling	U-2C 85,000 ft
	U-2R 90,000 ft
Electronics	U-2R Radar Homing And Warning System (RHAWS) pods and ELINT systems

RB-57

SAC flew two high-altitude, radar reconnaissance variants of the highly successful and ubiquitous Martin RB-57 Canberra from mid-1956 through 1960 (after which they continued in service with other USAF commands). The Canberra was Britain's first operational jet-propelled bomber; it was manufactured continuously for 12 years and has served a dozen nations in several roles. In the United States, Martin copied an English Electric Canberra B.2 to produce the B-57 as a tactical strike aircraft, with the first American-built unit flying on 20 July 1953. Subsequently, two strategic recce variants were manufactured. They retain the trim Canberra fuselage, but have disproportionately long wings and outsize engine nacelles. No weapons are carried. Six of the RB-57Ds were two-seat aircraft.

Wing structural problems grounded the RB-57Ds from 1963 to 1966. The RB-57F has a larger wing of an entirely new design (122 ft. span) and a pair of J60-P-9 turbojet engines in underwing pods (3,300 lbs. static thrust) to augment the two TF33-P-11 turbofans (18,000 lbs. static thrust).

Two RB-57Ds were transferred to Taiwan for overflights of Mainland China. Not listed below are several RB-57 tactical reconnaissance variants. Some RB-57Fs were later modified for weather reconnaissance (WB-57F).

Status: Retired.

Variants:

RB-57D   Reconnaissance variant; first flight January 1957; 20 built.
RB-57F   Reconnaissance variant; 2 crew; span 122 ft., wing area 2,000 ft.²; Pratt & Whitney TF33 turbofan engines; details differed; at least 23 converted from RB-57A, B-57B, and RB-57D by General Dynamics/Fort Worth.

Characteristics: (RB-57D)

Crew   1 (pilot)
Weight   27,876 lbs. empty; 36,610 lbs. combat takeoff; 46,355 lbs. maximum takeoff
Dimensions Span 106 ft., length 67.1 ft., height 14.8 ft., wing area 1,505 ft.²

RB-57D Canberra in foreground with conventional B-57 tactical bomber in background.

Engines	2 Pratt & Whitney J57-P-37A turbojet (10,500 lbs. static thrust maximum for 30 minutes; 9,000 lbst continuous) each
Fuel	2,740 gallons
Speed	530 mph at 60,000 ft.; 475 mph cruise
Range	1,512-mile radius; 3,024-mile ferry range
Ceiling	65,000 ft.
Electronics	APN-107 radar, APQ-56 radar

TR-1

The TR-1 is a variant of the U-2R used for tactical reconnaissance missions in Europe. It performs high-altitude standoff surveillance missions, providing the capability for day or night, all-weather surveillance without having to overfly the target.

The TR-1 is equipped to provide a battlefield surveillance system for theater and tactical commanders. It is capable of long loiter time and standoff surveillance from very high altitudes.

The TR-1 can also perform the Precision Location Strike System (PLSS), which uses three TR-1s to triangulate radar emissions and provide accurate targeting information for anti-radar strikes. Other equipment bays are located behind the cockpit, in the rear fuselage, and in the tailcone.

Designation: TR indicates Tactical Reconnaissance. The designation was reportedly adopted to imply a break from the covert operations connotation that the "U" indicated.

Status: First operational TR-1 received by SAC in August 1981. All 21 operational TR-1s are stationed at RAF Alconbury, England. Production of the TR-1 ended in October 1989 with a total of 37 TR-1A/TR-1B/ER-2 produced. All TR-1s are under the operational control of SAC.

Variants:

TR-1B	2-seat trainer version of TR-1; 2 built
ER-2	2 aircraft used by NASA for atmospheric research

Characteristics:

Crew	1
Weight	10,000 lbs empty; 40,000 lbs maximum takeoff
Dimensions	Span 104 ft, length 63 ft, height 16 ft, wing area 1,000 ft^2
Engines	1 Pratt & Whitney J75-P-13 turbojet (17,000 lbs static thrust)
Fuel	1,175 gal
Speed	over 430 mph
Range	over 3,000 miles
Ceiling	90,000 ft
Electronics	Synthetic Aperture Radar System (ASARS) that includes a Side-Looking Airborne Radar (SLAR); ASARS is also fitted with advanced Electronic Countermeasures (ECM), and passive Electronic Support Measures (ESM) including signal intelligence.

SR-71

The Lockheed SR-71 was a high-speed, high-altitude strategic reconnaissance variant of the A-11 design, developed as a high-altitude, Mach 3 aircraft for use as a fighter and strategic reconnaissance aircraft. The SR-71 was popularly known as the Blackbird because of its heat-emissive surface. The SR-71 was the intended successor to the Lockheed U-2 that was also a product of the famed Lockheed "Skunk Works." However, the SR-71 was retired from active service in March 1990 with the U-2 and its derivative, the TR-1, continuing in service.

The SR-71 had an unconventional design with a long, tapering fuselage of very small cross-section blending into a delta wing with rounded wingtips. The forward part of the fuselage was flattened and had sharp chines along each side. An engine nacelle was blended into the middle of each wing, each supporting a low tail fin, canted slightly inward. Skin temperatures on the fuselage would rise considerably during high-altitude, high-speed flight and the fuselage stretched 11 inches as a result.

The engines were continuous-bleed afterburning turbojets with large center-body cones and required special JP-7 fuel. The immense amount of fuel needed fills most of the fuselage and acts as a heat sink.

The Blackbird had no horizontal stabilizers, but had a relatively deep under-fuselage retracting ventral fin and two shallow underengine fins. Construction was mainly of titanium to resist the stresses of upper atmospheric flight, and composites were used in the remainder of the surface components.

Reconnaissance instrumentation was normally contained internally, with a minimum of bulges or blisters that add drag in flight. Side-Looking Airborne Radars (SLAR) and infrared linescanning equipment that can be interchanged were believed on-board. The two-seat tandem cockpit presented a minimal profile, with the systems officer position having side windows only.

The aircraft's sensors could survey over 100,000 square miles of the earth's surface in one hour from altitudes above 80,000 feet.

The SR-71 was involved in several confrontations while performing its photographic reconnaissance mission. In the 1960s, the Blackbird recorded China's first tests of a nuclear bomb; in 1982 it photographed the presence of Soviet MiGs in Nicaragua; in 1973 it provided verification photos for the Arab-Israeli war ceasefire; and in 1987 the plane flew bomb damage assessment missions following the U.S. bombing attack on Libya.

SR-71 Blackbird.

SR-71 Blackbird taking off.

Designation: Apparently SR-71 was meant to be RS-71, following the aborted RS-70 designation assigned to the abortive B-70 aircraft. President Lyndon Johnson was believed to have transposed the designation when he announced the plane's existence on 24 July 1964. SR is taken to mean Strategic Reconnaissance. Because the SR-71 evolved from the F-12 fighter aircraft, the reconnaissance variant should have been RF-12, or, in accord with the SR gambit, SR-12.

Status: Retired. In January 1989 the Air Force announced that it would retire all SR-71s. The final operational flight was on 18 January 1990 at Kadena AB, Okinawa. Initial operational capability was in 1966. The SR-71's first flight as the YF-12A was on 26 April 1962. Although actual numbers were not available, the best estimates suggested about 32 SR-71s were produced, including variants. Approximately 20 were in the inventory when the aircraft was retired; of that, 8 or 9 were operational at any one time.

On 6 March 1990, No. 17972 set four flight-time records while flying from Los Angeles to Washington D.C., in the final SR-71 flight.

Variants:

YF-12A	Development version in single-seat interceptor configuration; 3 built.
YF-12C	Prototype of SR-71A version; 1 built.
SR-71A	Production version. First flight 22 December 1964; estimated 25-30 built.
SR-71B	Two-seat, dual-control trainer version, with rear cockpit elevated and windscreen provided for forward view; two built.
SR-71C	Two-seat trainer modified from SR-71A; one converted after loss of SR-71B.

Characteristics: (SR-71A)

Crew	2 (pilot, reconnaissance systems officer)
Weight	60,000 lbs empty; up to 170,000 lbs maximum
Dimensions	Span 55.6 ft, length 107.4 ft, height 18.5 ft, wing area 1,800 ft^2
Engines	2 Pratt & Whitney JT11D-20B continuous-bleed turbojets (approx. 34,000 lbs static thrust each with afterburner; approx. 23,000 lbs continuous)
Fuel	8,000 gal maximum consumption per hour
Speed	Over 2,000 mph at 78,740 ft (Mach 3) maximum 207 mph approach; 173 mph at touchdown
Range	3,000 miles (approx); global with aerial refueling
Ceiling	80,000+ ft

RC-135

The Boeing RC-135 Stratolifter is used for strategic reconnaissance and was developed from the KC-135 Stratotanker. The RC-135 differs externally from the tanker with its turbofan engines, in-flight refueling receptacle, and additional aerials and radomes. Although the internal configuration of the RC-135 differs with the individual airplane, all have flight stations forward, followed by the equipment area, operator area, and rest area.

The RC-135 can detect, intercept, analyze, and record electronic transmissions. These data are provided to theater commanders, the Department of Defense, and National Command Authorities. The data are processed, analyzed, and stored by SAC, Electronic Security Command, and the National Security Agency. The information also is used by the Joint Strategic Target Planning Staff at Offutt AFB in the formulation of target lists and the Single Integrated Operational Plan.

Status: Operational

Variants:

RC-135   EW/ELINT variants, in 9 different configurations varying by EW/ELINT equipment carried.

RC-135A   An intelligence-reconnaissance aircraft not assigned to SAC.

RC-135B/C/D   Fitted with Side-Looking Airborne Radar (SLAR); RC-135D had thimble nose added. RC-135B/Cs converted to RC-135U/V; RC-135D reconfigured to KC-135A.

RC-135E   One KC-135A with JT3D-3B engines from the commercial Boeing 707. Military designation for the engines is TF-33-PW-102. Forward fuselage encircled by fiberglass band, pods suspended under wing roots. No longer in service.

RC-135M   6 modified C-135B with TF-33-P-5 engines. Thimble nose, double-lobe ventral fairing, teardrop antenna on rear fuselage. Some later converted to RC-135W.

RC-135S   A TF-33-P-5/9-powered C-135B used by Military Airlift Command for long-range weather reconnaissance.

RC-135T   1 KC-135R modified for command support and training.

RC-135U   3 aircraft modified with extensive external antenna fit including large SLAR "cheeks."

RC-135V   8 aircraft (7 RC-135C and 1 RC-135U) converted for electronic reconnaissance with SAC.

RC-135W/X   A TF-33-P-5-powered C-135B modified for electronic reconnaissance with SAC.

Characteristics:

Crew	3 (pilot, copilot, navigator) + 15 crew
Weight	299,000 lbs maximum takeoff; 147,859 lbs empty; 221,040 lbs combat takeoff
Dimensions	Span 130.8 ft, length 140.5 ft, height 41.7 ft, wing area 2,433 ft^2
Engines	4 Pratt & Whitney TF33-P-9 or TF33-P-5 turbofans (16,050 lbs static thrust continuous)
Fuel	22,246 gal (22,693 gal for ferry mission with 4-man crew)
Speed	530 mph cruise; 585 mph maximum
Range	2,675-mile radius; 5,639-mile ferry range
Ceiling	40,600 ft; 35,000 ft reconnaissance altitude
Electronics	ASD-1 electronic reconnaissance system, ALQ-70 ECM, ALA-6 direction finder, APR-17 reconnaissance

Strategic Tankers

KC-97

The KC-97 was derived from the B-29 Superfortress bomber, using the same wing, engine, and tail. The new fuselage had a double-bubble configuration. The C-97 served a varied mission when active; in addition to both troop and cargo transport and tanker roles, it was used for medical evacuation, Search And Rescue (SAR), and by the Israeli Air Force, as an Electronic Counter-measures (ECM) platform. Several transport variants were built for the Air Force with three C-97A transports serving as the prototype for the tanker. The trial units were fitted with the Boeing Flying-Boom refueling system. A total of 888 transports and tankers were built.

Status: Retired. First flight (XC-97) on 15 November 1944. The last KC-97 was removed from ground alert on 10 November 1965. The final flight of the KC-97 was on 21 December 1965 when two aircraft flew to the USAF storage facility at Davis-Monthan AFB, Arizona. Production ended in July 1956.

Variants:

XC-97	The original prototype originated from the B-29 Superfortress. Production started in 1945. Several different variants for military transport were built. Total of 888 C-97s built with 911 being the tanker variant (KC-)
KC-97A	3 converted from C-97A for tanker trials
KC-97E	Initial production version, beginning in 1951. Total of 60 built.
KC-97F	Later production, following the KC-97E; total of 159 built.
KC-97G	Total of 592 delivered to the Air Force; the last production version, ultimately replaced by the KC-135A. A total of 135 converted to the C-97G cargo configuration and 26 others assigned to SAC for passenger support. About 12 transferred to Israeli Air Force.
KC-97H	A single copy for hose tanker tests.
KC-97L	Converted from the KC-97G with a J47-GE-23 jet pod added beneath each wing. After the addition, assigned to Air Guard units.
TK-1	3 KC-97Ls transferred to the Spanish Air Force supporting F-4C Phantom squadrons.

Characteristics:

Crew   5 (pilot, copilot, navigator, flight engineer, boom operator)

Weight   82,490 lbs empty; 175,000 lbs maximum

Dimensions Span 141.25 ft, length 117.4 ft, height 38.25 ft, wing area approx 1,769 ft^2

Engines   KC-97G 4 Pratt & Whitney R-4360-59B

KC-97L with 2 underwing auxiliary J47-GE-25A jet engines (1 per wing)

Speed   375 mph maximum, 297 mph cruise

Range   4,300 miles

KC-135

The KC-135 Stratotanker is used for in-flight refueling operations in support of all U.S. Air Force refuelable aircraft, as well as aircraft of the U.S. Navy, and U.S. allies. Although related to the Boeing 707 commercial airliner series, the first KC-135 flew in August 1956, almost 18 months before the first B-707.

The 4 turbojet or turbofan engines are mounted on wing pylons. Most KC-135A are being refitted with CFM International F108-CF-100 engines (redesignated KC-135R), which give the aircraft a much needed 60 percent increase in take-off thrust while improving fuel efficiency by 27 percent. The KC-135A carries 31,300 gal of transferable fuel that is passed to receiving aircraft through a Boeing-designed "flying boom." The boom is controlled by an operator lying prone in a compartment under the fuselage near the tail.

Designation: The KC-135R designation was used for an early reconnaissance variant now out of service.

Status: First flight of the KC-135A was in August 1956; IOC in 1957. Production ceased in 1965.

Variants:

KC-135A Production tanker version. 732 were built before production ceased in 1964, about 595 remain in U.S. service. Surviving KC-135A aircraft are being upgraded to KC135R/E standard.

KC-135E Upgraded tanker version with service in the U.S. Air National Guard and Air Force Reserve units. Fuel consumption reduced by 14 percent, noise footprint by 85 percent, pollutant emissions by 90 percent. First delivery was 26 July 1982.

KC-135R Upgraded tanker version for U.S. Air Force with F108-CF-100 engines, strengthened landing gear, 2 Auxiliary Power Units (APU), and modifications to most major systems including installation of the Delco FSA/CAS. Greatly increased power allows the KC-135R to be climbing through 2,500 ft (762 m) before the KC-135A leaves the runway. 90 EPNdB Noise footprint is reduced by 98 percent. First flight on 4 August 1982,

	deliveries began in 1984; most expected to serve well into the 21st century.
C-135FR	Similar to KC-135R but for the French Air Force; 11 in service. First copy returned to service on 26 August 1985, the last on 13 April 1988.

Characteristics:

Crew	4 (aircraft commander, pilot, navigator, boom operator)
Weight	98,466 lbs empty;
	KC-135A 301,600 lbs maximum
	KC-135R 322,500 lbs maximum
Dimensions	Span 130.8 ft, length 134.5 ft, height 38.3 ft, wing area approximately 2,433 ft²
Engines	KC-135A 4 Pratt & Whitney J57-59W turbojets, KC-135R 4 CFM International F108-CF-100 turbofans
Speed	585 mph maximum
Range	1,150 miles with 120,000 lbs transfer fuel
	3,450 miles with 24,000 lbs transfer fuel
Ceiling	36,000 ft
Fuel Load	KC-135A 189,702 lbs maximum
	KC-135R 203,288 lbs maximum

KC-10

The KC-10 Extender is a military version of the McDonnell Douglas DC-10 "wide-body" civilian aircraft. It differs from the DC-10 mainly in the communications and avionics suite and the refueling equipment.

Fuel is stored in seven bladders on the lower deck, and there is a refueling station well aft with three positions for the boom operator, instructor (for training), and observer. The McDonnell Douglas refuelling boom is located under the centerline of the aft fuselage. It is longer than that of the KC-135 and has a maximum fuel transfer rate of 1,500 gallons/minute.

A General Electric turbofan engine is housed in a nacelle mounted on a pylon suspended from each wing. The third engine is located on the tail. The main landing gear consists of two 4-wheel bogies that retract inward into wing root bays and a centerline, 2-wheel assembly that is in line with the outboard bogies and retracts forward. The 2-wheel nose gear retracts forward.

The KC-10 program has been considered very successful, having been completed on time and within budget. Since entering service, the KC-10 has sustained Fully-Mission-Capable and Mission-Completion Success Rates of over 99 percent.

The Extender can transport up to 75 personnel and about 170,000 lbs of cargo, and can itself be air refueled.

Status: The IOC of the KC-10A was achieved in 1981; its first flight was on 12 July 1980. The first KC-10 was delivered on 17 March 1981 and the final, 60th, one was delivered on 4 April 1990. The Extender completed extensive flight testing that began in December 1988 and included the examination of the wing-mounted air refueling pod system. The underwing hose-and-drogue pods will allow the KC-10 to simultaneously refuel two to three aircraft.

Variants: None

Characteristics:

Crew	3 to 6 (pilot, copilot, flight engineer + 3 refueling crew)
Weight	241,027 lbs empty; 356,065 lbs fuel load; 590,000 lbs maximum takeoff
Dimensions	Span 165.3 ft, height 58 ft, length 181.6 ft, wing area 3,958 ft^2

Engines	3 General Electric CF6-50C2 turbofans (52,500 lbs. static thrust)
Speed	610 mph maximum, 564 mph cruise
Range	11,500 miles unrefueled
Ceiling	42,000 ft

Strategic Command and Control Aircraft

E-4B

The E-4B The Boeing E-4B National Emergency Airborne Command Post (NEACP) is a modified Boeing 747 fitted with communications equipment to act as the National Command Authority (NCA) operations center in the event of nuclear war.

Other than the markings, the only observable difference between the NEACP and a commercial 747 aircraft is the NEACP's array of antennas and a small radome bulge on the rear of the upper deck. Like the 747, the NEACP features a fuselage with a distinctive upper-deck bulge, wings mounted low at mid-fuselage, a high single tailfin, and four engines mounted on wing pylons.

Internal modifications are much more extensive. The 4,350 ft² interior of the NEACP has been divided into six working compartments: the NCA working area; a conference room; a briefing room; an operations staff area; communications control center; and a mission crew rest area. The upper deck houses the flight deck and flight crew rest area.

Communications capability spans the frequency spectrum from Very Low Frequency (VLF) to Super High Frequency (SHF) systems, permitting the NEACP staff to contact almost all nuclear delivery systems directly. The systems have been hardened against Electro-Magnetic Pulse (EMP) effects. The NEACPs are fitted with in-flight refueling capability to permit an endurance aloft of over 72 hours.

Automated data processing equipment provides the capability to process, store, display, and print critical command information. This system is interfaced with other command, control, and communications (C³) systems, and greatly increases the ability to direct strategic forces.

The alert force on board the NEACP consists of a JCS joint service operations team, a Defense Intelligence Agency element, the SAC flight crew, maintenance crew, and security forces, and a communications team from the Air Force Communications Command.

Status: Operational; initial operational capability (E-4A) in 1975; first flight in October 1974. Four E-4As are operational; probably stationed at Offutt AFB, Nebraska.

Variants:

E-4A First 3 aircraft procured; all have been upgraded to the E-4B standard.

E-4B   3 E-4A aircraft and 1 subsequently acquired aircraft with upgraded avionics, EMP hardening, in-flight refueling capability, and a larger staff working area than the original E-4A.

Characteristics:

Crew   4 (pilot, copilot, navigator, flight engineer), 31 battle staff and a varied number of command and technical support personnel
Weight   803,000 lbs maximum takeoff
Dimensions   Span 195.7 ft; length 225.2 ft; height 63.4 ft, wing area 5,500 ft^2
Engines   4 General Electric C56-50E turbojets (52,500 lbs static thrust each)
Fuel capacity   590,000 lbs
Speed   607 mph
Range   8,176 miles unrefueled
Ceiling   45,000 ft

EC-135

The Boeing EC-135 Looking Glass aircraft is a conversion of the basic C-135/KC-135 family of aircraft for the strategic command and control mission. This airborne command post function provides a survivable means of command and control in the event that SAC underground command center, alternate command posts, or ground-based communications are lost. It also provides an alternate method to launch the Minuteman/Peacekeeper missiles if ground launch control centers are destroyed.

Each airborne command post aircraft carries a battle staff and variety of communications equipment. The SAC Airborne Command Post has been on airborne alert around the clock since 3 February 1961.

When airborne, the battle staff, headed by a SAC general officer, monitors several communications systems and maintains contact with the SAC underground and alternate command posts, the national Military Command Centers, and the SAC alert forces.

Status: Operational. The aircraft, flight crews, and battle staff that support the missions are provided by the 2nd Airborne Command Control Squadron (ACCS), Offutt AFB, Nebraska, the 4th ACCS at Ellsworth AFB, South Dakota, and the 70th Air Refueling Squadron, Grissom AFB, Indiana.

Variants:

EC-135	Worldwide Airborne Command Post System (WWABNCP) variants, in 10 different configurations varying by communications equipment fitted; 39 aircraft representing 7 versions are active and being upgraded under the Pacer Link program (see below).
EC-135A/G/H/P	Command posts fitted with J57 turbojets; the EC-135G aircraft were earmarked for ICBM launch control. All retained the refueling boom and were fitted with the Air Refueling Receiver (ARR).
EC-135C/J	Command posts fitted with TF-33 turbofans; 13 EC-135C have capability to control SAC bomber and ICBM forces and are known as Looking Glass aircraft; EC-135J aircraft are Pacific Air Force command posts.
EC-135E	TF-33-powered C-135A modified for electronic command and control missions.

EC-135K	J57-powered KC-135A modified for the Tactical Air Command to provide overseas control of their fighters when deploying
EC-135L	J57-powered KC-135A modified for radio relay and dropout capability in support of SAC.
EC-135Y	Former J57-powered NKC-135 modified for commander-in-chief central command as command, control, and communications (C^3) aircraft.

Characteristics:

Crew	5 (aircraft commander, pilot, crew instructor, navigator, boom operator), 7 communications personnel and 15 battle staff (including the airborne emergency actions officer, airborne launch control system officer, communications control officer, 2 operational planning officers, 2 intelligence officers, weather officer, logistics officer, and engineering officer) and 1 spare staff position
Weight	300,000 lbs maximum takeoff
Dimensions	Span 130 ft, length 128 ft, height 42 ft
Engines	4 Pratt & Whitney TF33-P-9 (18,000 lbs static thrust each maximum)
Speed	600 mph maximum
Range	over 5,000 miles

Strategic Missiles

ACM

The Advanced Cruise Missile (ACM) is a low-observable (stealth) missile intended for launching by strategic bomber aircraft. Most of the ACM's characteristics were secret when this edition went to press. It has a turbofan engine, a rounded airframe with a pointed nose, rear folding fins, and an air inlet at the underside of the rear fuselage. The ACM uses both composite materials and design characteristics to lessen its radar signature.

The ACM has been plagued with problems during its development. The missile was behind schedule and suffered from several technical and management problems. Most of the missile's problems were traced to quality control at General Dynamics. Congress stipulated that the Air Force must conduct six successful free-flight tests before production of the missile could continue. In December 1989 the Air Force announced that the flight tests had been conducted successfully and that production would resume.

Designation: AGM-129

Status: IOC was originally scheduled for the early 1990s. Low-rate production started in 1986, but was curtailed in 1989 due to problems and resumed in 1990. Full-rate production is scheduled for 1992. The missile was originally produced by General Dynamics, but in November 1987 the Air Force chose McDonnell Douglas as a second source to produce the missile in an effort to overcome some of the development problems.

Procurement of approximately 1,100 AGM-129s is planned. Full production is scheduled for fiscal year 1992.

Characteristics: (estimated; most details are classified)

Weight	2,756 lbs launch
Dimensions	Length 19.7 ft, height 1.5 ft, width 2.8 ft
Propulsion	Williams International F112-WR-100 turbofan
Speed	No estimate
Range	2,300 miles maximum
Warhead	W-80 nuclear, 5-150 kiloton

ALCM

The Boeing Air-Launched Cruise Missile (ALCM) is a long-range, air-to-ground cruise missile for attacking strategic ground targets at distances of 1,500 miles. The ALCM flies at a very low altitude, permitted by the Terrain Contour Matching (TERCOM) guidance system, relying on its small radar signature and surrounding ground clutter to defeat enemy air defenses.

The ALCM was developed from the earlier Subsonic Cruise Armed Decoy (SCAD), a weapon designed to confuse and overwhelm enemy air defenses while the bombers launched their supersonic Short-Range Attack Missiles (SRAM). Both SCADs and SRAMs were to fit on the same rotary launchers. SCAD development ended in 1973 when the Air Force elected the ALCM-A, an attack weapon that was essentially the SCAD with improved guidance.

ALCM-A, which first flew in March 1976, was rapidly superseded by the ALCM-B. Unlike ALCM-A, the later missile, stretched by 30 percent to achieve a 100 percent increase in range, is too long to fit in B-52 or B-1 weapons bays. The ALCM-B is carried on wing pylons on the B-52G/H and on the B-1B, and the bombers' weapons bay designs have been modified to accommodate 8 ALCMs internally on a rotary launcher.

Designation: AGM-86B

Status: IOC was achieved in December 1982. Production ended in October 1986 with 1,715 built. 98 B-52G aircraft have been modified to carry 12 ALCM-B on external pylons; 96 B-52Hs are being modified to carry a total of 20 ALCMs and SRAMs. 98 B-1B bombers can carry up to 22 ALCMs.

Characteristics:

Weight	Approx 3,200 lbs
Dimensions	Span 12 ft, length 20.8 ft, diameter 2 ft
Propulsion	Williams Research F-107-WR-100 (600-lb static thrust turbofan)
Speed	Mach 0.7
Range	Over 1,500 miles
Warhead	1 × 200-kiloton W-80-1 nuclear

AGM-68A Air Launched Cruise Missile (ALCM) released from B-52.

AGM-86A ALCM with wings and tail fins extended.

Six AGM-86B ALCMs fitted on pylons under each wing of a B-52G.

Atlas ICBM launch.

Atlas

The Atlas (SM-65/HGM-19), was the first U.S. Intercontinental Ballistic Missile (ICBM) to achieve operational status. The Convair division of General Dynamics had initiated the project in 1946, with a goal of delivering a nuclear warhead to targets 5,000 miles from the launching point. A USAF contract was not awarded for actual development of the missile until January 1955. Early Atlas variants reached a limited operational capability in September 1958, with the definitive Atlas-D becoming operational in 1960. The last Atlas missiles—E and F models—were phased out in 1965, having been replaced by Titan and Minuteman missiles.

The Atlas was considered a "1½ stage" missile, with two booster engines and one sustainer engine, plus two small vernier engines on the sides of the missile. All five engines drew propellants from the main tanks and all were ignited prior to liftoff.

After withdrawal from SAC, some 200 Atlas missiles were made available for use as space launch vehicles. (On 18 December 1958 an unarmed Atlas test vehicle was placed in orbit for 34 days in Project Score.)

Designation: Originally SM-65 (for Strategic Missile). Subsequently changed to HGM-19 (silo stored/surface attack/missile).

Status: Retired; first flight 1957; operational in SAC from 1958 until 1965.

Characteristics:

Weight	Atlas-D 255,000 lbs.; Atlas-E/F 260,000 lbs.
Dimensions	Length 75.1 ft. with Mk 2 re-entry vehicle, 82.5 ft. with Mk 3 RV; diameter 120 in.
Propulsion	1 North American Rocketdyne LR89 sustainer engine (57,-000 lbs. static thrust); 2 LR105 booster engines (150,000 lbst each); 2 LR101 vernier engines (1,000 lbst each); liquid oxygen fuel
Range	Atlas-D 10,360 miles; Atlas-E/F 11,500 miles.
Warhead	Nuclear (single RV)

Hound Dog

The Hound Dog (GAM-77/AGM-28) was a standoff, air-to-surface attack missile operational with the Strategic Air Command from 1961 to 1976. The missile, built by North American Aviation, was initiated in the mid-1950s to increase the ability of B-52s to attack heavily defended targets by striking anti-aircraft defenses in the path of the aircraft. All B-52G/H aircraft were equipped to carry two Hound Dog missiles on wing pylons between their fuselage and inboard engine nacelles. The B-52 could use the Hound Dog engines for added power on takeoff or while in flight, and then refuel them from the aircraft's tanks before launching. The first Hound Dog was delivered to SAC in late 1959, with an initial operational capability being achieved in early 1961. Production ceased in 1963, with the SAC inventory reaching a peak of 593 in that year.

The missile had a sleek aerodynamically attractive configuration with small canard foreplanes, a delta wing, and a small tail fin with rudder. A turbojet engine was mounted in a pod under the after fuselage. The Hound Dog had an inertial navigation system, updated before launching by the B-52's system, and some models were fitted with anti-radar and terrain-following systems. Maximum speed was Mach 2.1 with an altitude spectrum ranging from 55,000 feet down to tree-top level.

Designation: Originally designated GAM-77 (for Ground Attack Missile); subsequently changed to AGM-28 (for Air-to-Ground Missile).

Status: Retired; first flight 1959; operational in SAC from 1961 until 1976.

Characteristics:

Weight	10,140 lbs.
Dimensions	Span 12 ft., length 42.5 ft., diameter 28 in.
Propulsion	1 Pratt & Whitney J52-6 turbojet (7,500 lbs. static thrust)
Range	500+ miles on most flight profiles; 700 miles on hi-hi flight profile
Warhead	Nuclear (W-28, yield approx. 1 megaton)

Two AGM-28 Hound Dog missiles on B-52 wing pylons.

Jupiter

The Jupiter was one of two Intermediate Range Ballistic Missiles (IRBM) deployed by the United States, the other being the Thor. The missile was developed by the ex-German team under Wernher von Braun at Redstone Arsenal. It was envisioned as an Army missile and in late 1955 the Navy was directed to adapt the missile for launching from surface ships and possibly submarines. This was considered most hazardous with respect to handling liquid fuels aboard ship and the effects of ship motion in handling a 60-foot-long missile. In early 1957, Secretary of Defense Robert McNamara assigned all weapons with a range of more than 200 miles to the Air Force, and the Navy subsequently abandoned Jupiter in favor of the solid-propellant Polaris missile. From 1960 onward, 30 missiles were deployed to Italy and another 30 to Turkey for joint USAF-local operation within NATO. However, the missiles in Turkey were never fully operational, and the entire program was disbanded in 1965.

The missile had a conventional configuration with inertial navigation. It was produced at the Army's Michigan Missile Plant, operated by the Chrysler Corporation, with production deliveries beginning in November 1957. Components were tested on modified Redstone missiles called Jupiter-A.

Designation: Originally designated SM-78 in the Strategic Missile series, the Jupiter later became PGM-19 (soft pad/surface attack/missile).

Status: Retired; first flight 1957; operational from 1960 to 1965 (forward based in Italy and Turkey).

Characteristics:

Weight	110,000 lbs.
Dimensions	Length 60.1 ft., diameter 105 in.
Propulsion	1 North American Rocketdyne S-3 (150,000 lbs. static thrust); liquid oxygen fuel
Range	1,976 miles
Warhead	Nuclear (single RV, yield approx. 1 megaton)

Jupiter IRBM launch.

MM

The Minuteman LGM-130 ICBM is the primary U.S. strategic missile, providing 50 percent of the available Single Integrated Operational Plan weapons, with 950 missiles deployed in fixed silos. The Minuteman force numbered 1,000 missiles at its peak until 50 Peacekeeper (MX) missiles became operational in late 1988, replacing an equal number of Minuteman missiles. The Minuteman was the first U.S. Air Force solid-fuel rocket ICBM and the first with Multiple Independently targetable Re-entry Vehicles (MIRVs).

The first version was the single-warhead Minuteman I, none of which remain in service. Two later variants are still deployed, 450 single-warhead Minuteman II and 500 triple-warhead Minuteman III. The 300 Minuteman IIIs with the highly accurate Mk 12A MIRVs are the most modern of the deployed Minuteman force.

Minuteman I ICBM launch.

Fifty Minuteman IIIs with Mk 12 warheads were deactivated to make room for the MX Peacekeeper missiles. The Minuteman III silos were easier to convert to MX than were the older Minuteman II silos.

Modifications to the command and control system and launch facilities, the development of a new third-stage rocket motor for Minuteman II, and the development of new penetration aids are intended to maintain Minuteman's deterrent credibility to the year 2000.

The deployment of Minuteman-equipped strategic missile wings in 1990 was:

Location: Malmstrom AFB, Montana: 150 Minuteman II, 50 Minuteman III. Ellsworth AFB, South Dakota: 150 Minuteman II. Minot AFB, North Dakota: 150 Minuteman III. Whiteman AFB, Missouri: 150 Minuteman II. F. E. Warren AFB, Wyoming: 150 Minuteman III. Grand Forks AFB, North Dakota: 150 Minuteman III.

Designation: See variants.

Status: Operational. First flight 1959. Initial operational capability, Minuteman I (LGM-30A/B) in 1963, Minuteman II (LGM-30F) in 1966, Minuteman III (LGM-30G) in 1970; Mk 12A MIRVs IOC in 1979. Production ended in 1977.

Minuteman ICBM in test launch silo; note technician at right of missile.

Minuteman ICBM is launched from a C-5A transport aircraft during airborne test launch.

Minuteman ICBM is lowered by parachute after being test launched from C-5A aircraft. Moments later the missile's engines were ignited.

Variants:

Minuteman I (LGM-30A/B)	World's first operational solid-fuel ICBM. Over 600 deployed, most as LGM-30B, which had increased range. None now in service, the last having been replaced by the Minuteman III in 1974.
Minuteman II (LGM-30F)	Larger, heavier missile with longer range and greater accuracy. 450 deployed; all remain in service.
Minuteman III (LGM-30G)	Introduced more accurate NS-20 guidance system, Mk 12 MIRVs, the first MIRVs on an ICBM and their deployment was as significant as the fielding of the first ICBM. A total of 550 Minuteman IIIs with Mk 12 warheads were deployed. 300 were retrofitted with Mk 12A warheads, and 50 were replaced with the MX Peacekeeper.

Characteristics:

Weight   Minuteman II approx 73,000 lbs
                       Minuteman III approx 78,000 lbs
                       Throwweight:
                             Minuteman II 1,625 lbs
                             Minuteman III 2,400 lbs

Dimensions   Minuteman II length 56 ft, diameter 6 ft
                       Minuteman III length 60 ft, diameter 6 ft

Propulsion   First stage:
                             Thiokol TU-122 (M-55), approx 210,000 lbs st
                       Second stage:
                       Aerojet SR19-AJ-1, approx 60,300 lbs st
                       Third stage:
                             Minuteman II
                             Hercules M57A1, approx 34,400 lbs st
                             Minuteman III
                             Thiokol SR73-AJ-1, approx 34,400 lb st with fluid-injection thrust vector control for greater range and accuracy
                       Post-boost vehicle:
                             Minuteman III
                             Bell Aerospace package of 11 small rockets for post-boost control

Speed   Over 15,000 mph
Range   8,000 miles
Warhead   Minuteman II
                             1 Avco Mk 11C RV with a W56 1.2-megaton warhead
                             Minuteman III
                             3 General Electric (GE) Mk 12 MIRVs with W-62 170-kiloton warheads; or
                             3 GE Mk 12A MIRVs with W-78 330-kiloton warheads

MX

The Peacekeeper was developed to replace the Minuteman as the U.S. land-based ICBM. The Peacekeeper, better known under its development name MX, is a large and highly accurate missile now in place in Minuteman silos.

The MX reflects 20 years of U.S. ICBM design with the most significant improvements coming in guidance and warhead technology. The solid-propellant missile has three boost stages and a powered Post-Boost Vehicle (PBV). Synthetic rubber-based solid-propellants with aluminum and oxidizer additives fuel the first two stages; the third stage solid-propellant is a synthetic polymer plastic-based fuel with the same additives. All three motor cases are made of wound Kevlar aramid fibers.

The Air Force originally planned 200 Peacekeepers; 90 were funded between FY 1984-1989, with another 12 requested in FY 1990.

All 50 Peacekeepers are in silos located in existing Minuteman silos at F. E. Warren AFB. Seven SAC bases have been identified as sites for the rail garrison MX: F. E. Warren AFB, Wyoming; Little Rock, Arkansas; Barksdale AFB, Louisiana; Wurtsmith AFB, Michigan; Grand Forks AFB, North Dakota; Fairchild AFB, Washington; Dyess AFB, Texas.

The PBV is powered by liquid bi-propellant fuel and can carry up to 10 Multiple Independently targetable Reentry Vehicles (MIRVs). The missile is guided by a Rockwell Autonetics Missile Guidance and Control Set (MCGS).

The MX is a "cold-launched" missile. A small gas generator pops the missile out of its silo after which the first stage ignites. This technique, never before used to launch a U.S. ICBM, was developed to enable the MX to be deployed as a mobile system.

Currently, the MXs are deployed in fixed silos. The Air Force intends to move the MXs to a "rail garrison." The MX trains, each consisting of two missile cars, control, and maintenance cars, would be housed in protective "igloos" located in garrisons on bases already served by commercial railroad lines. The cars would measure 88.7 ft long, 9.5 ft wide, and 15.8 ft high. With the missile embarked, maximum weight is 550,000 lb (249,480 kg). If a higher alert status were declared, the trains could move out onto the U.S. rail network to "hide" from enemy ICBMs.

An MX Peacekeper being successfully launched from a modified Minuteman silo at Vandenberg AFB, California.

Designation: LGM-118

Status: Operational. Initial Operational Capability (IOC) in December 1986. Rail garrison MX IOC scheduled for June 1992. Full-scale development began in 1979; first test flight on 17 June 1983. The 50 MX missiles achieved full operational capability on 30 December 1988, with additional missiles being procured for tests and proofing. The first test of a rail garrison MX is planned for Vandenberg AFB, California, in 1991.

Characteristics:

Weight	Approx 195,000 lbs (total missile weight)
	first stage 108,000 lbs
	second stage 60,000 lbs
	third stage 17,000 lbs
	post-boost vehicle 3,000 lbs
	throwweight 8,000 lbs
Dimensions	Approx 71 ft overall length
	first stage 30 ft
	second stage 18 ft
	third stage 8 ft
	PBV 4 ft
	diameter 7.7 ft
Propulsion	First stage
	Morton-Thiokol solid-propellant rocket
	Second stage
	Aerojet solid-propellant rocket
	Third stage
	Hercules solid-propellant rocket
	Fourth stage
	Rocketdyne storable-liquid rocket
Range	6,909 miles maximum
Warheads	10 Avco Mk 21 Multiple Independently targetable Reentry Vehicles (MIRV); each armed with 1 W-87 300-475 kiloton nuclear warhead

Quail

The McDonnell Quail (GAM-72/ADM-20) was a decoy missile carried in SAC bombers to confuse enemy radars. Each Quail produced a radar "blip" similar to that produced by a B-52. Speed and altitude capabilities were similar to that of a B-52. Two Quails were carried in special racks in B-52 weapon bays without degrading the aircraft's weapon capability.

The Quail was fabricated of fiberglass and had small fins that remained in a folded position until it was ready for launching.

Designation: Originally GAM-72 in the USAF's missile designation series. Later changed to ADM-20 (Air/Decoy/Missile).

Status: Retired; first flight 1958; operational in SAC from 1960 until 1978.

Characteristics:

Weight	1,100 lbs.
Dimensions	Span 5.5 ft., length 13 ft.
Propulsion	1 General Electric J85-7 turbojet (2,850 lbs. static thrust)
Range	265 miles
Warhead	None

ADM-20 Quail in flight.

Snark

The Northrop Snark (SM-62) was an Intercontinental Cruise Missile (ICM), the only weapon of its type to be deployed in the strategic role by any nation. (The Germans had a development program for such a missile, designated A-10, during World War II.) Snark development began in 1946 and flight test vehicles began flying in 1951. In essence, the Snark was a pilotless bomber with a high-altitude, subsonic (615-mph) flight profile. Compared to contemporary bomber aircraft, the Snark offered low investment and operating costs, a small radar cross section, and a relatively large warhead. A major Snark development was planned. The first missile was declared operationally ready at Presque Isle AFB, Maine, on 18 March 1961. However, less than four months later, on 25 June 1961, the Snark force was deactivated, having been made obsolescent by the large U.S. strategic bomber and missile programs.

The missile had a long, sleek configuration with swept-back wings and a vertical fin stabilizer without any horizontal tail surfaces. Its guidance was self-contained, pre-set with inertial updating and thus unjammable. It had turbojet propulsion with two solid-propellant boosters for "zero-length"

SM-62 Snark in flight.

SM-62 Snark being readied for flight.

launching. As the missile approached the target the warhead was ejected from the airframe, achieving an ultimate velocity of about Mach 1 (the airframe would then begin to tumble and break up).

Status: Retired; first flight 1956; operational in 1961 with 30 missiles completed.

Characteristics:

Weight	59,936 lbs.
Dimensions	Span 42.25 ft., length 75.9 ft. (including sensing probe), height 15 ft.
Propulsion	1 Pratt & Whitney J57-P-17 turbojet (10,500 lbs. static thrust); 2 solid-fuel rocket boosters (130,000 lbst each)
Range	Approx. 6,000 miles
Warhead	Nuclear (yield approx. 20 megatons)

SICBM

The "Midgetman" is a single-warhead mobile ICBM that will consist of a three-stage missile and a hardened mobile launcher. It is in the research and development stage, being studied alongside a mobile version of the MX as an alternative to the silo-based MX Peacekeeper and Minuteman II and III land-based strategic missiles.

The missile shares similar technology and several components with the Peacekeeper. Both are cold-launched, 3-stage missiles that are guided by the Northrop Inertial Measurement Unit (IMU) and armed with the W87 nuclear warhead. The mobile launcher for the Midgetman is still in the prototype stage.

Initial deployment is planned for existing Minuteman sites at Malmstrom AFB, Montana. Other sites will be Warren AFB, Wyoming, and Ellsworth AFB, South Dakota. Some missiles will also be randomly based at Air Force installations in the southwest United States.

The development of the Midgetman has been controversial, particularly in light of a decreasing Soviet military threat. The Air Force has favored a 100 MX missile program in lieu of the Midgetman. The Bush administration decided to continue both the MX rebasing and the Midgetman development; in the U.S. Congress, the Senate backed the administration but the House voted in early 1990 to cancel funding of the Midgetman.

Designation: MGM-134A

Status: Under development. Development began in 1984 and IOC is scheduled for 1997. Procurement plans include 500 missiles and launchers.

First test flight on 11 May 1989 was unsuccessful. During 1987–88 there was a successful series of 40 ground firings of the missile.

Characteristics:

Weight	37,000 lbs missile; 200,000 lbs launcher
Dimensions	missile: length 46 ft, diameter 3.8 ft; launcher: length 100 ft
Propulsion	Stage I, Morton Thiokol; Stage II, Aerojet; Stage III, Hercules
Range	6,000 miles
Warhead	GE single Mk21 Re-entry Vehicle (RV); W87 300–475 kiloton warhead

SRAM

The Boeing Short-Range Attack Missile (SRAM) is a guided nuclear weapon launched from strategic bombers against air defense systems during a bomber's final approach to its target. It is inertially guided and has a very small radar cross-section.

The SRAM was originally conceived as a stand-off weapon for fighter aircraft but its use has been restricted to strategic bombers and FB-111A deep-strike aircraft. The missile is capable of terrain-following, semi-ballistic, pop-up and dive, and a combination of inertial and terrain-following flight paths. It can also adjust its path laterally and attack targets in any direction after launch.

B-52G/H bombers can carry a maximum of 20 SRAMs: eight on an internal rotary launcher in the weapons bay and six on each inboard wing pylon. Three rotary launchers can be fitted in the planes. The B-1B can carry a maximum of 38 SRAMs, 24 internally and 14 on external pylons. However, the B-52 and B-1B usually will carry a mixture of SRAMs in the weapons bay and Air-Launched Cruise Missiles (ALCM) on the wing pylons. Operational considerations would determine the bombers to carry less than the maximum load.

Designation: AGM-69

Status: Operational. IOC in 1972. First flight in 1969. Production deliveries began in March 1972; the 42nd Bomb Wing, Loring AFB, Maine was the first to receive the missile. The last SRAM was delivered on 20 August 1975 to the 320th Bomb Wing, Mather AFB, California. Approximately 1,500 were produced.

Variants:

SRAM-B   Designed for the B-1 bomber; to have been nuclear-hardened; Thiokol HTPB-propellant motor; expanded computer memory; W-80 nuclear warhead. Cancelled when B-1 program was cancelled in 1977.

SRAM-II   In lieu of developing the Advanced Air-to-Surface Missile (AASM), the SRAM-II contract was awarded to Boeing in December 1986. See separate listing.

AGM-69A Short Range Attack Missiles on rotary dispenser in B-52 bomb bay.

Characteristics:

Weight   2,240 lbs
Dimensions   Length 14 ft, diameter 17.5 in.
Propulsion   SR75-LP-1 two-stage solid-fuel rocket motor
Speed   Mach 3.5 maximum
Range   35–50 miles low altitude
                 100–137.5 miles high altitude
Warhead   1 × 200-kt W-69 nuclear (contact or preset altitude air-
                 burst fuze)

SRAM-II

The Boeing SRAM-II is the planned successor to the SRAM (Short-Range Attack Missile), for launch from strategic bombers against air defense systems during a bomber's final attack on target. The SRAM-II is being developed as a lighter, longer-range missile with a new nuclear warhead that will be capable of penetrating improved enemy air defenses more effectively than its predecessor.

The SRAM-II is expected to make use of composite materials to achieve a lighter weight and lower degree of susceptibility to enemy radars. The guidance system will also be upgraded through the use of a ring laser gyro. FB-111As are slated to carry up to 6 SRAM-IIs while the B-1Bs and B-2s are expected to carry 12 each. The SRAM-II will be launched from a rotary launcher.

Designation: AGM-131

Status: Under development. IOC planned in 1994. Boeing Aerospace of Seattle, Washington, was selected as prime contractor in December 1986; current production plans allow for a total of 1,633 missiles. Also, the SRAM-II is being considered by Great Britain to replace the WE-177 nuclear bomb on their Tornado aircraft.

Characteristics:

Weight	1,933 lbs launch weight, 584 lbs warhead
Dimensions	Length 14 ft, diameter 1.3 ft
Propulsion	Solid-propellant motor
Speed	Approx Mach 3.5
Range	250 miles maximum
Warhead	W-80 nuclear, 200 kt yield; W-90 nuclear (under development)

Thor

The Douglas Thor was one of two IRBMs developed by the United States, being a USAF weapon developed after the Army's Jupiter IRBM. (The Jupiter was deployed under the auspices of the USAF.) Formal development of the Thor, SM-75/PGM-17, began in late 1955 having been given a high national priority. The contract for development of the Thor was awarded to Douglas Aircraft on 27 December 1955, and the first missile was delivered to the Air Force in October 1956—a record development schedule for a modern weapon system. The first Thor missiles became operational in England in December 1959 under a joint USAF-Royal Air Force "two-key" program. The entire force of 20 squadrons, each with three missiles, was operational by 1961. The subsequent U.S. intercontinental missile program and the British decision to deploy Polaris submarines as that nation's primary deterrent force led to the phasing out of the Thor program, with the last missiles being deactivated on 20 December 1963.

The Thor was developed with the employment of Atlas ICBM technology where possible to reduce development time. The use of an Atlas-C re-entry

SM-75 Thor IRBM.

vehicle resulted in the Thor having a "flat-top" configuration. The single, liquid-propellant booster was supplemented by two vernier rockets on the side to control roll and adjustment of velocity after engine cutoff. Inertial guidance was provided.

Designation: The Thor was initially assigned the designation SM-75 (Strategic Missile); subsequently changed to PGM-17 (soft pad/surface attack/missile).

Status: Retired; first flight 1956; operational from 1959 to 1963 (forward based in England).

Characteristics:

Weight	105,000 lbs.
Dimensions	Length 65 ft., diameter 8 ft.
Propulsion	1 North American Rocketdyne LR-79 (150,000 lbs. static thrust); liquid oxygen fuel
Range	2,000 miles
Warhead	Nuclear (single RV)

Titan

The Martin Titan is a highly sophisticated, second-generation ICBM that remains in SAC service in the Titan II variant, supplementing 1,000 Minuteman ICBMs in the nation's land-based strategic deterrence force. Development of the Titan, (SM-68/LGM-25), began in 1955 to take advantage of technological opportunities not being incorporated in the Atlas ICBM. Development problems slowed the Titan's progress, and the first missile did not fly until 6 February 1959. The first Titan I became operational in April 1962. In 1958, Martin initiated an improved Titan missile which was significantly larger (almost 50 percent heavier), with improved liquid propellants providing more range and double the payload, yet still being able to fit inside the Titan I launch silo. Also, the Titan I's radio command guidance, susceptible to jamming, was replaced by an all-inertial system. The first Titan II was launched in November 1961 and the weapon became operational in 1963. Titan II deployment reached a peak of 64 missiles in 1967, with 54 weapons now silo-based at Davis-Monthan AFB in Arizona, McConnell AFB in Kansas, and Little Rock AFB in Arkansas. The Titan II will be retained well

SM-68 Titan I ICBM being raised from underground silo.

SM-68 Titan II ICBM launch.

into the 1980s because of its large yield that provides a hard-target kill capability. (Titan I deployments peaked at 63 missiles in 1963, the last being phased out early in 1965.)

The Titan II is a two-stage missile with a cylindrical body (the Titan I had a ten-foot diameter first stage and eight-foot diameter second stage.) There are four small vernier rockets on the second stage to correct speed and trajectory. Inertial guidance is fitted, with periodic updates having been made to improve reliability and accuracy. The warhead is the largest ever fitted in a U.S. missile.

Designation: The Titan was originally designated SM-65 (Strategic Missile); changed to HGM-19 (silo stored/surface attack/missile). The Titan I was SM-65A/HGM-19A), and the Titan II had the -B and -C variants.

Status: Titan I first flight 1959, Titan II first flight 1961; 54 Titan IIs operational with SAC.

Characteristics: (LGM-25C)

Weight	330,000 lbs.
Dimensions	Length 103 ft., diameter 10 ft.
Propulsion	1 Aerojet General LR91 sustainer engine (100,000 lbs. static thrust); 1 Aerojet General LR87 booster engine (430,000 lbst); liquid fuel
Range	9,300 miles
Warhead	Nuclear (single RV Mk-6, yield approx. 10 megatons)

Tomahawk

The General Dynamics AGM-109 Tomahawk is a Navy-developed missile suitable for launching from surface ships, submarines, and aircraft in the anti-ship or strategic roles. The missile is an alternative to the Boeing AGM-86B ALCM for use by the B-52G as a stand-off attack weapon during the 1980s. (See ALCM listing for potential program size and schedule.) Tomahawk development began in the early 1970s to provide a long-range missile in two variants for the anti-ship and strategic attack roles. The latter variant has the Harpoon's active radar/homing guidance, a 1,000-pound conventional warhead, and a range greater than 300 miles. Both versions have the same mid and after bodies and a Williams turbofan engine, providing a high subsonic speed and a low-altitude flight profile. The ship/submarine launched BGM-109 is in advanced development, although no deployment decisions had been made when this book went to press.

The requirement for multi-platform launch gives the Tomahawk a torpedo-shaped configuration that is compatible with standard 21-inch-diameter submarine tubes and launch tubes that can be fitted on the decks of warships.

BGM-109 Tomahawk in flight. (U.S. Navy photo)

The missile has a combination inertial and Terrain Contour Matching (TERCOM) guidance. After launching, the engine inlet extends down from the after fuselage, and stub wings and four tail fins emerge to provide aerodynamic lift and control.

Status: Development; first flight (anti-ship and land-attack variants): 1976; competitor with AGM-86B ALCM for use by SAC B-52G force and possible advanced Cruise Missile Carrier Aircraft (CMCA).

Characteristics: (AGM-109)

Weight	Approx. 3,200 lbs.
Dimensions	Span 8.3 ft., length 20.5 ft., diameter 20.9 in.
Propulsion	1 Williams F107-WR-400 turbofan (approx. 600 lbs. static thrust)
Range	Approx. 2,300 miles
Warhead	Nuclear (W-80, yield approx. 200 kilotons)

BGM-109 Tomahawk with wings and tail fins extended.

Glossary

AAM	Air-to-Air Missile
AB	Air Base
ACCS	Airborne Command and Control Squadron
ACM	Advanced Cruise Missile
ADC	Air Defense Command; later Aerospace Command
AFB	Air Force Base
AFCON	Headquarters USAF Controlled (unit)
AFS	Air Force Station
AGM	Air-to-Ground Missile
ALCM	Air-Launched Cruise Missile
AMSA	Advanced Manned Strategic Aircraft
BMEWS	Ballistic Missile Early Warning System
CINCSAC	Commander-in-Chief Strategic Air Command
CONUS	Continental United States
ECM	Electronic Countermeasures
EW	Electronic Warfare
FEAF	Far East Air Force
GAM	Ground-to-Air Missile
ICBM	Intercontinental Ballistic Missile
ICM	Intercontinental Missile
IOC	Initial Operational Capability
IRBM	Intermediate Range Ballistic Missile
JSTPS	Joint Strategic Target Planning Staff
MAJCOM	Major Air Command
MM	Minuteman
MX	Peacekeeper
NASA	National Aeronautics and Space Administration
NEAC	Northeast Air Command
NEACP	National Emergency Airborne Command Post
NOA	Non-operational Aircraft
NORAD	North American Air Defense Command
O&M	Operations and Maintenance
PAA	Primary Aircraft Authorization
PACAF	Pacific Air Forces
PACCS	Post Attack Command Control System
POL	Petroleum, Oil, and Lubricants
RAF	Royal Air Force
RAS	Radar Absorbent Structure
RCS	Radar Cross Section
RTU	Replacement Training Unit
SAC	Strategic Air Command
SACCS	SAC Automated Command Control System
SAM	Surface-to-Air Missile

SEA	Southeast Asia
SICBM	Small ICBM
SIOP	Single Integrated Operational Plan
SRAM	Short-Range Attack Missile
TAC	Tactical Air Command
TDY	Temporary Duty
UE	Unit Equipment
USAF	U.S. Air Force
USAFE	U.S. Air Forces Europe